"In December 1991, my daughter's harp was stolen; we got it back. But it came back in a way that irrevocably changed my familiar world of science and rational thinking. It changed the way I go about living in that world. It changed the way I perceive the world and try to make sense of it.

"This book is about what unfolded as I attempted to explain what happened."

—Elizabeth Lloyd Mayer

EXTRAORDINARY KNOWING

"A book to rejoice in. Mayer opens thrilling new possibilities for science and its applications."
—Larry Dossey, M.D.,
author of *Healing Words* and *Reinventing Medicine*

"A fascinating exploration of the mind and of what it might be to be human. Mayer opens up intriguing new vistas for thinking about our deeper connectedness."
—Adam Phillips, author of *Going Sane* and *Side Effects*

"Marvelous ... the most exciting and important work I've seen in a long time. Mayer has courage as well as brilliance."
—Louis Sander, M.D., Professor Emeritus, Boston University School of Medicine

Extraordinary Knowing

Science, Skepticism, and the Inexplicable Powers

of the Human Mind

ELIZABETH LLOYD MAYER, PH.D.

BANTAM BOOKS
New York Toronto London Sydney Auckland

EXTRAORDINARY KNOWING
A Bantam Book / March 2007

Published by Bantam Dell
A Division of Random House, Inc.
New York, New York

The account by Patrick Casement in Chapter 2 has been retold and adapted from *Learning from Life: Becoming a Psychoanalyst* (London: Routledge, 2006), with the kind permission of the author.

The photograph on page 144 by R. C. James is reprinted from *Vision Science* by Stephen Palmer, with the kind permission of MIT Press.

Book design by Sabrina Bowers

Bantam Books is a registered trademark of Random House, Inc., and the colophon is a trademark of Random House, Inc.

LIBRARY OF CONGRESS CATALOGING-IN-PUBLICATION DATA
Mayer, Elizabeth Lloyd.
Extraordinary knowing : science, skepticism, and the inexplicable powers of the human mind / Elizabeth Lloyd Mayer.
p. cm.
ISBN-13: 978-0-553-80335-8 (hardcover)
1. Subconsciousness. 2. Cognition. 3. Parapsychology. I. Title.
BF315.M39 2007
133.8—dc22   2006025661

Printed in the United States of America
Published simultaneously in Canada

www.bantamdell.com

10 9 8 7 6 5 4 3 2 1
BVG

Contents

Foreword by Freeman Dyson   vii
Foreword by Carol Gilligan   xi

1   The Harp That Came Back
My Journey Begins   1

2   Going Public with Private Knowing
Breaking the Silence   11

3   Disavowing the Extraordinary
Personal Cost and Public Consequences   25

4   States of Mind
Knowing That Doesn't Feel Like Knowing   39

5   Intuitive Intelligence
The Art and Science of Union   57

6   Starting—and Stopping—the Conversation
The Strange History of Paranormal Research   69

7   Tossing Out Meteorites
Science, Fear, and Anxiety   97

8   Nighttime Eyes
Learning to Live with Paradox   133

9 Measuring the Power of Prayer
   Is God in the Equation?   153

10 Listening Harder
   Tuning In to Dreams and Telepathy   185

11 Three Seconds into the Future
   The New Science of the Unconscious   213

12 Quantum Uncertainty
   A Working Model of Reality   237

   Epilogue: To Begin Again
   The Challenge of the Extraordinary   263

   Acknowledgments   273

   Endnotes   275

   Index   291

   About the Author   301

Foreword

by Freeman Dyson,
Institute for Advanced Study,
Princeton, New Jersey

This book begins with an extraordinary story about a harp—one that is typical of thousands of others in which somebody knows something without having any normal way of knowing. This kind of extraordinary knowing is commonly called extrasensory perception, or ESP. Since I am a scientist, the story puts me in a difficult position. As a scientist I don't believe the story, but as a human being I want to believe it. As a scientist, I don't believe anything that is not based on solid evidence. As a scientist, I have to consider it possible that Elizabeth Mayer and Harold McCoy might have concocted the story or deluded themselves into believing it. Scientists call such stories "anecdotal," meaning that they are scientifically worthless.

On the other hand, as a human being I find the story convincing. I am impressed by the fact that Elizabeth Mayer is herself a scientist and would normally be skeptical of such anecdotal evidence. She understands why the majority of scientists do not believe her story. She is eager to maintain a friendly dialogue between skeptics and believers in ESP. She feels herself in many ways closer to the skeptics. But she does not have the luxury of not believing the harp story, because it happened to her and she knows it is true. I am convinced, not by the story itself, but by the portrait that

Elizabeth paints of herself as a scientist confronting a mystery that orthodox science cannot grasp.

The greater part of this book describes the history of ESP research, some of it based on anecdotal evidence and some based on scientific experiments. The Society for Psychical Research, with branches in England and America, has been the main collector and publisher of anecdotal evidence. The society has been active for more than a century. It has published a large number of well-documented stories in its journal and in a famous book with the title *Phantasms of the Living*. A phantasm of the living is an episode in which person A at a moment of extreme crisis or danger is seen by person B hundreds of miles away. The society documented these episodes with firsthand testimony from A and B, recorded as soon as possible after the events. The evidence is of very uneven quality, and all of it is anecdotal.

The scientific investigations of ESP have been pursued with dogged determination for long periods of time, initially by Joseph Rhine at Duke University, later by Harold Puthoff at Stanford Research Institute, and recently by many other groups. The history of these efforts is murky, partly because there were some accusations of cheating in Rhine's laboratory, and partly because much of Puthoff's work was sponsored by the Central Intelligence Agency under conditions of secrecy. Elizabeth Mayer gives us the clearest account of ESP research that I have seen, with an excellent bibliography of relevant documents. The results of the scientific investigations were in the end disappointing. Investigators claimed to have positive and statistically significant evidence of ESP, but the positive results were always marginal, large enough to be statistically significant but not large enough to convince a skeptical critic.

There are three possible positions that one may take concerning the evidence for ESP. First, the position of orthodox scientists, who believe that ESP does not exist. Second, the position of true believers, who believe that ESP is real and can be proved to exist by scientific methods. Third, my own position, that ESP is real, as the anecdotal evidence suggests, but cannot be tested with the clumsy tools of science. These positions also imply different views concerning the proper scope of science. If one believes, as many of my scientific colleagues believe, that the scope of science is unlimited, then science can ultimately explain everything in the universe, and ESP must either be nonexistent or scientifically explainable. If one believes, as I do, that ESP exists but is scientifically untestable, one must believe that the scope of science is limited. I put forward, as a working hypothesis, that ESP is real but belongs to a mental universe that is too fluid and evanescent to fit within the rigid protocols of controlled scientific testing. I do not claim that this hypothesis is true. I claim only that it is consistent with the evidence and worthy of consideration.

I was asked to write this preface because I published in *The New York Review of Books* a review of a book about ESP with the title *Debunked!,* by Georges Charpak and Henri Broch. Elizabeth Mayer read my review and refers to it in her Chapter 12. In my review I said that ESP only occurs, according to the anecdotal evidence, when a person is experiencing intense stress and strong emotions. Under the conditions of a controlled scientific experiment, intense stress and strong emotions are excluded; the person experiences boredom rather than excitement, and so the evidence for ESP disappears. That, I wrote, is why scientific investigation of ESP fails. The experiment necessarily excludes the human emotions that make ESP possible.

After my review was published, I received a large number of angry letters in response. Orthodox scientists were angry because I said ESP might be real. True believers in ESP were angry because I said ESP could not be scientifically proved.

What I like best about Elizabeth Mayer is her eagerness, throughout this book, to maintain a friendly working dialogue between believers and skeptics. I am happy that she and I can disagree and still stay friends.

Foreword

by Carol Gilligan

I met Lisby over a story of extraordinary knowing—the one she tells in the first chapter of this book. A mutual friend who works in the theater, determined to bring us together, had set up the date and place: a café in Harvard Square. I see her across the small wooden table, the coffee cups, packets of sugar ripped open next to her plate, her face lit, her eyes eagerly searching mine. Our friendship would hinge on this conversation.

Her daughter's harp had disappeared in Oakland, California. As a last resort, Lisby called a dowser in Arkansas. In recounting his response, she took on his accent, his slow country drawl. All he needed was a map of the city and the light given off by a precious object. There was nothing unusual about this. What was in one framework extraordinary knowing was in another ordinary. Matter-of-fact.

I have had the experience many times—thinking of someone I haven't seen for ages and then they call on the phone, knowing something without any way of explaining how I knew. Knowing it viscerally, knowing it intuitively, knowing in a way that challenges long-standing assumptions about separateness and the impossibility of reading other minds. Knowing through *connectedness*—the word that would join us, bridging Lisby's work and mine. It is how children know. And then, when connectedness is shattered or discounted or overridden, they come not to know.

The next time I went to San Francisco, I spent an afternoon with Lisby, sitting in her garden. She wanted to talk about Erik Erikson, another link between us. She wanted to talk about the assumptions we make about ourselves and the universe we live in. She wanted to talk about psychoanalysis, physics, music, empathy, Bell's theorem, action (seemingly) at a distance, like the pull of the moon on the tides. There were many experiences we shared in common, ranging from our fascination with the figure-ground reversals of Gestalt psychology to raising children and running a household. Our conversations extended over the years as we met in Cambridge, Berkeley, Vermont, and the Bershires, our friendship widening to include our families, circling back to the question: What happens when you shift framework? When you examine seemingly extraordinary events through a different lens?

We organized a study group at the psychoanalytic meetings, we taught a seminar together at Harvard, presented together at conferences, ran a writing workshop one Saturday for Radcliffe students. I watched Lisby enliven every scene she entered, inviting enthusiasm, welcoming skepticism, her generosity extraordinary, her curiosity boundless.

"Ineluctable modality of the visible," Joyce wrote. To Lisby, lines and boundaries could be deceptive. She was drawn to those whose seeing challenged perception: psychics, card-players who knew what was in other hands, surgeons guided by white light. I had never been interested in ESP, but I am fascinated by what people know, gripped by knowing that seems extraordinary. In our study group, we invited psychoanalysts to share such experiences.

Over and over again, the analysts came forward, often shyly, sometimes fearfully, to describe incidents where they or their patients knew something that they had no way to account for. The question of explanation became pressing. At the same time, I was struck by the judgments hedging their revelations and by the intensity of emotion aroused by these conversations, as if we were breaking a taboo.

This book is an invitation to think with Lisby about the inexplicable powers of the human mind. To open ourselves to the possibility, as Hamlet tells his friend Horatio, that "there are more things in heaven and earth than are dreamt of in your philosophy." The vision is at once stunning and daunting: "Once we open the door to mind-matter anomalies, who knows what the rules are? . . . Can minds touch each other in ways that transcend [the boundaries of] mind and space as we understand them? . . . What if the perceptions we now label extra-sensory . . . could be reliably trained to deepen people's ordinary knowing of each other, extending our capacities for empathy and compassion? . . . What if we took possibilities like that seriously—seriously enough to subject them to our best scientific scrutiny?" This is a book that ends with questions.

At the close of my first encounter with Lisby, she handed me two cards. One identified her as a psychoanalyst, the other as director of San Francisco Bay Revels. The Christmas Revels, which began in Cambridge and she then took to the West Coast, is a celebration of the winter solstice, the darkest day of the year, the moment when the earth turns back toward the light. *Extraordinary Knowing,* written by someone with one foot in the arts, the other in science, captures a hope common to both: of finding light in darkness. I took Lisby's two cards and placed them in my wallet.

Carol Gilligan is the author of *In a Different Voice* and, most recently, *The Birth of Pleasure.* She is University Professor at New York University.

Extraordinary Knowing

The Harp That Came Back:

My Journey Begins

IN DECEMBER OF 1991, my daughter's harp was stolen; we got it back. But it came back in a way that irrevocably changed my familiar world of science and rational thinking. It changed the way I go about living in that world. It changed the way I perceive the world and try to make sense out of it.

This book is about what unfolded as I attempted to explain what happened. I encountered questions: huge and disconcerting questions about the world as we know it. They held radical import not just for science but for the ways we live our everyday lives. This is a book about those questions and some of the surprising answers I encountered along the way.

In 1991 I was teaching in the psychology department of the University of California at Berkeley and at the University Medical Center in San Francisco. I was doing research on female development and seeing patients in my psychoanalysis practice. I was a member of numerous professional associations, doing committee work, attending international meetings, functioning on editorial boards, and lecturing all over the country. I was a training and supervising analyst in the American Psychoanalytic Association. I was busy and fulfilled, and life was running along the way it does.

My eleven-year-old daughter, Meg, who'd fallen in love with the harp at age six, had begun performing. She wasn't playing a classical pedal harp but a smaller, extremely valuable instrument built and carved by a master harp maker. After a Christmas concert, her harp was stolen from the theater where she was playing. For two months we went through every conceivable channel trying to locate it: the police, instrument dealers across the country, the American Harp Society newsletters—even a CBS TV news story. Nothing worked.

Finally, a wise and devoted friend told me, "If you really want that harp back, you should be willing to try anything. Try calling a dowser." The only thing I knew about dowsers were that they were that strange breed who locate underground water with forked sticks. But according to my friend, the "really good" dowsers can locate not just water but lost objects as well.

Finding lost objects with *forked sticks*? Well, nothing was happening on the police front, and my daughter, spoiled by several years of playing an extraordinary instrument, had found the series of commercial harps we'd rented simply unplayable. So, half-embarrassed but desperate, I decided to take my friend's dare. I asked her if she could locate a really good dowser—the best, I said. She promptly called the American Society of Dowsers and came back with the phone number of the society's current president: Harold McCoy, in Fayetteville, Arkansas.[1]

I called him that day. Harold picked up the phone—friendly, cheerful, heavy Arkansas accent. I told him I'd heard he could dowse for lost objects and that I'd had a valuable harp stolen in Oakland, California. Could he help locate it?

"Give me a second," he said. "I'll tell you if it's still in Oakland." He paused, then: "Well, it's still there. Send me a street map of Oakland and I'll locate that harp for you." Skeptical—but what, after all, did I have to lose?—I promptly overnighted him a map.

Two days later, he called back. "Well, I got that harp located," he said. "It's in the second house on the right on D—— Street, just off L—— Avenue."

I'd never heard of either street. But I did like the sound of the man's voice—whoever he was. And I don't like backing down on a dare. Why not drive to the house he'd identified? At least I'd get the address. I looked on an Oakland map and found the neighborhood. It was miles from anywhere I'd ever been. I got in my car, drove into Oakland, located the house, wrote down the number, called the police, and told them I'd gotten a tip that the harp might be at that house. Not good enough for a search warrant, they said. They were going to close the case—there was no way this unique, portable, and highly marketable item hadn't already been sold; it was gone forever.

But I found I couldn't quite let it go. Was it the dare? Was it my admiration for the friend who'd instigated the whole thing? Was it my devastated daughter? Or was it just that I had genuinely liked the sound of that voice on the other end of the line?

I decided to post flyers in a two-block area around the house, offering a reward for the harp's return. It was a crazy idea, but why not? I put up flyers in those two blocks, and only those two blocks. I was embarrassed enough about what I was doing to tell just a couple of close friends about it.

Three days later, my phone rang. A man's voice told me he'd seen a flyer outside his house describing a stolen harp. He said it was exactly the harp his next-door neighbor had recently obtained and showed him. He wouldn't give me his name or number, but offered to get the harp returned to me. And two weeks later, after a series of circuitous telephone calls, he told me to meet a teenage boy at 10:00 P.M., in the rear parking lot of an all-night Safeway. I arrived to find a young man loitering in the lot. He looked at me, and said, "The harp?" I nodded. Within minutes, the harp was in the back of my station wagon and I drove off.

Twenty-five minutes later, as I turned into my driveway, I had the thought, *This changes everything.*

I was right. The harp changed how I work as a clinician and psychoanalyst. It changed the nature of the research I pursued. It changed my sense of what's ordinary and what's extraordinary. Most of all, it changed my relatively established, relatively contented, relatively secure sense of how the world adds up. If Harold McCoy did what he appeared to have done, I had to face the fact that my notions of space, time, reality, and the nature of the human mind were stunningly inadequate. Disturbing as that recognition was, there was something intriguing, even exciting, about it as well.

Over the ensuing months I spent a lot of sleepless nights. I argued with myself a lot. I regularly woke up at 3:00 A.M. certain that with just a little more effort, a little more clear thinking, I'd come up with some comfortably rational way to explain how that harp had ended up back in my living room where it belonged. Finally a friend of mine, a statistics professor at Berkeley, listened to my conflicted ranting and said in exasperation, "Get *over* it and get some sleep, Lisby. As a statistician, I can promise you the odds that dowsing works are a lot greater than the odds that this could have been coincidence."

I decided it was time to consider what it might mean if I started taking the whole thing seriously. *What if,* I began wondering. *What if* I stopped trying to explain it all away but instead tried to consider how on earth a dowser, over the phone and from two thousand miles away, could pinpoint the exact location of my stolen harp within the vast metropolitan San Francisco Bay Area?

I began to look into the scientific evidence for dowsing. That quickly led to reports from some very respectable scientific minds about all kinds of other, possibly related anomalous phenomena. I was discovering a vast, strange new territory of research regarding anomalous mind-matter interactions—interactions between mind and matter that simply cannot be contained inside what we call normal science.

Of course, I also discovered that the world of anomalous mind-matter interactions is filled with shoddy research, flaky research, and research based on questions that are neither particularly interesting nor rooted in a solid grasp of science, scientific method, or scientific thinking. Yet as I delved more deeply, what most impressed me was the significant bank of well-conducted, scientifically impeccable research that imposes enormous questions on anyone interested in making sense of the world from a Western scientific point of view. I began to wonder, why had so much of this excellent research been overlooked, its conclusions dismissed?

Weeks after I'd published my first tentative foray into exploring mind-matter anomalies, a physician I barely knew came up to me at a professional meeting. He'd read my article and wanted to tell me something. The story poured out. He'd been diagnosed twenty years earlier with fatal bone cancer and had become deeply depressed. As a marathon runner, he'd found relief from despair only while he ran. Early one morning, two hours into his run, he'd been suddenly overcome by what he described as "a sensation of light—clear, soft light, as though light was filling my bones, as though light and air were infusing each bone. I saw it—light penetrating those bones, right through to the marrow."

The next week his X-rays were clean. "I've never told another colleague," he said. "I told my wife when it happened—no one else. And this part I didn't tell anyone: I know that's what cured me. The light crowded out the cancer cells. I don't know how, but I know it did."

As word of my new interest spread, my medical and psychoanalytic colleagues began to inundate me with accounts of their own anomalous experiences, personal as well as clinical. As with the physician, the stories they shared with me were often ones they'd never revealed to another professional associate. Their accounts—by e-mail, snail mail, at conferences, in seminars, in hall corridors, or at dinner—made as little sense to me as they did to the colleagues telling me about them. The stories were all about knowing things in bizarrely inexplicable ways:

"My patient walked in and I knew her mother had died—no clues—I just knew, instantly."

"I woke up in the middle of the night like I heard a shot; the next day I found out it was exactly when my patient took a gun and tried to kill herself."

"I suddenly felt that my partner's son was in trouble. I called my partner; it worried him enough that he tracked down his son. His son had been in a bad car accident and my partner got there just in time to make a decision about surgery that probably saved his life."

I was particularly fascinated by how eagerly my colleagues shared even the most weirdly personal stories with me. Their eagerness puzzled me, until I realized how badly people wanted to reintegrate corners of experience they'd walled off from their public lives for fear of being disbelieved.

"I was on a bus and all of a sudden found myself smelling the perfume my brother's ex-wife used to wear. When the bus stopped, she got on. I hadn't smelled that perfume or seen her in thirty years."

"My husband and I fell in love with a house in London on our honeymoon—very distinctive, across from a park. Fourteen years later, living in Boston, I woke up one day, and thought, maybe we could buy it. I tracked down a realtor in London, asked if she could figure out the address and find out if it was for sale. Crazy! But she did. The man who'd been living there had just died; the For Sale sign wasn't even up yet. We bought it the next week."

I began taking notes, word for word and with every detail I could catch. I couldn't figure out what else to do. I couldn't ignore the things people were telling me, but I couldn't find ways to make sense of them either. The stories were from credible people, backed up by enough hard facts that I couldn't reject them out of hand.

As my files of all these notes grew, I found myself pursuing the odd, unexpected conversation with a new kind of curiosity, not just with colleagues but also with friends, students, and even first-time acquaintances. I began asking different questions. Someone would mention an unusual outcome of a friend's illness; instead of letting it pass, I'd ask what was so unusual. In return, I'd often hear accounts of apparently anomalous healing or treatment or even diagnoses: perhaps a stranger delivering an accurate, complex diagnosis of a medical condition over the phone, without any background information. Or someone would describe knowing something but having no idea how they knew it, and I'd probe gently. Peculiar stories would follow: a woman wakened by a sudden ache in her chest just as her father suffered a heart attack three thousand miles away; a man assaulted by shooting leg pain at the moment an identical twin fractured his leg; a student instantly guessing to four decimal places the exact strength of a chemical solution that should have taken hours to work out; a mother seized by panic at the exact moment her baby across town took a bad fall.

My new focus also encouraged me to tune in to my patients in a new way. I gradually had to face the realization that there were things my patients had been only half telling me for years, things they viewed as too weird or risky to reveal for fear I wouldn't believe them or—worse—would think they really were crazy. Now when my patients began to hint at strange incidents, odd images, or funny coincidences, I worked harder to encourage them to explore their meaning. And I began hearing some remarkable things.

I was somewhat stalled with one deeply troubled patient, a woman who was isolated and very frightened of the world. For years she'd insisted she couldn't remember any of her dreams, and indeed she'd reported almost none to me through our work together. Then, during one session, she told me that the night before she'd dreamed of my going to Arizona. I had indeed been planning a trip to Arizona that week, but I'd told none of my colleagues or patients about it. I asked her, why Arizona? She had no idea, no associations. I told her that I was in fact going to Arizona and wondered if she'd somehow picked that up. For a moment, she was quiet. Then she hesitantly told me that she often had dreams in which she knew where people were going, and it turned out she was right. She couldn't begin to explain it. She'd learned not to tell people; it was too weird. She had had dreams like that as a child and her parents had raged at her and called her crazy. They would sometimes beat her until she said she'd made it all up. So she'd learned to shut up and started pretending that she didn't have dreams, that a lot of things she experienced weren't real. Pretending to others, to herself, had made her feel safe, but it had also made her feel that she wasn't very real.

That exchange with my patient was a turning point in her psychotherapy. It was also a turning point for me. My evident curiosity about her dream had liberated a flood of experiences. As my patient started believing that I could believe her—and considered her neither crazy nor dangerous—a new world opened up between us. She began for the first time telling me about other bizarrely intuitive experiences, and about how they terrified her. Bit by bit, her comfort in the world took new root. Her life changed in profoundly positive ways. She told me that she started feeling she could be real.

M y patient's fear—of being unable to credit the evidence before her eyes, of being thought crazy, of losing the comfort of being believed—began to take on an enormous resonance for me. I still wanted to make sense of my own experience with the harp. But I also wanted to understand more about why our culture is so fearful about anomalous experiences. Could this be why so much well-conducted research in the United States hasn't been given more attention? What is the nature of that discomfort and the conflicts that underlie it? What does our collective and individual fear of these unknowns cost us? How might we start to relieve that discomfort while working to resolve the conflicts? And—very important to me—is it possible to investigate apparently anomalous experiences while remaining firmly grounded in rational thought?

I dearly value the rational world and all it enables, while facing the awareness that it's a world with no room for experiences like the harp's return. We need to address what it may take to acknowledge and appreciate both worlds, and manage to live in both at the same time. I don't insist that any reader swallow the stories in these pages as true; I consider myself a skeptical, highly trained scientific professional, and feel that that perspective is essential if we're to make any creditable analysis of anomalous events. After fourteen years of studying such phenomena with my skepticism firmly in place, I believe that these vast arrays of experiences deserve our serious attention.

The stories in this book, along with the questions they raise, have led me to consider an inescapable possibility. As human beings, might we be capable of a connectedness with other people and every other aspect of our material world so profound that it breaks all the rules of nature as we know it? If so, it's a connectedness so radical as to be practically inconceivable. In this book, I'll suggest how we can start to render such a radical connectedness more conceivable by making a new kind of sense out of it. We can begin by looking to certain transactions that we haven't conceptualized before, transactions that take place between the realms we call mental and material. They're transactions that occur between the realm of unconscious mental processing—as understood by contemporary psychology, neuroscience, and cognitive science—and the realm of intangible physical dynamics, which fields such as quantum physics are beginning to explore.

I'll suggest that these transactions are characterized by a paradox that helps explain why we haven't acknowledged them, much less found ways to understand them. They reflect human capacities to which we can't gain access in the customary ways. They're peculiar capacities in that they're *least* likely to become available when we deliberately try to access them. We cannot reach these new sources of information simply by "tuning in" to something new; paradoxically, we must also "tune out" much of the ordinary information that continually bombards our senses. While some people appear born with an innate gift for doing that, it may be possible for the rest of us to learn to develop precisely that same quality of awareness, an awareness that might result in a subjectively felt state of profound connectedness to other human beings and to every aspect of the material world around us. If that state exists and we can achieve it, we may also develop distinct perceptual capacities, including an intuitive intelligence whose development and training our culture has largely overlooked. Refining and educating such an intelligence has huge implications for how we see the world because it changes what we're able to see, changing what we're able to know as a result. It may render the intuitive knowing we currently call extraordinary and anomalous not only possible but downright ordinary.

Ultimately, this is a book about what we know and how we know it. As I've come to believe, extraordinary knowing may not be so extraordinary after all, but part of ordinary knowing that we simply haven't known how to account for. If that's true, we might start inhabiting our world with a different, radically more hopeful outlook for our future.

2

Going Public with Private Knowing:

Breaking the Silence

A NEUROSURGEON of world-class reputation calls me. He's been suffering from intractable headaches. Despite exhaustive medical workups, no physiological cause for them can be found. In desperation, he's called for a psychological consultation—a last resort, in his view.

During our first appointment, he begins to describe his work. He's passionate about it. He is also supremely successful. When heads of state need brain surgery, he's flown in to operate. His reputation rests not just on the brilliance of his technique but even more on his astonishing track record. He undertakes one dangerously life-threatening surgery after another, yet he tells me, humbly and with quiet gratitude, "I never seem to lose a patient." He has a loving marriage and wonderful children. He can't think of anything troubling him, no obvious subconscious source for the crippling headaches that are destroying his life.

I probe a little, looking for some hint of possible conflict, anxiety, or pain. He, on the other hand, keeps going back to his work, lighting up as he talks about it.

And then it occurs to me that he hasn't mentioned doing any teaching, even though he's on the staff of a big university hospital. So I ask: Does he teach residents? He looks away, suddenly silent. Finally, he speaks:

"No, I don't teach at all anymore."

"But you did? What happened?"

"I had to stop."

"You *had* to?"

"Yes...I couldn't keep it up....But I miss it. I loved teaching. As much as surgery itself, I loved it....But I had to stop...."

He falls silent again. Gently I probe further. *Why* did he have to stop? And then slowly, reluctantly, the surgeon tells me what he's never told anyone. He can't teach anymore because he doesn't believe he can teach what he's really doing. He tells me why his patients don't die on him. As soon as he learns that someone needs surgery, he gets himself to the patient's bedside. He sits at the patient's head, sometimes for thirty seconds, sometimes for hours at a stretch. He waits—for something he couldn't possibly admit to surgery residents, much less teach. He waits for a distinctive white light to appear around his patient's head. Until it appears, he knows it's not safe to operate. Once it appears, he knows he can go ahead and the patient will survive.

How, he asks me, could he possibly reveal that? What would the residents think? They'd think he was crazy. Maybe he *is* crazy. But crazy or not, he knows that seeing the white light is what saves his surgeries from disaster. So how can he teach and *not* talk about it? It's a horrible dilemma. He's adopted the only possible solution: he's quit teaching.

And when did your headaches begin? I ask him. Startled, he looks up at me. It hits him and hits him hard.

"*That's* interesting," he says. "The headaches started two years ago. And I remember when I noticed the first one. It was the day I resigned from teaching, right after I told the dean...."

The neurosurgeon and his white light exemplify a conflict.

What happens when you have an anomalous experience, but you're afraid to acknowledge it? If you admit to the experience, you run the risk of being disbelieved or thought crazy. It's a profoundly destructive conflict, one that stops us as a society from looking for ways to discover and develop new knowledge. And one that stops us as individuals from embracing our reality.

We pay a price for denying our personal experiences of what's real. Our self-betrayal becomes a slippery slope. We begin to feel helpless and dishonest; we don't allow ourselves to think certain thoughts. We reject any reminders of the inadmissible. We develop troubling symptoms as our minds work overtime to keep firmly outside our conscious awareness what we dare not admit. Our lives shrink as a result. The neurosurgeon with his headaches was an emphatic demonstration of how the fear of appearing credulous or crazy leads many people to disavow their reality, which can paralyze their creativity, conscience, and freedom to be themselves.

Freud himself grappled with this issue. He had an early fascination with the idea that thoughts from one person's mind could somehow be transferred to the mind of another, and had engaged in an extensive correspondence with Hungarian psychiatrist Sándor Ferenczi on the subject. Throughout that correspondence, Freud asserted that "thought transference"—his term for telepathy or ESP—was a thoroughly real and important aspect of how humans communicate. But he also insisted it was too politically dangerous even to discuss in public, much less credit. He repeatedly warned Ferenczi to keep the issue quiet to preserve their reputations as men of science.[1] (It's impossible not to wonder how the course of research into anomalous events would have been affected had Freud chosen to publicly embrace this avenue of exploration. I'll discuss this fascinating correspondence in greater depth in Chapter 6.)

For several years, I continued to record my colleagues' experiences and to use my broadening understanding of such anomalies to help my patients. Then, in 1997, I took a step further. Carol Gilligan, Ph.D., a member of the faculty at Harvard, invited me to join her in teaching an advanced graduate seminar where we would discuss theories of knowledge. Carol is an internationally renowned psychologist and author, most famously of the pioneering book *In a Different Voice: Psychological Theory and Women's Development*. Carol and I had often discussed Harold and the harp, along with other stories I'd heard. What, we asked ourselves, could those stories teach us about how we know what we know? How might they affect clinical practice? How does the eagerness to tell such stories, as well as the attending embarrassment, reflect on the culture of public conversation in which we live? Carol and I decided to start a discussion group to consider these questions at the biannual meeting of the American Psychoanalytic Association. With a nod to Freud, we called our group "Intuition, Unconscious Communication, and 'Thought Transference.'" We wanted only participants who were actively engaged in the issues, not voyeurs, so we made attendance contingent on submitting a written account of an apparently anomalous experience, personal or clinical.

We were promptly inundated. We accepted the first sixty people who signed up and sent letters to the other applicants saying the group was filled to capacity. Three days after the letters went out, the scientific program director for the APA left me a message: "Lisby—*do* something! Our office is overwhelmed with calls from people saying they *have* to get into this group. Call me!"

We decided to open the group to more attendees. Meantime, the accounts kept pouring in. One came from Susan Coates, Ph.D., a world authority on early childhood and a brilliant clinician. She reported the following:

> Some years ago I treated a very young girl who was four years old. In the second year of her treatment, I saw her on October second, which is the anniversary of my brother's death. He drowned while saving someone's life when I was twenty-five years old and it was a profoundly painful loss for me. It's still very much with me, especially on October second. My young patient was playing out a theme that had preoccupied her for some time when out of the blue she suddenly turned to me, and said, "Your brother is drowning—you have to save him!" The hair stood up on the back of my neck and I said to her, "No one is going to drown because we will save them,"

and she went right back to the play that she'd been involved in that had no relationship to drowning or even to being overwhelmed. I hadn't been aware of thinking about my brother at that moment, but he's often on my mind on the anniversary of the day he died. There was no way that this child could have known about this fact of my life. I believe this kind of thing happens, though infrequently, and I also think you're right to use the word "anomalous" for it. It has happened only one other time in my practice and that was with an adult who is a therapist.

Paula Hamm, a psychoanalyst who practices in Washington, D.C., submitted this vignette.

As part of my routine in the course of a week, I try to make time to sit quietly. Recently, during one of these moments, I closed my eyes and the image of a little boy came to mind. He was toddler age and was putting a plastic bag over his head. There was a sense of distress surrounding the little boy. I didn't recognize the child or the situation in this disturbing image.

Two hours later, a patient came in and started the session by saying he'd experienced a distressing situation over the weekend. He'd been busy preparing dinner in the kitchen when his little boy walked into the kitchen with a plastic bag over his head, holding the bag tight around his neck. When his father went to reach for the boy, the son ran to another part of the house. The situation became chaotic and my patient was yelling with fear for his wife. They got the bag off the child's head in time. The little boy said he'd been trying to eat the cotton candy off the inside surface of the bag.

Robert Pyles, M.D., at that time president elect of the American Psychoanalytic Association, sent in a story he'd never before revealed to colleagues:

Some years ago I was diagnosed with a viral meningoencephalitis. Over the course of my being worked up, they discovered a large mass in my chest along with infiltrate throughout my lungs. It turned out to be disseminated sarcoidosis. I lost forty-five pounds and the disease seemed to be taking its expectable course—invasion of other organs and a high probability of death not too far off. I began meditating, then running, mostly to calm myself down. I had young kids, an active career—I wasn't handling the prospect of an early death well at all. Without knowing what I was doing, I felt the impulse to focus on my actual cells—my literal physical cells—as I ran. Then I began focusing on the lesions. And something very strange began happening. It will sound hallucinatory and crazy—I thought it was totally crazy at the time—but all I can say is, it was also very real and powerful. What started happening was I literally *became* those cells and those lesions while I ran. And once that happened, the lesions started getting smaller. I *became* the lesions resolving. I watched them resolving and I *was* them resolving.

And sure enough, the mass started decreasing and after three years the infiltrate was gone. *Gone.* Eventually the mass totally disappeared. In fact, I was written up in a medical journal—a spontaneous resolution of a disseminated sarcoidosis that was entirely unexpected and unexplained.

The evidence for what happened is medically irrefutable. I myself am sure that running got me into a state of mind that enabled me to affect those cells and those lesions by—strange as it sounds— becoming them. That experience didn't just change my life because I was cured—it also opened a world of possibilities about connections between things we're normally unaware of, connections rooted in access to certain states of mind.

The APA discussion group teemed with impeccably creden-tialed professionals eager to tell stories like these, stories they nor-mally didn't feel safe enough to divulge. We all recognized that we needed an ongoing forum for systematic consideration and investi-gation of apparently anomalous experiences, and agreed to con-tinue to meet.

Soon thereafter, I was introduced by a mutual friend to Carole W. Morgan, Ph.D., a psychologist from Los Angeles. Carole had a paper written by her friend Robert J. Stoller, M.D. Stoller was a psychoanalyst, psychoanalytic theorist, and researcher, as well as professor of psychiatry at UCLA Medical School. He'd authored eleven books and innumerable scholarly articles covering topics from cross-cultural studies to pornography to gender identity to revolutionary work on female development before his death in a traffic accident in 1991. His perspectives were invariably bold and innovative. I'd admired his work for years and told Morgan I was eager to see the paper.

The paper was titled "Telepathic Dreams?" Stoller had written it in 1973, but never attempted to publish it. Instead, he'd shown it to Ralph Greenson, his mentor and an icon in the history of American psychoanalysis. Greenson had read it, sprinkled it with his own handwritten notes, and then given Stoller his advice: if Stoller valued his professional future, he would put the paper away in a drawer and forget about it. At the same time, Greenson told Stoller that he'd found the paper utterly convincing, was shaken by reading it, and that his own thinking about the human mind had been permanently affected by it.[2]

The paper started this way:

> ... Although these experiences began in 1960, I have hesitated ever since to report them, they having as yet no respectable explanation. I am not intrigued with the subject of telepathy nor a devotee of that literature, usually feeling the reports I chance upon to be foolish or fraud. Having finally decided to present these data, I shall not like having directed at me the sort of derogatory thoughts I often have when others broach the subject. But the data—seemingly telepathic dreams—appear more than coincidental; perhaps it is time to take a look....

One Thursday in 1960, Stoller continued, he'd gone to see Greenson, for whom he was then doing supervisory work as a candidate. He'd walked in, offered his usual perfunctory greeting, and inquired after Greenson's health. Greenson replied that he was fine, but that over the weekend he'd had a terrible experience. His son, Danny, had lost control of a motorcycle in San Francisco and been admitted to the hospital with a compound comminuted fracture of his left leg; he now might not be able to start medical school on time.

Stoller was, as he put it, absolutely astonished. That previous Saturday night, he'd dreamed that he was back in the emergency room of the San Francisco hospital where he'd worked as an intern. The dream was a vivid one, and the emergency room appeared just as he remembered it. But the central action entailed something that had never happened while he'd been there: a medical student was brought in with a compound comminuted fracture of the left leg.

The Monday following Stoller's dream, he'd described it in detail to his own analyst, who, Stoller wrote, had reason to note its resemblance to the weekend's events, since he was a close personal friend of Greenson's and knew about the accident, although he said nothing to Stoller at the time.

That was the first in a series of bewildering experiences for Stoller. A pattern soon emerged. Typically, a patient would come in for a Monday session, report dreams he or she had had over the weekend, and the dreams would turn out uncannily to duplicate events in Stoller's life over the same weekend. Stoller began taking copious verbatim notes on his patients' dreams, from which he quoted at length in his paper.

DREAM 1:
There was a party going on at somebody's home. There was a big crowd of people milling around in a large room, which instead of having a wall had one whole side made of glass. An older man whom I do not know but who was very kindly was there. He walked by me carrying some large object and suddenly smashed through the glass. I was terribly frightened that he was hurt, and yet in some strange manner he was not. There was glass all around.

Over that same weekend, Stoller had been at a party where someone had given a speech. After the talk, he'd offered to help move chairs through the sliding glass doors on one side of the room. Stoller, not recognizing that one panel was closed, crashed through it. No one was hurt, though the floor was covered with shattered glass.

The pattern continued, as patients told him dream after dream.

DREAM 2:

A man explained to me a new invention. It's a new way to build and market homes. What he showed me was a big, central concrete pole. On this could be hung individual rooms that one could buy at the store, in any number and in any style.

The day before, Stoller had spoken with a friend about an innovative architectural scheme. It involved plans to market a central concrete core, upon which could be hung prefabricated rooms of any size and number.

DREAM 3:

I'm walking through a house that is under construction. I walk from one end to the other; I get to the part that is to be the bathroom and see that they are building a sunken bath. Someone had put an initial in the still-soft cement.

Unbeknownst to the patient, Stoller was in the midst of building a new house. Over the weekend, he'd been inspecting work done the day before. He discovered that the terrazzo surrounding a newly installed sunken bath had been vandalized, with an initial inscribed in the drying cement.

As patient after patient reported dreams with striking correspondence to Stoller's waking life, he grew increasingly uncomfortable about the situation. Yet it took him thirteen years after that first dream about Greenson's son to write his paper, which he ended on a highly tentative and inconclusive note: "Besides finding the whole subject [of telepathy] alien to my scientific beliefs, I have also hesitated to write this up because of not knowing if something right or wrong is going on in me. If, someday, it is found that such experiences reflect an ordinary enough function of human psychology, it will seem quaint that I was uneasy."

After I'd read the paper, I called Stoller's widow. She told me that Stoller had overcome his uneasiness and returned to the paper in the years prior to his sudden death, a fact Carole Morgan confirmed. He'd become convinced that the far reaches of unconscious communication, telepathy included, were the single most exciting frontier awaiting a Western science of mind. He regretted having abandoned the paper I'd just read. Mrs. Stoller wanted to see a respectable journal publish the paper, so long as there was no damage to her husband's reputation.

I offered to help. Here was a paper on a controversial topic from a distinguished and revered scholar, one that offered a glimpse into a part of Stoller's mind that he'd kept hidden from public view while he was alive. The paper was clearly unfinished. Had Stoller tried to publish it during his lifetime, reviewers would certainly have seen plenty to question, not to mention plenty that begged for revision. But as a posthumous work, such unanswered questions and potential revisions were beside the point. The paper would stand exactly as Stoller originally intended: an inconclusive and exceedingly tentative look at a mass of utterly puzzling data.

I submitted Stoller's paper to the *Journal of the American Psychoanalytic Association,* the flagship journal of American psychoanalysis, with my own introduction and epilogue to place it in the context of other work on unconscious communication. When it was published in 2001, it drew a host of letters and e-mails, most with their own accounts of personal anomalous experiences, with the now-typical comments that the writers had rarely before, if ever, revealed these experiences in a professional forum. I added these accounts to my growing files.

While I was readying the Stoller article for publication, I went to Barcelona for a conference. There I met Patrick Casement, a distinguished psychoanalyst from London whose books on clinical technique are considered classics the world over. He'd heard about my experience with the harp and asked if I wanted to hear about an experience he'd once had. It wasn't long before I was writing down every word of his account:

> In 1952, when I was seventeen, I was staying with my father's mother for my Easter holidays. That week, my grandmother told me she had only one real regret in her life. During the war, when people kept

moving from one address to another, she lost touch with her dearest friend. Many attempts to trace her had resulted only in returned letters.

My grandmother lived about four miles from the little church my parents usually attended. I was to go to the service there on Easter Day. Afterwards, I decided to walk the four miles back rather than wait forty minutes for the bus, because I was wanting to test out my solution to a familiar school mathematics question. I had worked out exactly how fast I would have to walk so the bus wouldn't catch me up. If my calculations were wrong, I would admit defeat by taking the bus for the rest of the journey. I was absolutely determined to walk those four miles at just the right pace, to prove that I'd worked it all out correctly.

However, after about twenty minutes, I was shocked to find that—in what I can only call a reflex action, as though my right arm had suddenly taken on a life of its own—I put out my right hand to thumb down one particular car. I was utterly astonished to watch myself defeating my own purpose. To my relief, the car drove past— my race against the bus was, I thought, not to be spoilt. But a moment later the car suddenly stopped. Since, regrettably, I had thumbed it down, I felt I had to accept the offered lift.

I got into the front beside the chauffeur. I imagined he had first driven by and chosen to ignore me, but had then been told to stop by the lady in back. So I turned to her, and simply said, "Thank you."

She immediately asked, "Were you at Winchester?" I had no idea what had prompted the question but I replied that, in fact, I was currently at that school.

She replied, "If you are there now, you won't know the person I am thinking of. He was called Roddie Casement and he went to Winchester, but that must have been a long time ago now." When I told her that she was actually speaking of *my father,* the lady was delighted, and immediately asked, "Is his mother still alive?" I informed her that she was, and that we would soon be driving past her door, two miles down the road we were on. The lady then told me a story almost exactly parallel to the one I had been hearing from my grandmother all week. This lady had been trying to trace her very close friend—my grandmother—ever since they had lost touch during the war. She was, in fact, the friend my grandmother had been seeking for ten years. They spent that day together—probably their last chance, as my grandmother died soon thereafter.

Perhaps this lady saw a physical similarity between myself at seventeen and my father at a similar age. But that does not explain why my arm took on a life of its own and suddenly thumbed a lift from that particular car, forcing me to abandon my carefully calculated walk, the last thing I wanted to do. What I do know is accepting that lift meant my grandmother died happily, having finally met up with her beloved friend.

Over the next six hours, Casement shared numerous other accounts of anomalous experiences he'd had, including several with his own patients. When we finally got up to return to the conference, I asked him: Given his prolific clinical writing, didn't he feel pressure to make these stories part of what he put out to the world? His reply was graceful but unequivocal. "I'm a reserved sort," he explained. "I feel no such pressure. These are the kinds of experiences people generally don't talk about. I accept that."

The case examples that pepper Casement's books are remarkably compelling. That's part of why people read him—they find his clinical descriptions invaluable. Instructors regularly assign his work to help students develop a keenly attuned clinical ear. Now I couldn't help wondering: how much of that compelling material was the result of listening with the clinical ear I was only now hearing about—an attunement Casement typically didn't reveal at all?

Why were so many men and women with sterling scientific pedigrees—the very cohort best qualified to undertake rigorous investigation into the phenomena—so reluctant to speak out publicly about their experiences?

At the next meeting of the APA discussion group, the power of that question came home to me. I mentioned that, while Patrick Casement hadn't written about anomalous experience, he was interested in the topic. Two younger members of the group were astonished. They'd both named him as an author by whom they'd been especially influenced. They'd both given accounts of apparently anomalous experiences they'd found troubling. Neither had revealed those clinical experiences to their supervisors; they were sure they'd be dismissed out of hand.

I reflected that, had Casement been among their supervisors, he wouldn't have dismissed them—but these admirers of his work wouldn't have known that. So students stay silent but so do their teachers, along with others who carry authority, and each side's silence reinforces the other. The people in our APA discussion group commented on exactly that phenomenon:

> I can't believe I'm finally talking about this. Why don't we talk like this in training . . . or in study groups . . . or somewhere!? I feel so invigorated by being open about these things, finally.

> There are colleagues in this room I've known for thirty years and it never occurred to me they'd be sympathetic to hearing about these experiences. This is a first for me, talking this freely.

> I was in analysis myself at the time this happened with my patient. I tried to tell my analyst about it. Eventually I realized it was no good: he simply didn't buy it. I never mentioned it again. But it was hugely important to me and I compromised myself by not talking about it. I left it out of my analysis, but as a result, my work with that analyst was limited.

> I'm Indian. In Asian culture, all this is perfectly normal, nothing anomalous about it. In medical school I found out how not-normal the things I'm describing seem to Westerners.

Our group wasn't close to making sense out of the stories we were encountering, but we were starting to come up with interesting speculations, even a few plausible hypotheses. We noticed, for example, how frequently people telling these stories used the word "attunement." That sent us to research on earliest mother-infant interaction, an arena where patterns of exquisitely coordinated mutual responsivity—attunement—have been extensively investigated.

We wondered if there might be something in the mother-infant bond that could help us explain the kind of bond that apparently facilitates anomalous communication.

We examined research on mental states associated with creativity, heightened emotional receptivity, and alterations in consciousness. We looked at research on identical twins apparently able to communicate across vast distances without any identifiable means. Several people who attended the group were experts on psychological tests of intuition. We looked at the variables associated with top scores on intuitive ability to see whether those variables were especially characteristic of people who report anomalous experiences. We invited neuroscientists to join the discussion group and help us consider which areas of the brain might conceivably process perceptual cues that feed purportedly anomalous experiences.

We were far from any definitive answers, but some of those avenues looked promising, and at least we were establishing a forum for serious exploration of extraordinary knowing. What began as a venue for raising systemic scientific questions was fast becoming a repository for a growing mass of insistently puzzling data. We were becoming a place where rational people could go public with experiences they'd previously kept to themselves—experiences they'd sequestered out of shame and anxiety—and know that their stories would receive a thoughtful, respectful hearing from other professionals.

It was a beginning.

3

Disavowing the Extraordinary:

Personal Cost and Public Consequences

W E SUFFER FROM an underlying cultural disinclination for publicly acknowledging certain highly subjective, highly personal experiences. We're especially reluctant to credit those personal and subjective factors when it comes to things we prefer to be dictated by rational and objective thinking—for example, how we do science. Or practice medicine. Or talk about exactly what enables us to know what we know. We end up exaggerating our apparent reliance on the logical reasoning that emerges from evidence we all agree is legitimate. Inevitably, we tiptoe around anomalies.

Some time ago I met a couple at a dinner party. They'd been married for over forty years. Not long into dinner, they disagreed, gently and politely, about their current crisis in dealing with the husband's aging parents. After a few minutes, the wife backed off and turned to me, slightly embarrassed that their disagreement had been aired in public. In fact, I was impressed by how she and her husband managed to stay so respectful and kind, despite viewing things differently, and I told her so. Heartened, she volunteered more:

> Everything he's just said is perfectly logical—it usually is. But I get a gut feeling sometimes I can't explain and I'll know it's right—more right than anything I can argue for. We have a good marriage because he knows the same thing. We keep it to ourselves, but he'll go home tonight and come up with a long list of reasons why he should change his mind and do just what I've said. We won't talk about it, and he has no idea how I get there, but when I get those gut feelings deep inside, he knows to go with them as much as I do. By next week we'll agree about exactly what we need to do. He'll explain it to his brothers and they'll be impressed with how clearly he thinks about things. But the solution doesn't really come from his clear thinking. That's just how he'll justify it after the fact. I don't mind because it's okay between us. He respects my gut.

In one regard, this was an ordinary bargain between members of a couple. But in this context of looking at a broad cultural tendency to disavow certain kinds of knowing, I wonder if the bargain might ultimately turn costly.

With her permission, I'd been scrawling the wife's remarks on my napkin. I asked if her arrangement with her husband ever bothered her. She shrugged.

> If he didn't respect me, it would. But he does, so who cares? He's out there in the world and I'm not. He thinks the way the world says you should think. He's good at it. I'm not, so if he goes out and does it, I don't have to try. I get to stay home and paint. I don't mind.

She doesn't mind? Again, I wonder. There's nothing anomalous about trusting your gut feelings. On the other hand, the ease with which their influence stays hidden, credited only in private—isn't that in part what keeps the neurosurgeon from publicly exposing how he relies on cues he can't justify as remotely rational? What has the young women in our discussion group carefully editing their accounts to supervisors? Ultimately, isn't this to some degree why we don't investigate apparently anomalous experience carefully, rigorously?

Halfway through our dinner, people started discussing their children. Again the wife turned to me, adding an unexpected piece to our prior conversation:

> It's funny you asked if I mind the way my husband and I have worked things out. I never used to—I never even thought about it. But in the last few weeks, I did start thinking about it, because of our daughter. She's in her thirties and her husband just walked out on her. She has small children and no career, no way of earning money, no confidence about how she's going to make it in the world. She's wise and competent and has lots of skills. *I* see that but she doesn't. She's like me—she knows plenty about all kinds of things but she keeps what she knows to herself. She doesn't know how to talk about what she knows and she's never staked out her own place in the world. She's sure she doesn't know how. She's never claimed recognition for who she is. She let her husband do all that for her— like me.
>
> Now she's terrified and I'm thinking it's partly my fault. What's worked for me isn't working for her. She's not prepared for life without a husband who does all the things my husband does for me. He's my face to the world. Maybe I could have helped her be more prepared if I hadn't been so content to hide behind my husband and his ease with thinking the way the world wants you to think.

Ultimately, this wife is talking about disempowerment. Privately, with her husband, she feels valued and loved, and that mitigates and maybe even eradicates whatever sense of disempowerment she might personally have had to face. But suddenly her daughter's dilemma has put her own lifetime bargain in a new light. She's seeing how that bargain can cost.

Most of us recognize what it's like to disavow some piece of knowing that feels rationally indefensible, whether or not we've ever come close to an apparently anomalous experience. I began to think about how these disavowals fall along a spectrum. At one end of that spectrum lies our refusal to go public with any mildly unusual experiences until they've been translated into the appearance of logic. At the far end comes our disavowal of events as apparently weird and extraordinary as that neurosurgeon's white light. Or the panicked outburst from Susan Coates's child patient—"Your brother is drowning—you have to save him!" Or Patrick Casement's impulse to hail a ride he's sure he doesn't want, but that enables his grandmother to rediscover her long-lost friend.

Maybe, regardless of where along the spectrum our personal disavowals happen to fall, examining what they have in common can help us grapple with the extraordinary knowings at the far end, those that trouble us the most.

I decided to ask other medical professionals whether they routinely sequestered certain things from public exposure when they talked about their work, and if so, what and why.

I started by meeting with a nurse's assistant who cares for premature infants. I'd heard she was remarkably gifted at what she did. Under her eye, highly stressed babies thrive with an ease far beyond their prognosis. I told her I was interested in whether she understood what made her so unusually good at her work, and whether she ever talked about that with co-workers. She was prompt and emphatic in her reply: "Girl, you think I'm crazy?"

She saves babies' lives, she says, because she's often able to sense just when a baby's about to hit serious trouble. But she never tries to explain that to supervisors anymore. She'd tried when she was younger, but she couldn't come up with explanations anyone found satisfying—they just criticized everything she said. So she'd made the decision to waffle instead, saying a change in the baby's color or pulse rate tipped her off. In other words, she decided to lie.

> I just get a hunch. I *know.* I have no idea how I know. The more I've learned to trust those hunches, the more I get them. There are some nurses and some doctors who say, "You *go* with your hunches, girl—your hunches are *good!*" They trust my hunches. But I know who

likes hunches on the unit and who wants facts. If they want facts, they mostly don't want to hear about my hunches. . . .

I'm good. I'm better than lots of the people who like facts. They know I'm good but they trust me more if I lie about the facts than if I'm honest about my hunches. That's pretty strange, but it's true. I like facts, too, but lots of the time they don't tell me what I need to know. My hunches have saved a lot of babies.

One doctor tells me my hunches are facts. I think he might be right. But they're not facts I ever learned. He's unusual. I think he might get hunches like I do. Once I tried to ask him, but he just joked back at me. He wouldn't tell me. I thought it was funny he can call my hunches facts, but not *his* hunches. . . . Maybe that comes from being a doctor.

I shared my notes from the nurse's assistant with Bette Flushman, infant development specialist at the Neonatal Intensive Care Unit of Children's Hospital and Research Center at Oakland, California. She wasn't surprised.

When medical conditions are extreme, the infant's subtle cues really matter. These cues are the infant's language, a language that is very hard for most of us to recognize or understand. The infant tries to tell us of comfort and stress levels often before the medical technology alerts us. That nurse's assistant probably does save babies. Her hunches are about intuition, or more precisely, her ability to understand and interpret the infant's subtle language and her ability to communicate with the tiny, medically fragile infants in her care.

Intuition is a daunting challenge to articulate because it's not objective. In an intensive care environment, it may show up like this: Two infants weighing two pounds are in incubators next to each other. The first gets changed and bathed by a nurse who is highly skilled and manages one effective move right after another. But five minutes later, that baby's monitor alarms go off, indicating that she is medically stressed. The nurse with the other baby executes all the same caregiving tasks, but she is in tune with the baby, letting her hand nestle the baby's foot or stopping during the bath to cradle the baby's head with her hand, adjusting her touch to the baby's apparent need for comforting during and even after each task. And just that touch, at just those moments, with just that pressure, at just that place, leads to some tiny, tiny relaxation in the baby's foot, in the baby's body, in the baby's being. The baby relaxes and mobilizes her resources to cope with what is happening and with what comes next. A caregiver who knows how to look for this kind of communication can make all the difference.... There's nothing anomalous about it... and it does save babies.

I'd bet your nurse's assistant relates this way to babies all the time. She's telling you that her supervisors don't want to hear about her understanding of the babies, her knowing. She must answer staff in ways that are certain, reliable, prescriptive, with facts.

Yet that doctor she talked to, he is right. Her hunches *are* facts— just different facts.... In a highly technological environment such as a neonatal intensive care unit, it can be hard, or nearly impossible, to recognize what we see and know on a human level with these tiny infants. The learning that is objective and task based has such importance that it becomes easy to ignore or doubt the hunches, or as I prefer to say, the understanding of the very subtle language of the baby. It is people like this nurse's assistant who bring so much to the medical care and development of the tiny, fragile infants in intensive care.

Michael Ripley, D.C., DACBSP, is an alternative medicine sports physician who is a treating doctor for members of the U.S. Olympic track and field team. (He helps with performance enhancement and deep tissue work, among other interventions.) He works with an approach to treating injury without surgery whenever possible and instead relies on various forms of exceedingly subtle tissue release, what he calls working internally, which he does by dividing the body into three planes of movement based on the internal anatomy of connective tissue. Using this method, his success rates greatly improved.

Dr. Ripley has been extraordinarily effective in treating overuse syndromes of many kinds. Nineteen athletes whom he's treated have gone on to win Olympic medals. He's treated forty-six world champions in all. He says that with his techniques, which meld conventional, alternative, and intuitive medicine, resolution rates with peripheral nerve entrapment and carpal tunnel syndrome run at roughly 90 to 95 percent, versus the more conventional 25 percent success rate with surgery.

When I got in touch with Dr. Ripley to discuss his work, he told me he'd left the public hospital where he'd seen patients for a number of years. It wasn't the best environment for him, he said tactfully. When I asked him why, he replied:

> Frankly, I do things that simply aren't part of ordinary orthopedic medicine in this country. I'm regularly asked to consult to the U.S. Army, major HMOs, and medical training programs all over the world. I work with tissue release with actual physical manipulation but at a very intuitive, very nuanced, very subtle level. My colleagues and I figured out a new methodology for physical release of muscle tension based on cutting-edge science, and it was really effective. But sometimes all the scientific methods we knew wouldn't work, and I'd try something new and it would get results. I'd get an intuitive conceptualization of how something might work and I'd try it; I worked with intuitive information I received. I used my intuition to improve the scientific information. I was in a perpetually compromised situation with the top surgical group at my hospital. The younger doctors were more open to alternative medicine; the older, more dogmatic doctors weren't. Frankly, I got tired of it. I've moved away from the hard-core, dogmatic, more rigid sides of medicine. Now I only see people privately. I prefer to work one-on-one with athletes. I've trained plenty of people, so the work I do gets out there.... But it's not the way it should be. People don't get the best care. They don't get *honest* care. It's not good for anybody.
>
> Whenever I have a problem I can't resolve, I always turn to my intuition. I've always had pretty good success in this line of work, using intuition and persistence.

Ripley didn't have the kind of internal conflict that tormented the neurosurgeon who saw white light around his patients' heads, nor did he have the surgeon's debilitating headaches, because he was open about his way of knowing. He'd simply grown tired of dealing with senior colleagues on a daily basis who, while sending him patients and lauding his work in private, wouldn't go public with how they relied on him. His colleagues' silence sprang from their reluctance publicly to acknowledge a form of knowing that appeared inexplicable—and inexplicably effective.

A young physician from the Midwest contacted me for advice. She'd been practicing medicine for six years and had decided to take time off. She wanted to learn about complementary approaches—acupuncture, meditation, visualization. She wasn't sure what she was after, but she knew she needed a change in professional direction. She wasn't loving medicine anymore; she'd found herself retreating from her work and questioning everything. She'd recently taken a staff position at the medical center where she'd trained and continued to work closely with a senior member of her department whom she greatly admired. Recently, however, she'd had several disconcerting experiences with him:

> He's a great doctor. Wise, skilled, good with patients, but he's senior and used to being right. He doesn't like being wrong—at all. He's always urged me to have more confidence in myself, to go with what I think. I *have* gotten more confident over time, mostly about how I talk to patients and how I listen to them. That's the best part of practicing medicine for me. I get to know my patients better than a lot of attending physicians do. I'm really there for them and because of that my patients connect to me very strongly. It's very close and personal. I like how that feels, it's personally satisfying. But I also think it helps me pick up on things about my patients' conditions. Because I'm so involved in getting to know them, it's like I have a sense of smell—a literal *smell*—for how things are with them.
>
> I certainly smell death. That's not uncommon, though; I've heard other doctors say that. For me, it's more. I even smell—it sounds strange—just where in the body disease is. It's odd. It comes with a kind of certainty that is like smell, any smell that's strong and overpowering. You *know* you smell it, there's no doubt.

But the thing I get—it's ephemeral, too, like smell. It comes and then it's gone. I try to hold on to it and pin it down but I can't.

Over the past year, there've been a few times that's happened when it gave me a different impression about a patient than my boss had. I tried being confident like he'd encouraged me to be, but that meant telling him I thought he was wrong. He didn't like it and I backed down. Once, the one time it really mattered, the patient died. My boss's diagnosis was wrong and mine was right.

But I couldn't explain myself. What could I say—I got a *smell?* I want to know more about whatever the thing I'm calling smell is. I'm picking up on something I can't explain and I know it's important. I want to know more about it so I don't keep getting scared into backing down and doubting myself.

I told this young doctor that what especially interested me about her story was the pressure that she, like many other people, felt to disclaim something she was sure she knew but couldn't adequately explain. I told her I was writing about just that and that I found her account moving and evocative. Would she give me permission to quote her? She replied with an easy yes and seemed pleased.

But some weeks later I got a phone message from her. She'd rethought things. She was worried that her quote might get back to her mentor and hurt her career. The more she thought about it, the more she started doubting what had really happened—so much so that she'd looked up the medical records from each patient about whom she and her boss had disagreed. That helped a little—it turned out she *was* remembering everything correctly. She'd been right and he hadn't. But she still worried it might cause trouble to say so. I was welcome to use her story but only if I disguised her identity. She still hoped that anything I said about her, anonymously, might somehow be helpful to other people.

I was most struck by how very poignant this doctor's message was. She wanted her story told, she was just afraid to be held accountable for it.

There couldn't be better evidence for our disavowals—and their cost.

The stories from medical professionals were sounding the same notes over and over. Each was about deeply personal, deeply subjective moments of intuitive knowing, and about a sense that it isn't always acceptable or safe to reveal that knowing.

What if more highly regarded professionals were to speak openly about their experiences, including those we haven't yet managed satisfactorily to include inside Western science? Things, in fact, that science regularly dismisses out of hand? Wouldn't that encourage others to step forward? Including precisely the kind of highly trained, highly creative minds who could help move us forward with rational, scientific consideration of apparently anomalous experience?

I thought back to my sessions with the neurosurgeon plagued by headaches after he'd given up teaching. He told me that he'd been trained by a brilliant chief of surgery who was happy to teach him crucial technical skills, but who shied away from discussing what he considered the art of surgery. Whenever a resident probed him about it, the chief would say, "Don't ask! Forty years' experience and you'll know what you're doing like I do. I can't tell you what I do and if I could, you wouldn't know what to make of it. Shut up and watch." The neurosurgeon was beginning to appreciate how he'd participated in a medical subculture that robs clinical wisdom of its guts, its intuition. He said of his chief of surgery, "I know chances are he never saw anything like my white light. That happens to be my weird thing. But he gave us a killer message anyway—don't talk about whatever you know that makes you really good. Keep that to yourself. He wasn't just telling us how it's a damn hard thing to talk about. The killer was how he told us: don't even try."

Then the neurosurgeon tried to imagine himself confiding his white light story to a colleague, and asking, "What do you make of it?" He told me:

That chief of surgery is the last guy I'd tell. He says he's got his own secrets. Does that make him the guy I'd pick? Does that make him easier? Not on your life. I'll bet dollars against nickels that guy's scared to death the stuff he doesn't talk about might be just as crazy as my white light. Whatever makes him a genius—and he is, no question—I'm not sure he wants to know what's behind it. But I can promise you, what he really doesn't want is to discover anything in himself that makes him feel as crazy as that white light makes me feel. . . . It could upset—and I mean seriously upset—a lot of apple carts.

This neurosurgeon had hit on a truth that's larger than a particular form of anomalous knowing. He'd come upon the spectrum of disavowals. He was linking the secrecy with which he himself had shrouded his own experience to the chief of surgery's injunction—don't ask questions about apparently inexplicable knowing. The primrose path of disavowal begins with our decision not to talk about intuitive knowledge that appears thoroughly routine: the normal, expectable consequence of accumulated clinical experience. But the path becomes steeper and thornier as we begin to disavow the knowing that seems more private, more anomalous, and the disavowals take more and more mental work, more inner compromise, to maintain. We cut off increasingly larger segments of ourselves, giving up anything that reminds us of what we don't want to know. The farther down that path we travel, the more disempowered we're likely to feel, the more we lose a sense of our own authenticity. That's troubling but it's also potentially illuminating. It may help us see how, starting at the earliest and most accessible end of that path, we can begin to reverse the pattern.

But there's another implication to this spectrum of disavowals. If the neurosurgeon was right about the underlying fear he attributed to his chief of surgery, it suggests that we are motivated to disavow events at the more ordinary end of the spectrum because we're even more afraid of the strange happenings at the further end. If we insist on cloaking even the most ordinary intuition with silence, we're much less likely to have to acknowledge knowing that might, as the neurosurgeon put it, "upset a lot of apple carts."

To look behind those disavowals, even the ordinary ones, we must examine a kind of data that isn't our usual scientific fare, the deeply personal, highly subjective, and insistently private ways in which intuitive knowing manifests itself.

There's something startling about the idea that examining what's most personal, subjective, and private constitutes the way into any scientific exploration. But that may be exactly why we've made so little progress investigating the extraordinary. I was struck with this again and again as I moved deeper into the existing science on phenomena such as remote perception or telepathy. In their efforts to study anomalous phenomena, researchers have largely resorted to studying things like whether a person in one room can, with odds significantly beyond chance, accurately guess whether someone in another room is holding a red or black card. They've been looking for the objective, something characterized by simple yes/no, right/wrong answers. Those are hardly the data we can designate as most personal, subjective, or private. In that sense, the vast banks of accumulated data about, say, card reading, *may be essentially irrelevant to the actual experiences that most interest us.* They may miss the point.

To study those objective, digitizable data simply because we know how is like looking for our keys under a lamppost because that's where the light is instead of trying to find them where we actually lost them. If our real data—the data in those hundreds of stories I've been collecting—are distinguished by how *personal and personally meaningful they feel to the people reporting them, that personal quality becomes a critical feature of the data.* If we're designing studies that omit that personal element because we're at a loss to study it, we're dumping science firmly under a lamppost, and we'll never locate any keys.

And if that personal quality does prove critical, no wonder most people, even those passionately committed to understanding apparently anomalous knowing, find all the card-reading studies (and their ilk) dreary in the extreme. If we're going to study the real data, we'll have to apply some version of scientific method to the data where they really live and as they really are. We'll need to take on the daunting, even unnerving task of systematically investigating singular, subjective, profoundly personal experience.

Tackling that forward-looking challenge may also help us look backward, by opening a fascinating window on the history of science.

That window opens first on Galileo, the father of modern scientific empiricism. Every schoolchild learns that Galileo's ideas were revolutionary and that the Church viewed them as so threatening to established knowledge that he was censured, placed under house arrest, and threatened with torture as well as excommunication.

Yet the central idea for which Galileo was attacked, the notion that the earth revolved around the sun rather than vice versa, had been publicly and officially proclaimed ninety years earlier by Nicolaus Copernicus. In fact, it was at the urging of the Church and with the Church's blessing that Copernicus published his treatise proposing a heliocentric planetary system: *On the Revolution of Heavenly Bodies*. The Church was actually very grateful to Copernicus for his thesis. His ideas—no surprise—made it much easier to accurately calculate dates for Easter and other movable feasts determined by the full moon. Unlike Galileo, Copernicus enjoyed a ripe and comfortable old age, neither censured nor placed under house arrest, nor threatened with torture and excommunication.

How to explain the difference in how these two men were treated? The difference lay in each man's relationship to empiricism, in the sense for which we still honor Galileo: *knowledge based in experience*. As environmental scientist William Eddy pointed out in a visionary essay, Galileo declared that he knew what he knew based on his own personal sense experience. Copernicus set forth precisely the same ideas, but based his claims on hypothesis alone. Galileo changed the face of science forever by proclaiming that personal experience could lead to knowledge of the truth. Not surprisingly, the Church—the established authority, which laid claim to all knowledge by fiat—reacted full force, with unremitting determination to make Galileo disavow *not his ideas but the basis on which he asserted them to be true.*[1]

Galileo initiated a revolution not just in how we pursue *theory about theory* but in how we pursue *knowing about knowing*. This revolution has profound relevance for investigation of apparently anomalous experience. We must follow Galileo's lead and start with an empiricism grounded in personal experience, as we most honestly, most authentically are able to locate it. That means starting with data that, for the moment, show up largely in deeply personal accounts of knowing that don't appear to play by our usual scientific rules. It means rejecting the temptation to substitute other data that are easier to study, but that excise crucial features of exactly what we're trying to understand. And it means giving up the disavowals that currently sequester our real data, keeping them immune from consensual, open, and public scrutiny.

Science no longer lives inside official domination by the Catholic Church. Contemporary disavowals of knowing that challenge established knowledge are no longer enforced by threats of literal excommunication. But established knowledge hasn't stopped exerting its influence. Nor has it stopped exercising its constraints.

The nursing assistant lies. The sports doctor limits his practice. The young physician dissembles. The neurosurgeon stops teaching. The famous psychiatrist hides his paper in a drawer to his subsequent and permanent regret. They've all betrayed their own quintessential empiricism—knowing based in their own deeply personal, privately valued sense-experience.

At the moment, the stories these people tell, like my story of Harold and the harp, *are* our empirical data. Yes, they're preliminary, chaotic, and difficult to bring under systematic review. But right now they're what we have to work with. The challenge ahead entails figuring out how we can possibly begin making scientific sense out of them.

4

States of Mind:

Knowing That Doesn't Feel Like Knowing

EVERAL YEARS AGO, I was invited to a dinner where I was seated next to a champion poker player. Across from us was the owner of a large casino. Conversation between the two men was peppered with references to my neighbor's astonishing record of wins. At a certain point I joined in, addressing the casino owner: "He *can't* win all the time! You don't mean it, do you?"

Suddenly serious, the casino owner looked me in the eye: "In fact, he *does* win consistently. It's remarkable. We figure he pays his way because people line up thirty deep to watch him. But I have no idea how he does it."

I turned to my neighbor. "How *do* you do it?" He smiled, shrugged, and told me he just enjoyed playing. I pursued it. "No," I said, "really. I'm interested. If it's true, what can you tell me about it? How do you think you do it?"

The poker player sized me up; I could feel him weighing his choices about how to answer me. Then he made his decision.

"Okay," he said. "Okay, I'll tell you the real truth about how I win. It's simple. I know what the other guy's cards are. And not because I remember what's already been played. I know because I *see* his cards; I know exactly what he's holding. But here's the key. *I know—but I know that I don't know at the same time.* That's the truth about how I do it."

The poker player was a prominent West Coast medical professional, someone eminently rooted in rational thinking. He'd given a lot of attention to understanding—in fact, writing about—the brain and its functions. But the state of mind in which he knows exactly what cards his opponent is holding is a state neither he nor any neuroscientists have devoted much time to mapping. It's a state he felt frankly unable to comprehend, because it bears no relationship to the brain-mind models with which he's familiar. This paradoxical state of mind felt so bizarre that he'd even found himself refusing to believe it existed, much less should be taken seriously.

Four years after our dinner, the poker player wrote me a letter. He was still living with paradox, but had adopted a different approach toward it:

> At the time that we had that dinner, it was true that I consistently won, often despite bad odds. However, subsequently, I had a period in which I never could "see" the cards. As a result, I stopped playing. Every few months I'd go back and test the waters, but to date, the "feeling" has not returned.
>
> Mind you, I had this "feeling" intermittently for many years, and its absence could be merely a statistically temporary event, but it feels distinctly different, as though I no longer have access to this "information." Conversely, I began to feel as though I knew that the other player was going to get a card that would beat me. As a result, I stopped playing nearly a year ago.
>
> Now, looking back, I'm not sure that I had any true knowledge, as opposed to riding a wave of remarkable coincidence. On the other hand, my sense that the cards were going against me could also be seen as a different form of the same knowledge.

What also is of interest is that, during such periods of positive "feeling," I have had the sense that more was coming—i.e., positive feedback. Now it all seems like a distant dream.

Perhaps this is why I'm working on understanding ignorance and the limits of knowledge (neurologically as opposed to just logically).

I called the poker player after I got his letter. He tried to articulate his ambivalence about his experience: "Part of me says to you, *prove* it was true! Prove it wasn't just a run of good luck, statistically unlikely but perfectly explicable. Another part of me feels nostalgia. Something different *was* happening then; I did feel I had access to something. It was good, it was real, but now I'm not sure. I wish it were true . . . but I don't know."

What was the "it" for which this man was so nostalgic? I didn't sense he was yearning to win again at poker, nor even for a certainty he once had and had now lost. Instead, he seemed to be yearning to dance once again with that paradoxical state of mind he inhabited. While he was playing poker, he'd played with the paradox. He'd surrendered to it, acted on it, watched himself acting on it, shrugged at how little he'd understood it, and gone ahead anyway, amazing himself and everybody else with what unfolded. Now he was fighting to be certain it had ever really happened and it pained him that he couldn't hold on to that certainty. The more he tried, the more he failed and the more he questioned whether any of it could really have happened at all.

The poker player's second-guessing himself reflects one of the first predicaments we face when we have an apparently anomalous experience. Looking back on it, it seems unbelievable. And when something seems unbelievable, we usually try to make it happen again. That's how we prove it really did happen in the first place. That's why we replicate experiments in science. We try for the same in everyday life. *"Do it again!"* roar children at a party, poised between belief and unbelief as they watch a magician pull rabbits out of a hat. *"Can* he do it again?" they wonder. *"Show* us—show us *again! Then* we'll believe it!"

But our instinct for replication sets us up for a huge problem in the effort to understand anomalous knowing. We can only set the stage for replication by instigating control. Experimental controls are an attempt to do away with chance and random interference. They aim at giving us certainty: we *know* that we know, because we can count on making it happen again. We strive to move away from the uncertain terrain of the poker player, who can claim only, *"I know—but I know that I don't know at the same time."*

However, if we want to study anomalous knowing seriously, we'll have to reconceive our notion of replication and control. The control to which we're accustomed appears antithetical to the state of mind in which we say, *"I know—but I know that I don't know at the same time."* It's an elusive state: difficult to regulate at will, and even harder to command. It requires suspension between ordinary polarities of certainty and uncertainty, active thought and receptive attention.

As I continued to examine research on extraordinary knowing, it was easy to dismiss much of it out of hand. But I was gradually building a file of reports from some very respectable scientific minds about what appeared to be some very respectable experiments that went far beyond simple card reading. They attempted to investigate the kind of personal, subjective data I'd begun to suspect might lie at the core of understanding anomalous experience.

Every once in a while, I'd also hear about individuals who purported to excel at some form of intuitive knowing. If an account was compelling enough, I followed it up. That meant putting myself out on what felt like a highly personal limb. It meant talking with people who do this thing called clairvoyance, people who not only didn't disavow their anomalous experience, but actually embraced it in all its paradoxes. What might they teach us about a different way to think about "knowing without knowing"? I received no end of referrals from friends and acquaintances aware of my search, but the majority of them didn't pan out; these people with purported extraordinary abilities more often than not simply didn't hold up to my scrutiny. Then came a situation that encouraged me to put one of them to the test.

I'd been interviewing candidates for a managing director position, someone to run an arts organization. I'd narrowed it down to two women but was stuck between them. They couldn't have been more different. Each had great strengths and noticeable weaknesses. They'd guide the organization in utterly different directions. I did what I usually do with a tough decision: I weighed the options. It got me nowhere. I'd wake up one morning certain one would be better; the next morning, I'd be sure I should pick the other.

In the middle of my dilemma, an old friend called. He told me he'd just received an astonishingly accurate diagnosis of his medical condition—over the phone, from a woman who had no information about him except his first name. He'd called her out of the blue, on a friend's recommendation. He described in great detail what she told him. It was fascinating, and he was a friend I trusted. I ended up asking for the woman's number.

The woman, Deb Mangelus, lived on Cape Cod. I called her, leaving my number and requesting a session with her, feeling just the way I'd felt when I called Harold to find the harp: what's to lose? I got a message back: call her at 10:00 A.M., the following Saturday.[1]

I called at the appointed hour. Like my friend, I gave her only my first name. I didn't tell her anything about why I was calling, except that I'd heard of her and that I was curious about what she did. Deb moved right into an obviously rehearsed introduction. Sometimes, she said, people call her and lay out a problem they want help with. Then she focuses on the problem. Sometimes people ask her simply to tell them what she sees. They give her no background information and she just goes ahead and talks.

Skepticism at the ready, I chose the latter option. Not a word, not a hint about my managing director dilemma—in fact, it wasn't even on my mind. I was much more interested in the question of whether this woman could really do what my friend said she did.

"Fine," Deb replied. "I'll take a few seconds to be sure it's you I'm seeing. Then I'll say whatever comes to me. The whole session will be tape recorded. I'll mail you the tape when we're done."

Briefly, she was quiet. Then she said, "You're in the middle of a decision. There are two women involved. They're very different.

One is fiery, playful, someone you can have fun with. She has trouble with words. Maybe she's not always reliable. Fire is a big part of the image; I see the two of you holding hands like children, dancing around a campfire." She pauses. "The other woman is different—really different. She's very responsible. Dutiful. Orderly. The funniest thing is happening.... I keep seeing her hands and they're clasped in her lap. I simply *can't* get her to unclasp her hands."

I got that same strange, dissociative feeling I'd gotten the night I'd loaded my daughter's harp into my car at the all-night Safeway, the same sudden sensation of my world shifting in some irrevocable way. For starters, Deb's description of each woman struck me as unbelievably accurate. I'd liked the first woman a lot. She seemed like she'd be enormous fun to work with, though her writing samples were terrible and I wondered how she'd handle details. I'd been less drawn to the other woman. She seemed great on details, but I doubted if she ever got excited about what she was doing. She struck me as boring. Even more to the point was this: The second woman had managed to sit through our entire two-hour interview *holding her hands firmly clasped in her lap.* At the time I had repeatedly wondered to myself, "How can anyone possibly keep her hands so solidly clasped for this long?" After she left, I'd turned to the colleague with whom I was conducting the interview and said just that, engraving the image in both our minds.

And the fire image? The first woman had a huge head of bright red hair. I'd joked with her as she'd walked out the door, "*Now* I know what fiery red hair really means!"

Anomalous knowing? It certainly seemed that way. Clasped hands and fiery red hair? Both were notably beyond the garden-variety cliché that keeps circus fortune-tellers and weekly astrology columns in business.

Over the next two years I talked to Deb a few more times. It wasn't the shock value, even the credibility value, of details such as the image of clasped hands that kept me engaged. I told Deb nothing, or as close to nothing as I could consciously manage. But within minutes, she would tell me things that made me feel that she saw my life with a clarity my closest friends couldn't match, things I knew but hadn't yet recognized that I knew. They rang extraordinarily true and were also extraordinarily important. She pinpointed the central dilemmas, choices, situations, and desires in my life. Deb was somehow breaking every mold I recognized about how people achieve insight about themselves. She *knew* me. And I couldn't begin to explain how. Whenever I started to wonder if any of it could possibly be true, Deb tossed off another image as specific, concrete, and thoroughly unlikely as those clasped hands. And the crack in my familiar picture of things widened a little more.

After several sessions, I asked Deb if she'd talk with me about the state of mind in which she sees what she sees. Were the images really visual? Where did she think they came from? Was she seeing into my mind? Was she seeing some objective reality outside my mind?

Deb was responsive: thoughtful, interested, tentative, but willing to wonder and explore. She told me she wasn't at all sure what she was seeing. She was even less sure how she did it. Some image would just cross her mind—once it was my youngest daughter and the word *sprite*. In fact, a friend had just been watching that same daughter in our garden and remarked on her being a "real flower sprite." Amused, I'd told him it wasn't the first time the word had been used to describe her. Her fourth-grade teacher, trying vainly to help her see that her effervescence could use some control in class, had once compared her to a can of Sprite that had been violently shaken and suddenly opened. The image sent my daughter into gales of laughter for months afterward—during class. And it stuck. For years our entire family dubbed that daughter our sprite.

Another time, Deb told me I needed nourishment. I hadn't told her anything about it, but in fact I'd been off solid food for two days and had been counting the hours until I could eat again. Deb had me thinking about the word *clairvoyance. Clear seeing.*

She wasn't always right. Sometimes she'd report an image and it wouldn't ring true; I'd tell her so with an irritation I promptly regretted. My extreme sharpness made me realize that I was like my poker-playing friend: I wanted certainty. I wanted Deb to be consistently wrong—or right. No half measures. I recalled how, in my first phone call to Harold about the missing harp, he'd started off with a cheerful warning: *"I'm pretty good, maybe ninety percent, but I gotta tell you, I'm not a hundred percent.*" So much for replication. So much for the reliability and predictability I like to count on.

I explained to Deb that I was grappling with my poker player's paradoxical state of mind: *"I know—but I know that I don't know at the same time."* She began building me a picture of a different relationship to knowing: "It's true that I try to see what I see, but then I stop trying," she told me. "It takes me over—no, don't ask what 'it' is, I don't know. There isn't an 'it': it's not me, that's the point. Except it is, because it comes from deep inside me."

I asked Deb when she started seeing this way.

> It has everything to do with my mother and her many sisters. . . .
> When I was a small child and the phone rang, my mother would say,
> "Deborah, answer the phone, it's your aunt Rosie." Well, my aunt
> lived in Yonkers and we lived in Connecticut and we wouldn't speak
> to her for months. But with absolute belief, I'd pick up the phone,
> and say, "Hi, Aunt Rosie." Without surprise, my aunt Rosie would
> reply, "Hi, Deborah, how are you, baby? Is your mommy there?"
>
> I believe I was taught a certain channel of communication that I
> didn't realize was out of the ordinary until I got to first grade. I would
> answer to what I thought my teacher was saying, but it would turn
> out I was responding to what she was thinking. So I was in the hall a
> lot in first grade. . . . What my teacher thought and what she said
> were very different and I quickly learned to keep my mouth shut. . . .
> The painful environment of my childhood narrowed it down to
> hypervigilance. . . . I used the way I knew things to detect danger in
> the environment, to keep myself safe. The channel was honed by
> insecurity. The danger detector became well used when I worked as a
> nurse in high-risk settings. I intuited danger, then validated it with
> machines and scientific scrutiny.

I'd heard about other people reputed to have intuitive capacities as remarkable as Deb's. Three stood out as both exceptional in their ability to know things inexplicably and convincing in their capacity to talk about what they knew in a sane, grounded way. I scheduled times to talk with them at length: Ellen Tadd in Massachusetts, and John Huddleston and Helen Palmer, both from California.

S omeone I knew and respected had taken a workshop with Ellen Tadd and believed that her abilities held up under close inspection; she seemed worth further investigation.[2] During a trip east, I met with her in person. At the beginning of our first session, I gave her only my name, no more, and told her I just wanted her to tell me what she saw. Again, I felt every skeptical muscle in my body working.

Ellen started by looking at my right hand, which she said activated her clairvoyance, and began to describe my past lives. My wariness meter leaped into action. *Past lives?*

I said nothing, but Ellen must have sensed my resistance. "By the way," she told me, "don't worry if you don't believe in past lives. Just treat them as a metaphor. I personally find past lives a useful way to read people's histories and see how those histories influence their current lives, but it doesn't matter if you don't."

I calmed down. At least Ellen was a savvy clinician; she knew how to manage resistance. *Metaphor.* I could handle that. The conversation shifted to my daughters. Ellen said she saw that there was something out of balance between me and one of my children. That child, she said, was currently reworking a trauma from a prior life and I wasn't helping her with it. Ellen continued, "I see one of your children—a girl, I think?—as very careful, very serious about things. She seems much older than her age."

In fact, I would describe one of my daughters that way, but I quickly reminded myself that it's hardly a unique characterization. Ellen went on:

> You're trying to get her to lighten up. That's a mistake. She's reworking an experience she had many lives ago. That's what this lifetime is about for her. She was a feudal lord on the Scottish border. She'd built a little utopia there. People were well fed, content. She'd devoted her life to them. People were so content they got careless about watching the border. One night a band of Picts, some tribal group, came over the border and destroyed everything. The people were completely unprepared. All the women and children were raped,

tortured, killed. Your daughter is still carrying the terrible guilt she felt at letting her people get so comfortable they forgot how to fight.

When your daughter asks you whether she should paint the leaves on a tree light green or dark green, you think you're reassuring her when you tell her that whichever she chooses will be great. You're not reassuring her at all. For her, every decision is a decision about how to run her fiefdom, with all that consequence attached. It's life and death for her. All those people are on her shoulders. You won't help her lighten up by trying to convince her the color she chooses doesn't matter. For her, it matters totally. For her, it's not about paint, it's people's lives. You'd help her more by taking every one of her decisions just that seriously.

What Ellen told me didn't have the compelling specificity of Deb's image of clasped hands. On the other hand, the psychological truth Ellen had captured about my daughter and our relationship hit me as astonishingly apt. Even if I discounted completely the business about past lives, Ellen was absolutely right about my daughter's psychology. Even more to the point, she accurately discerned that my attempts to help my daughter worry less weren't working. That daughter does worry a lot. She loves to draw, but often asks my advice about every tiny detail of a picture. I typically tried to reassure her that any decision she made would be lovely, wonderful, good enough, but I'd been aware that the reassurance wasn't helping.

Suddenly, because of Ellen, I saw my daughter in a new way, with a clarity that was deeply illuminating and useful. I knew that what Ellen had told me was not just correct but important. No matter how petty the issue might seem to me, I was much more likely to help my daughter worry less by letting her know that I take her worries seriously. *Of course,* I think, *I should have known that.* Again I had the sense that Ellen was telling me, just as Deb did, exactly what I needed to know—what at some level I already knew, but hadn't quite let myself know that I knew.

In one sense, there's something completely familiar about the way Ellen's insight about my daughter hits home. I'm used to the way an insight feels when it's right. I've been a psychoanalyst for thirty years. I've spent thousands of hours with patients. I've experienced many thousands of moments when some truth makes all the difference because it's precisely on target, exactly what someone needs to hear. Much of my teaching is aimed at helping students hone their abilities to develop and articulate insights like that, insights that are precisely, exactly right. There's nothing more key to clinical skill. So I recognize the ingredients. I recognize insight when it feels right. What's not remotely familiar is getting there this way. How on earth did Ellen manage to get there? How did she get *me* there?

By the end of my second conversation with Ellen, I decided to ask her a specific question. I was planning a research project and had five people in mind as possible collaborators. I needed to choose one. I gave Ellen a list of all five names—only the names— and asked her to assess the virtues and liabilities of each.

Ellen was quick in her response on the first three; everything she said fit with what I already knew of them. She got to the fourth name on the list and stopped. This was a man I'd never met, but whose work I'd read; I'd planned to contact him when my research proposal was a little further along. Ellen asked his name again. She was quiet for a minute, then said she simply couldn't find him. This happens sometimes, she told me; she just couldn't make a connection. She moved on to the fifth name and once again had plenty to say.

A month or so later, I was ready to contact the man whose name had been fourth on my list. I tracked down his phone number and called; a woman answered. I told her who I was looking for. "I'm very sorry," she replied, "but he died unexpectedly about six weeks ago."

Coincidence? I compared the dates. He died exactly two weeks before Ellen and I had spoken.

I asked Ellen when she first became aware of her intuitive abilities.

I had many experiences as a child where I felt other people's feelings. I was often overwhelmed by the fact that what people were verbalizing and what I felt they were actually feeling were actually quite different. I also slept with my light on because I saw faces in the dark and I felt safer that way. I tried to talk to my father about my experiences. He was a physicist, but he felt only that I had a creative imagination. He didn't really understand what was happening to me. I sought out books for answers, but not another person. When I was nineteen, my dead mother came back and spoke to me and for the first time I realized that my sensitivity was a gift and not a problem. After that encounter I started to become comfortable with my sensitivity and worked to develop it.

I felt the crack in that familiar surface of things widen just a little more.

I next called John Huddleston, another on my list of people with purportedly unusual intuitive abilities.[3] I'd initially known John only as a member of a group of academics, scientists, and visionaries who got together once a month to exchange ideas. Some members dubbed us the Resonance Group. As John and I became better acquainted, I learned that he was a professional intuitive, and we discovered that we shared many overlapping interests.

John has been in private practice as an intuitive for thirty years, with clients throughout the country. For the past fifteen years, he has also been on the senior faculty of the Berkeley Psychic Institute, teaching others to develop their intuition. After a number of conversations, I scheduled a phone session with him. By now I was familiar with the uncanny sense, palpable throughout our conversation, that he somehow *knew* me. Half of me practically expected it.

Then something happened that I wasn't expecting. John came up with a description of a very close family member that was not only totally unlikely but profoundly disturbing. I knew this person so well that, before we ended our session, I told John that he'd been right on a lot of things, but was totally off the mark about that one person. It was simply impossible that this person would do what John told me he'd been doing.

John didn't hedge. He seemed relaxed and easy, admitting he could be wrong sometimes. But, he said, he'd stick to his guns on this one. I hung up, uneasy but refusing to doubt my sense of someone I knew and loved. Twelve days later, I received the news. Everything John had told me turned out to be accurate. I was as stunned as the rest of my family—but they didn't have to contend with the fact that someone had told me all about it twelve days earlier.

John was able to recall the first time he became aware of picking up information on a different level:

> It was in grammar school, in Wyomissing, Pennsylvania, when I was seven or eight years old. We were studying a textbook about world history. I remember the illustration in the chapter on ancient civilizations: a low-angle shot of the pyramids. Whenever I looked at it, I got light-headed, almost to the point of passing out. It was an extremely visceral experience, like being buried beneath a collapsing sand dune. If I turned the page, I would feel better immediately. The information came from a different realm, but I knew it was genuine. And the otherworldly shimmer of the experience was fascinating and compelling. Where did it come from? Jung's "universal unconscious"? Past-life recollection? I'd say the latter, because as children, each of us is much more closely knitted into that luminous world, which includes imaginary playmates, conversations with God, and glimpses of past lives. It also helped that I was raised in an atmosphere where the nonphysical was accepted. My mother was a widely respected artist, and I can recall her pausing before beginning a landscape of an old red mill, "waiting to hear what the landscape has to reveal to me," she explained. And my grandfather, who was a university professor and author, drove down from Harvard to Walden Pond in 1893 so he could read *Walden* at night by candlelight in the remains of the celebrated cabin, the better to commune with Henry David Thoreau. He also wrote verses about past-life glimpses.

I asked John to describe the state of mind he's in when he does his readings:

> It's *relaxed focus,* that's the best way to describe it. There's calm, clarity, and a receptive quality. There's also a physical component, and by that I mean I'm physically centered and grounded within

myself, not drifty and discorporate. I'm in communion with the client, the barriers are down, and they are very easy to see, but I don't merge with them in order to read them. This is not an out-of-body experience. In fact, my state of mind is surprisingly down to earth and ordinary.

I had a hard time accepting John's premise that what he was doing was by any stretch ordinary. John seemed amused at my consternation.

Ordinary? Oh yes, it's surprisingly ordinary. In fact, most people use aspects of this state of mind in their daily lives without realizing it. For instance, an important key to this state of mind is "no effort." And that's quite ordinary, because if you think of a time when you tried hard to remember something, you know the more you *tried* to remember it, the more you pushed it down within you. However, when you relaxed and *allowed* it to emerge, it bubbled right up. You accomplished that with no effort. That's how intuition works. Effortlessness. It's easier than you think. Doing a reading is as effortless as opening a garden gate and stepping into a new landscape. I simply observe the garden; I don't have to create it.

Another state of mind is discrimination. A reading is like observing a huge, moving, transforming mural: the client's health, relationships, family, joys and challenges, future—they're all there. So discerning what's important among all that is essential. Think of it as talking to a friend at a noisy, crowded party. You're able to screen out fifty other voices and hear the voice that's important. How do you do it? Well you just *do*. On a deeper level, spiritual discrimination is also what allows a mother to sleep through noisy trucks rumbling past, but awaken when her baby cries in the next room. And finally, a reading is also personally reflective, in the way psychotherapists are aware that they learn from their patients. Remember when you nurtured a friend when he or she experienced a death in the family? That was also an opportunity for you to uncover and heal some of your own unresolved grief. In a reading, both the client and the reader have an opportunity to learn, heal, grow.

The truth is that everyone is psychic. Everyone is intuitive. Most people just block it out. Parents teach their kids to be sensible. They stifle the kids, who learn that intuition is unacceptable behavior.

Helen Palmer was the last name on my list. I'd listened to a taped session she'd done with a client I knew well, and I'd been impressed by her description of people and family dynamics with which I was very familiar. She'd also written a number of best-selling books and taught courses and workshops on psychology and intuition.[4] I scheduled a phone session with her, once again telling her nothing beyond my name. She promptly focused on the fact that she saw me writing something. My first response was my familiar knee-jerk skepticism. *Lots of people write,* I said to myself. *My voice sounds educated. It's hardly a surprising guess. People write all the time. And if they don't, they feel flattered when someone tells them they're writers underneath. None of what she's saying counts as remarkable.*

Then Helen told me precisely how I was missing the boat on an article I'd been struggling to finish. And suddenly I was hearing just what I needed in order to shift gears entirely. By the end of our conversation, I had a mental outline of a brand-new paper. Two months later, it was off to the publishers. It was precisely the paper Helen told me I was wanting to write, *not* the one I thought I was writing. At the very least, she'd saved me months of unproductive work. At most, she'd salvaged a paper that was on its way to the junk heap.

Helen Palmer has written extensively about intuition and travels all over the world through her school, which teaches people to develop intuitive abilities. How does she access that intuition? I ask:

Maybe 75 percent of the process lies in getting empty enough to watch the different inputs of my mind. I follow my abdominal breath until thoughts and feelings recede. The emptiness feels very nourishing, very soft and intimate. You lose awareness of the room, your body, your face. That all goes, but there's a separate awareness that stays. I need time to get empty, so I'm not anticipating, not resisting anything that wants to appear, before I focus on anything. Otherwise I get confused about where I am inside and can't tell the difference between an accurate impression and my own fantasy projections.

Once you're internalized, you establish a focal object, not trying for anything. The focal object is an imagined representation of whatever you need to contact. It could be a meditation symbol that you want to unite with, or an inner picture of some real-world event. You focus, then wait. You doubt and you stay there anyway. You just keep shifting attention back to the focal object, until it starts to capture your attention. Then you're ready. The process is the same if you're focused on a "world" question or knowing about spiritual matters, but it takes very precise concentration for spiritual knowing.

I've used the same contemplative exercises for wrapping my imagination around a focal object for maybe thirty years. You just keep allowing the object to enhance in your imagination until it stops fluctuating. First the emptying phase, then the focusing phase. You clear the inner space, then target the object. I maintain concentration by imagining the object as beautiful until the picture in my mind becomes so vivid and believable that it starts to play itself out. I don't try for content or information. I just lose a sense of separation from the impression and take in whatever it shows. I think that focused imagination connects ordinary consciousness with a greater reality, so if you keep oscillating between enhancing the focus and receiving what it shows, a close relationship forms between the observer and the observed.

Meanwhile, you are so far removed from the room and yourself and the passage of time that you become whatever that focus is, so you know it from the inside. You participate with whatever you're reading in a certain sense. You read another person accurately because you *are* them; you know them from the inside because you've stopped being separate. Then the thing is to track how you yourself get in the way. You have to make sure your placements of attention are precise so you're not projecting. That's why my teaching is so focused on knowing yourself and what you're likely to project into a reading; that's the only way to get reliable with intuition.

Intuition operates from a different state than ordinary consciousness: quite decisively different from ordinary consciousness. If you don't know that, if you don't know how to shift back and forth between states, then you can start to feel very crazy, especially when you can't immediately verify what you know. You need a conceptual framework that keeps you feeling normal. That's essential. I did feel unstable early on, not about the states I went into, which were comforting, actually, but I felt such a terrible loneliness. I felt like a freak. As I learned more, I realized the amazing thing was to be so *located*. My clairvoyance could locate people at a distance or at different points in time, so any accuracy on my part automatically located us both in a greater reality that people need to know is kindly and real. Clairvoyance isn't a mind-to-mind thing, like reading people's thoughts. It lets us see a much larger pattern of existence.

Not every comment that Deb, Ellen, John, and Helen made had such startling impact as Deb's image of the clasped hands, Ellen's take on my daughter, John's prediction of the family member's surprising action, or Helen's course correction on my article, but there were enough of them that I was back to asking *"What if?"* What if people like Deb, Ellen, John, and Helen really could know things in ways that turn our usual definitions of time and space upside down? What if we seriously considered what that might mean, not just about what we know but also about how we gain access to knowing?

The ways these four people described the state of mind in which they access their intuitive knowing sounded strikingly similar. Even if they were doing nothing more than exercising some inconceivable acuity at reading tones of voice, the distinctive state of mind in which they did it seems worth learning more about. What *is* that state of mind? Is it really ordinary? Available to ordinary people? Might we all, in fact, have access to it?

What if?

5

Intuitive Intelligence:

The Art and Science of Union

A YOUNG FRIEND who's a rock singer drops by my house. She's very comfortable with the idea that life is filled with all kinds of strange things we'll never understand. She finds my determination to come up with ways to understand these things more peculiar than the things themselves. I'm in the middle of sorting piles of notes about the state of mind people associate with extraordinary knowing. I decide to read her a few bits.

She's delighted. She feels her view of the universe is confirmed. *"Yes!"* she says to me. *"Yes! Just try wrapping your mind around all *that*!"*

I reply, half-distracted by organizing my notes into the right folders. "No," I say, "no, it's not about wrapping my mind *around* it; it's about getting my mind *inside* it."

She looks at me with surprised interest.

"You just might be starting to get it," she says.

Am I getting it? I'm not sure. Maybe I'm closer to grasping the notion of a knowing so imbued with uncertainty that it doesn't feel like knowing at all. Maybe I'm grasping the idea of a knowing more facilitated by the knower's internal state than by our usual capacities to generate knowing on command. Maybe my offhand comment about getting my mind *inside* this kind of knowing rather than *around* it reflects something I'm learning. My young friend, who routinely relies on what she calls her "psychic antennae," seems to think so. Maybe I'm learning something about a kind of knowing more rooted in what Martin Buber called *knowing,* as opposed to *knowing about.* But I certainly don't know what it's like to know the way professional intuitives like Deb, Ellen, John, or Helen do.

Or do I?

Suddenly, bizarrely, I remember a strange, dissociated moment: a moment when, for the first and only time in my life, I might have experienced exactly what that knowing is like.

My youngest sister was living with my husband and me, finishing her last year of high school. My husband's aunt had given him an extremely showy gold watch, one he'd never wear. In a burst of generosity, he'd given it to my sister.

My sister wore it every day. But she was seventeen and careless. She'd leave it lying around in the kitchen, in the car, in the laundry room. One afternoon I was working in my bedroom when she burst in: "I can't find that watch!" We retraced where she'd been and when she'd last had it. No luck. My husband was due home in two hours. My sister was panicked; she was sure he'd be quick to notice that she wasn't wearing the watch and ask where it was. We circled back over all the places we'd already looked. We were about to give up.

And at that point something happened that was unlike anything I'd ever experienced. I was standing in our upstairs hall, near the door of my husband's study. I walked into his study: deliberately, intentionally, but with no awareness of volition on my part. It was as though I was watching myself in a slow-motion film. I walked straight to a closet in the far corner of the room, a closet I'd entered maybe twice—if that— over the course of our entire marriage. As I walked, I wasn't aware of thinking, of deciding, of choosing to do any of the things I was doing or about to do. I was just doing them. I bent down—again, it felt absolutely deliberate—and reached deep into the closet, behind a row of shoes, then behind some boxes behind the shoes. My hand went directly to a small leather case in the very back corner. I lifted out the case, stood up, and opened it. Inside was the watch.

Weirdly, I felt neither surprise nor excitement; I simply expected it. I walked out of my husband's study, called for my sister, and showed her the watch. "Where *was* it?" she demanded.

I tried to tell my sister what happened, but it was hard to find the words. She looked disbelieving. I hazarded a guess as to how the watch got into my husband's closet. Perhaps, annoyed at rescuing the watch from my careless sister one too many times, he'd taken it and hidden it away. My sister was skeptical, but couldn't come up with a more compelling suggestion.

I decided I'd save face for everyone. I put the watch back in the closet, and when my husband got home, I told him what a panic my sister had been in and how she'd spent all afternoon looking for it.

My husband was calm and casual in his reply. "I was wondering when she'd miss it," he said. "She left it in the bathroom after you'd gone to work this morning. You weren't here, so I thought I'd try teaching her a lesson. I put it away in my closet."

He went and got it, then handed it over to me. "Tell her to be more careful with it from now on."

In retrospect, two things amazed me. One was the fact that I somehow did what I did to locate that watch. But what struck me as equally peculiar was that I could have forgotten all about the experience for years. It wasn't until months after I'd begun thinking about people like Deb, Ellen, John, and Helen that the memory of finding that watch came back. And I realized what prompted me to remember. What these people had all been talking about—the state of mind characterizing their apparently anomalous knowing—finally woke me up to the fact that I dimly recognized what they were describing. They'd finally given me a context in which to locate and understand my memory.

I phoned Helen Palmer to tell her the story, groping for words. Finally I said, "I didn't *decide* to walk into my husband's study. Certainly I walked, but it feels more like I was *being* walked . . . walked, somehow, by the experience."

Helen was delighted. "That's impeccable: 'walked by.' *Exactly.* That's the state of mind that seems ordinary at the time, and you're simply taking actions that anyone would take."

Now that I had a context for the sensations that accompanied finding that watch, I realized that it was an oddly familiar state, one I recognized from peak moments in lessons with my voice coach or in the midst of a performance. Moments when I suddenly sang an aria I'd been working on and it came out absolutely right... *as though it were somehow singing me.*

I used to play varsity field hockey. In the last few minutes of one final game, I recalled running through the other team's entire defensive line as if I were slipping through water, evading each player as though I'd had an advance blueprint of exactly how each one would try to block me. Then I'd shot a goal from a wildly improbable position, promptly regained the ball and shot again—and watched the ball fly through the goal posts a second time, clinching an unbelievable victory... *as though the game were somehow playing me.*

I was starting to see, feel, taste the spectrum of extraordinary knowing. It seemed to depend on a state of mind that had a markedly sensory, absorbing, kinesthetic quality, one that linked my experience singing or playing hockey with that utterly weird moment of locating my sister's watch. It was a purely visceral state, one that bypassed conscious thought and paradoxically bound together absolute intention with lack of intention, a simple letting go and giving over.

I found the link immensely reassuring. If there really was a continuum that stretched from something as blessedly ordinary as singing or playing hockey to more extraordinary experiences, maybe I could grope my way from that reassuringly ordinary end to the peculiar state in which I found that watch. Maybe I could even fathom the state in which Harold found the harp, or the state in which people like Deb, Ellen, John, or Helen did their extraordinary work.

I immersed myself in accounts from the more familiar end of the spectrum, accounts from poets, athletes, musicians, artists, and dancers who described being "in the zone" or in "flow." As varied as these accounts were, they all centered on the paradoxical sensation that seems to release intention into a state of no-intention, when capacities beyond ordinary volition and ordinary conscious control appeared to take over.

I read what Michael Jordan said about his mind-defying dunks: "I never practice those moves. I don't know how to do them.... I'm taking off, like somebody put wings on me."[1] Here's Catfish Hunter after he pitched his perfect game against the Minnesota Twins in 1968: "I wasn't worried about a perfect game going into the ninth. It was like a dream. I was going on like I was in a daze. I never thought about it the whole time. If I'd thought about it, I wouldn't have thrown a perfect game—I know I wouldn't."[2] Pelé, describing his 1958 World Cup soccer game: "[I] played that whole game in a kind of trance, as if the future was unfolding before [my] own disinterested eyes."[3] And British golfer Tony Jacklin: "I'm absolutely engaged, *involved* in what I'm doing.... That's the difficult state to arrive at. It comes and it goes, and the pure fact that you go out on the first tee of a tournament and say, 'I must concentrate today,' is no good. It won't work."[4] The German philosopher Eugen Herrigel talked this way about learning Zen archery: "The shot will only go smoothly when it takes the archer himself by surprise.... You mustn't open the right hand on purpose."[5]

People in the arts described their experiences similarly. Here's Jacques d'Amboise on dancing at the top of his form: "When you're dancing like that, you seem to be removed. You can enjoy yourself doing it and watch yourself doing it at the same time."[6] Author Isabel Allende: "I have the feeling that I don't write my books, that the story is somewhere floating.... I don't know what I am writing."[7] Anne Sexton on being a poet: "All I am is the trick of words writing themselves."[8]

At the center of every account was the description of some radical extension of knowing, one that occupied body and soul, heart as well as mind. Now I began to reread with fresh eyes the vast body of recent research that explores knowing like that, knowing that emerges from beyond the intellect. The research comes from cognitive scientists, educators, neuroscientists, psychologists, and sociologists. None of it touches on knowing that's apparently anomalous, but perhaps established research about those "peak moments" could help us start thinking about what happens at the other end of the spectrum.

Research on knowing beyond the intellect gained enormous impetus in 1983, when psychologist Howard Gardner, a professor of cognition and education at Harvard, put forth a theory of multiple intelligences with his book *Frames of Mind*.[9] Gardner challenged the dominance of IQ, asserting that there were other crucial forms of intelligence that had no correlation with IQ. He specified seven distinct kinds: not only linguistic and logical-mathematical (the types measured by standard tests) but also musical, spatial, and bodily kinesthetic intelligences, plus two forms of personal intelligence, one directed toward other persons and one directed toward oneself. Gardner's perspective could be found in sources ranging from Plato to the Hindu Upanishads, but it had received short shrift in cognitive science until Gardner helped establish a formal, carefully documented, and thoroughly researched way of defining abilities that weren't limited to intellect. His ideas resonated to a degree he never expected, both within the psychology community and within popular culture. His book became an international bestseller. As a result, Gardner helped radically reconfigure the American view, and way, of knowing.

Gardner's portrayal of seven specific forms of intelligence was useful. But his greatest contribution was to get us *thinking* in terms of multiple intelligence. He himself anticipated that his breakdown of intelligences was far from absolute and would be refined and expanded over time.

Psychologist Daniel Goleman's book *Emotional Intelligence,* published in 1995, explored current research on yet another crucial form of intelligence, one that contributed more significantly to the development of competence and creativity than intellectual prowess or technical skill.[10] He argued that qualities such as empathy, self-awareness, and persistence were likewise crucial components of this intelligence, and that they could be taught. Like Gardner, Goleman pointed to the limits of IQ as a measure of intelligence and made a compelling argument that emotional intelligence, of which gut feelings are a component, enables a different kind of knowing. And like Gardner, Goleman hit a collective nerve. His book, which also became an international bestseller, resonated with what people knew from experience but hadn't been able to articulate scientifically. The term *emotional intelligence* continues to pepper daily conversations in fields from corporate management to marital counseling to preschool education.

My experience finding the watch pushed me into wondering if

there might be another intelligence at work, one we might call intuitive intelligence. Peak moments, no matter how subjectively extraordinary or brilliant beyond the norm, sit happily inside the various intelligences enumerated by Gardner and others who followed him. To whatever extent such moments are informed by intuition, their intuitive aspects are explicable. They're responses—mostly nonconscious responses—to skills we've systematically developed over time. They're thoroughly expectable as by-products of ordinary learning, even when they erupt most unexpectedly. But finding my sister's watch simply *wasn't* explicable as a by-product of ordinary learning. There had been no conventional cues to learn.

I turned to the *Oxford English Dictionary:* "*Intuit:* to receive or assimilate knowledge by direct perception or comprehension; to know anything immediately, without the intervention of any reasoning process." Beneath that definition I found another: "*Intuitive:* consists in direct and immediate looking upon an object, and seeing it as it is."

That last piece of the definition took me by surprise. "Seeing something as it is"? I thought about anticipating an opponent's moves in hockey or locating the unlikely spot where my sister's watch was hidden. Or Harold McCoy, over the phone and from two thousand miles away, identifying the exact location of the house in Oakland where a stolen harp lay hidden. Seeing something as it is? What if every one of these peculiar knowings was about activating an intelligence that facilitated a capacity to see things as they are, even as we're glaringly unable to understand it? Clairvoyance. Clear seeing.

Deb, Ellen, John, and Helen appeared to have access to information that belonged categorically inside me, not them. I remembered speaking with Deb, and thinking, *She knows me better than I know myself; she's gotten ahead of me in my own life.* And when I'd spoken with Ellen, I'd thought, *It's as though she's inside me looking out, and she's seeing my world, not hers.* If Deb and Ellen literally, actually knew what they seemed to know about me, what kind of perceptual capacity might give them access to such information? Such perceptual channels, if they existed, weren't any I recognized, and they relied on some sensory or neurobiological underpinning that was equally unfamiliar. Nor could these channels be remotely reconcilable with any conventional understanding of the human brain. With no way to conceptualize the neurobiological substructures that would explain what they seemed to be doing, I had reached an impasse.

Then in 2001, two physicians doing research at the University of Pennsylvania, radiologist Andrew Newberg and his colleague Eugene D'Aquili published a book called *Why God Won't Go Away*. Subtitled *Brain Science and the Biology of Belief*, it reported on studies of the brains of Buddhist meditators and Franciscan nuns during states of deep meditation or prayer.[11]

Newberg was expert in the use of brain-imaging techniques to examine how various portions of the brain function. D'Aquili had a long-standing interest in psychological correlates of spiritual experience. Together, the two developed a research design that was straightforward in its method but unusual in its promise for capturing the notoriously elusive phenomena they hoped to study.

They set up an experiment in which they were able to examine freeze-frame pictures of people's brains during moments of profound meditation or prayer. They settled on using SPECT (single photon emission computed tomography) technology to obtain the images they wanted. That choice immediately put their research in a category of its own—and an exceedingly clever one.

While there are other high-imaging techniques available for scanning the brain, such as positron emission tomography (PET) or functional magnetic resonance imaging (fMRI), SPECT technology is unique in allowing detailed examination of changing blood flow patterns in the brain while subjects are in a minimally invasive environment. Newberg and D'Aquili's subjects could sit or lie down alone in a quiet room, with access to any supplemental materials they found useful, and take as long as they liked to achieve a state of deep meditation or prayer. In other words, instead of having to meditate or pray on a predetermined schedule inside the confining, noisy machines required by other forms of brain imaging—conditions that are far from naturalistic—the subjects were studied in an environment that more closely resembled their ordinary lives.

During the actual experimental procedure, a long intravenous line was inserted into a subject's left arm. Each subject then went into a secluded room and engaged in his or her usual spiritual practice. The single unusual intervention was that the subjects were asked to give a brief tug on a string at the moment they felt they were in a state of deep meditation or prayer. When the subject pulled the string, Newberg, from a neighboring room, injected a radioactive tracer into the intravenous line. The radioactive tracer hit the brain almost immediately, measuring blood flow activity, and remained there for hours. Meanwhile, the subjects took as long as they wanted to conclude their meditating or praying. When they completed their practice, they went off to the University of Pennsylvania's nuclear medicine department, where SPECT scans of their brains were taken. Those scans produced highly detailed pictures of precisely the moments of deep prayer or meditation when people had pulled on their strings and the radioactive tracers had locked on to areas of increased blood flow in the brain.

Comparing these pictures with baseline scans taken under normal conditions, Newberg and D'Aquili came up with a number of findings that suggested something unusual was happening at the moments when the tracer was injected. One finding in particular grabbed me.[12] I expected that they would discover which regions of the brain "lit up" as a consequence of increased blood flow during moments of deep meditation or prayer, suggesting that those areas were especially active. Instead, Newberg and D'Aquili found that *certain areas of the brain went essentially dark,* meaning that they were *less* active than usual during a deep meditative state. What part of the brain was affected? Those bundles of neurons located in the posterior superior parietal lobe, the region of the brain that's critical to orienting us in the physical world. This part of the brain normally feeds us ongoing signals regarding the physical limits of our individual selves in relation to everything else, helping us separate "us" from "not us" with messages such as "I'm here, not there," "I'm next to my bed, not on it," or "I'm in my body, not hers." During the subjects' moments of deepest meditation and prayer, what stopped firing were all the signals that tell us where to locate the boundaries that separate us from everything that isn't us.

The neurons responsible for orienting each person in space hadn't been rendered any less capable of activity than they normally were; they simply seemed to have stopped receiving and decoding sensory information. Newberg and D'Aquili wanted to know why.

They postulated that they were simply seeing the end result of what happens when the brain is deprived of a specific kind of information to which our brains are normally habituated as a constant incoming flow. The neurons responsible for transmitting perpetual awareness of our individual boundedness in space had stopped doing their jobs.

On a purely neurobiological basis, the SPECT scans led to a fascinating speculation. They suggested that anybody whose posterior superior parietal lobe quieted down would experience the same subjective sensation. They wouldn't feel separate and boundaried from the rest of the world in all the ways we consider normal. Instead, they would probably experience a subjective sense of oneness or connectedness with everything around them.

In fact, that's precisely the subjective experience reported by Newburg and D'Aquili's subjects at the moments when they pulled their strings, as well as by generations of meditators and mystics before them. The essence of that experience, which many have described as "being one with the universe" or "united with God," seems to be the literal evaporation of any sense of separation from others or the surrounding world. Evelyn Underhill, one of the great interpreters of meditative and mystical experience, articulated all mystical experience as fundamentally "the art of union with reality."[13]

Newburg and D'Aquili's experiment suggests there may be a neurobiological basis for achieving that art of union with reality, not by achieving access to new sources of sensory information but rather by learning how to *tune down* the flow of incoming sensory information that constitutes our daily and habitual diet. And that is absolutely consistent with what meditators and mystics have told us over centuries about how they gain access to the states they engage.

Newburg and D'Aquili's work also offers a potentially startling hint about where to start looking for the substrate of sensory, perceptual, and neurobiological functioning that could generate a capacity for anomalous knowing. A subjective sensation of oneness characterizes not just the states that D'Aquili and Newberg were studying but also the felt state out of which intuitive knowing appears to emerge, whether anomalous or nonanomalous. Their work might give us a basis for conceptualizing the knowing that occurs along the whole spectrum of what we might call intuitive intelligence.

I went back to the accounts of athletes and artists describing their peak moments. Jimmy Clark, one of the all-time great automobile racers: "I don't drive a car, really. The car happens to be under me and I'm controlling it, but it's as much a part of me as I am of it."[14] Explorer Richard Byrd describing his sojourn in the Arctic: "I could feel no doubt of man's oneness with the universe. It was a feeling that transcended reason...."[15] Champion French skier and mountain guide Patrick Vallençant: "At the beginning of any steep descent... there is man, and a slope of snow, in unison.... I become a part of this cosmic dimension."[16]

Again, Jiichi Watanabe and Lindy Avakian, in *The Secrets of Judo*: "You and your opponent will no longer be two bodies separated physically from each other but a single entity, physically, mentally, and spiritually inseparable."[17]

Charles Lindbergh famously described his epic flight across the Atlantic: "There's no limit to my sight—my skull is one great eye, seeing everywhere at once... all-seeing, all-knowing...."[18]

Those descriptions took me back to my own experiences singing and playing hockey. Even my best attempts at describing those experiences—"the aria was singing me" or "the hockey game was playing me"—separated me from the thing itself. But Clark, Byrd, Lindbergh, and the others weren't describing what a subject did to an object or vice versa. Clark wasn't *doing* something to his car, nor Byrd to the wilderness, nor Vallençant to the slope, nor judo artists to their opponents. Subject and object were one. I realized that what made for an experience of the extraordinary, of knowing just what to do as well as how and when to do it, came out of the fact that *all of a sudden there was no separation*. The aria and I were one. The game and I were one. For a peculiar, bizarre instant, even those opposing players and I were one. That's why it felt like I had an advance blueprint of their moves. I knew how they'd move because I *was* them.

And that took me straight to the anomalous end of the spectrum of intuitive intelligence. Every "professional intuitive" to whom I spoke characterized their mental state in the same way. As Helen Palmer put it, "You read the other person accurately because you *are* them; you know them from the inside because you've stopped being separate." Deb Mangelus: "I know what I know about the other person because I go where they are. I draw on how connected we all are so I really am seeing with their eyes when I read them." According to John Huddleston, "It's ordinary because it's just there, all that information about the other person. All you have to do is get yourself out of the way. We're all connected, that's the point. We don't know it most of the time because we think we'd rather feel separate." And Ellen Tadd: "It's a state of oneness, really—from that oneness, you get a very profound knowing."

From nonanomalous to anomalous, every one of those descriptions of intuitive knowing corresponded to what Newberg and D'Aquili's subjects reported. And there was a further link as well. In every spiritual tradition, people highly practiced in deep meditation or prayer regularly report experiences of *exactly the kinds of anomalous knowing Deb and the others described.* They regard these experiences as ordinary by-products of spiritual practice and consider them an actual distraction from the real point: the art of union itself. In short, clairvoyance, telepathy, and similar phenomena are entirely expectable, but nothing to get excited about. Such capacities merely reflect the way things *are* during the union with reality.

Perhaps, then, the patterns of neural activity identified by Newburg and D'Aquili can help us begin to localize a neural and perceptual substrate for anomalous intuitive knowing. Perhaps, if the ordinary flow of perpetual input feeding our habitual awareness of separateness is damped down, we gain access to information that is, under ordinary circumstances, utterly out of reach. Out of that perception might come an unaccustomed and startling ability to see everything around us in totally different ways—ways that transcend the boundaries established by our usual rules about how space and time delineate separateness. In a perceptual model like that, anomalous knowing might stop looking so anomalous. It might instead start looking like the perfectly ordinary result of *seeing things as they are* when connectedness, rather than separateness, moves to the foreground of our awareness.

6

Starting—and Stopping— the Conversation:

The Strange History of Paranormal Research

"SCIENCE," WERNER HEISENBERG ONCE REMARKED, "is rooted in conversation."[1] As I was increasingly drawn into conversation with colleagues about anomalous experience, I wondered what sort of science might be rooted in these new conversations I was having? Maybe more challenging, what sort of science was rooted in the *absence* of those conversations?

The stories I was hearing were pointedly absent from the science with which I'd grown up. And most of the people telling me their stories found that absence as troubling as I did. What would it take to enter their stories into serious scientific conversation? *Could* they be entered, with respect not just for the stories but for science? What would happen to the stories? What would happen to a science that rigorously considered them?

Such a field has inhabited the outer edges of mainstream science for a very long time. I began discovering mountains of research and a vast relevant literature I hadn't known existed. As astonished as I was by the sheer quantity, I was equally astonished by the high caliber. Much of the research not only met but far exceeded ordinary standards of rigorous mainstream science.

Every good scientist knows the famous dictum first enunciated by sociologist Marcello Truzzi and later popularized by astronomer and author Carl Sagan: "Extraordinary claims require extraordinary evidence."[2] The claims made by the research I was reading were plenty extraordinary. They suggest the existence of mental capacities that defy space, time, and the basic boundaries of individual identity. Anything less than superb evidence won't begin to justify claims like that. As a result, a good deal of research on anomalous mental capacities—certainly not all, but enough to be startling—adheres to stunningly high standards. Outside assessments of that research have repeatedly determined, often to the significant surprise of the evaluators, that the studies are overall scrupulously controlled, rigorously designed, and carefully regulated by masked and double-blind procedures.[3]

The more I looked, the more I discovered the extent to which scientific curiosity about anomalous mental capacities had been around for a long time. But I also discovered how often that curiosity was thwarted as it tried to enter mainstream scientific conversation. To explore the reasons why, I decided to go back to the beginnings of modern science.

I went all the way back to seventeenth-century scientist Sir Robert Boyle, hailed as the father of modern chemistry. Boyle was a vastly accomplished scientific visionary. He was among the first to argue that all basic physical properties were due to the motion of atoms. He introduced a variety of new methods for determining the chemical composition of substances. He was a founder of the Royal Society of London, then and still among the world's foremost scientific organizations. Chemistry students today, however, know him primarily as the author of Boyle's law, which states the inverse relationship between pressure and volume in gases under constant temperature. However, I discovered that he played a central role in a drama regarding anomalous mental capacities that unfolded during the midseventeenth century.

Born in 1627, Boyle's illustrious career was thoroughly established by 1666, when a contentious political activist, Dr. Henry Stubbe, published a short book in the form of a letter addressed to the Honorable Robert Boyle. The book was called *The Miraculous Conformist* and described the purportedly miraculous cures of a popular Irish healer, Valentine Greatrakes, who "stroked" people's afflicted body parts to cure them. According to Stubbe's book, Greatrakes was able to cure deafness by stroking the afflicted person's ears; he was said to cure tuberculosis by stroking people "until the pain were driven out the toes' ends."[4] As one contemporary account put it, "All England and Ireland were excited by the marvelous cures wrought by Valentine Greatrakes."[5]

Boyle was outraged by Stubbe's use of his name on his book with no permission. In Boyle's opinion, Greatrakes's alleged abilities defied the proper relation of man to nature as well as God. He immediately wrote Stubbe saying that he wanted nothing to do with Greatrakes or Stubbe's claims about Greatrakes's purported miracles.

On the other hand, Boyle was a scientist and a mere letter of protest didn't satisfy him. He decided to tackle Stubbe's claims head-on. Armed with a list of seventeen questions, Sir Robert set himself to observe a series of Greatrakes's strokings. His list of questions would do credit to any modern medical investigation. For example, he wondered, "Can he cure men of different religions as Roman Catholics, ... Jews, etc. as well as infants, or distracted persons to whose recovery the faith of the patient cannot concur?" "How many times must he touch the patients, and at what intervals between those times?" "What are the diseases that Mr. G. cannot at all cure? Among those which he sometimes cures, which are they that he succeeds best, and which he succeeds worst with? Among the former, which complexions, ages, sexes, etc., do the most favor, or disfavor his cures?"[6]

On Easter Sunday of 1666, Boyle wrote a letter in which he described watching Greatrakes at work. He described how he watched Greatrakes restore a deaf woman's hearing after the healer "put his fingers in her ears, and (as I remember) a little stroked them ... she went away joyful." Presented with Boyle's sister's servant, who suffered with a "tedious and violent fit of the headache,"

Greatrakes stroked the "middle of her head without taking off her hood" and the woman walked away cured, "leaving Mr. G. to resume his discourse, which he pursued as unconcernedly as if nothing had happened at all to interrupt it."[7] After a number of such observations and after subjecting them to his own list of questions, Boyle publicly retracted his prior denunciations of Greatrakes's apparently extraordinary abilities. He became one of the healer's most ardent supporters, signing seven sworn affidavits testifying as an eyewitness to the astonishing efficaciousness of Greatrakes's cures, which included curing patients of blindness, deafness, and paralysis.

The Boyle-Greatrakes controversy was front-page news in its time—widely publicized, widely discussed, and Boyle's name was heavily featured in the furor. But when I searched through modern scientific accounts of Sir Robert Boyle, I found mostly silence. A few mentioned Stubbe's book as well as Boyle's protest at having his name attached to it. But none referred to Boyle's subsequent investigations of Greatrakes. Nor his sworn affidavits, nor his eventual change of opinion about Greatrakes's abilities based on observing the healer at work. I called an academic friend, a specialist in the history of chemistry. He knew nothing about any of it, but promptly added that Boyle wasn't in his period since he wasn't an early modernist. As he put it, an episode so "evidently arcane" would fall outside his purview.

Evidently arcane? Maybe. I imagined high school students hearing about this other side of Boyle, maybe even registering a provocative lesson about the value of subjecting skepticism to open-minded review, and a great scientist's dedication to systematic observation in the face of claims he doesn't believe are possible. But instead the story has been buried as a piece of arcana.

Over the next two centuries, there were many more carefully documented inquiries into apparently anomalous phenomena by leading members of the scientific community. Like Sir Robert Boyle's investigation of Greatrakes, they were often extensive and widely publicized, but like Boyle's inquiries, they've languished as historical footnotes.

By the nineteenth century, that was starting to change. Scientists across Europe and the United States began regularly convening to pursue scientific discussion of anomalous mental phenomena. They collaborated on experiments and collected masses of anecdotal reports. Investigators included such notables as Parisian physicists Marie and Pierre Curie (winners of three Nobel Prizes for their work on radioactivity), the British physicist Sir Oliver Lodge (whose work on oscillations of electric waves led to development of the radio), and British chemist-physicist Sir William Crookes (developer of the cathode-ray tube, the radiometer, and the spinthariscope for observing high-energy particles emitted from radioactive substances).

In 1882, collective scientific interest finally consolidated in the establishment of the first formal scientific organization to study anomalous mental capacities. Numerous eminent scientists and philosophers gathered in London "to investigate that large body of debatable phenomena...without prejudice or prepossession of any kind and in the same spirit of exact and unimpassioned inquiry which has enabled Science to solve so many problems."[8] Those meetings resulted in the founding of the British Society for Psychical Research. In 1885, a sister organization in the United States, the American Society for Psychical Research, was formed.

The growing weight of scientific curiosity was significantly responsible for the founding of both the American and the British societies. But mere curiosity hadn't previously been enough to break through taboos on public scientific acknowledgment of anomalous mental capacities. The fact was, by the late nineteenth century, a number of other forces had converged as well.

One such force was phrenology, imported from Vienna in the early 1800s to England. Phrenology postulated a relationship between the shape of the face and skull and mental capacity; later proponents taught eager audiences that they could improve their mental abilities through specific exercises. The 1830s in Victorian England saw the rise of mesmerism, invented by a Viennese doctor named Franz Mesmer, who proposed that a person endowed with healing powers could cure another by staring into his eyes. He later refined his theory that such a person could affect "animal gravity"—the influence of the planets on earthly bodies—by manipulating the fluid in the patients, sending them into a healing hypnotic trance. The belief that the mind could be manipulated and improved saw its acme in the growth of Spiritualism, a movement that declared that the human spirit could survive physical death. By the 1850s, Spiritualism claimed to have more than 2 million adherents in America.[9]

The growth of these three movements, among others, spawned a vast industry of people purporting to have anomalous mental abilities and a fascinated public eager to believe them. By the late 1800s, the United States was home to thirty thousand so-called mediums (people purported to communicate with the dead), and in Philadelphia alone there were over three hundred "magnetic circles" (gatherings with a medium) convening on a regular basis.[10] Anomalous mental capacities were thoroughly in vogue, and séances, where mediums purported to facilitate the appearance of the dead to commune with the living, were a popular social event. While reports from credible scientists emerged testifying to the abilities of some individuals, it was perhaps inevitable that the field would be overrun by fakers eager to trade on the credulousness and grief of mourning family members eager to reconnect with a loved one after death.

A giant of late nineteenth-century psychology, William James, ventured boldly into the public arena to help separate legitimate fields of inquiry from quackery. James, who spent his entire professional career teaching psychology at Harvard, beginning in 1876, had first studied anatomy and physiology at the Harvard Medical School. He was firmly committed to scientific study of human beings in their completeness—body, mind, and soul—and viewed systematic investigation of anomalous mental capacities as a critical piece of that study. James managed the rare feat of retaining his Harvard colleagues' respect while consistently going public with his view that anomalous mental capacities mattered.

In 1890, James's *Principles of Psychology* had "burst upon the world like a volcanic eruption,"[11] promptly receiving international acclaim. He was well on his way to becoming the person many still view as the most important psychologist America ever produced. Five years earlier, however, he'd been a prime mover in founding the American Society for Psychical Research.

James was determined that the American society, like its British counterpart, would remain impeccable in adherence to rigorous standards of science. It would also be deliberately elite in its membership. James was fully aware that the scientific skepticism directed at the SPR would be somewhat mitigated by the roster of preeminent scientists and thinkers of the day on its board. With tongue in cheek but serious intent, James wrote, "We are founding here a 'Society for Psychical Research,' under which innocent sounding name ghosts, second sight, spiritualism and all sorts of hobgoblins are going to be 'investigated' by the most high-toned and 'cultured' members of the community."[12] James was all too aware that prospects for the society's eventual acceptance would be inextricably linked to the credibility of those participating.

The original American society included 250 members. They were the cream of American intellectual life at the time. The five vice presidents were Granville Stanley Hall (a psychologist at Johns Hopkins University who founded the *American Journal of Psychology* and was the first president of the American Psychological Association); Henry Pickering Bowditch and Charles Sedgwick Minot, both at the Harvard Medical School; George Stuart Fullerton, a philosopher at the University of Pennsylvania; and Edward Charles Pickering, an astronomer at the Harvard College Observatory. By 1890, the American society was well established and the two groups, American and British, decided to merge. The American society became a branch of the British, and a single society, known as the SPR, was born.

The SPR undertook myriad investigations of purportedly psychic phenomena, using the most rigorous of standards.[13] The poet William Butler Yeats no sooner became a member than he complained, "It's my belief that if you psychical researchers had been about when God Almighty was creating the world, He couldn't have done the job."[14]

Among the first tasks the SPR shouldered was the investigation of countless people advertising themselves as mediums. Perhaps the most famous was Madame Blavatsky, founder of the hugely popular Theosophical Society, which boasted close to 100,000 active members during the late 1880s. The SPR carefully examined Blavatsky's purported psychic achievements and finally pronounced them fraudulent, calling her "one of the most accomplished, ingenious and interesting impostors in history."[15]

But the SPR did more than discredit quacks and frauds. They also sponsored vast amounts of research into thought transference, automatic writing, communication with the dead—the full gamut of purportedly psychic phenomena.

Among the SPR's most impressive achievements was a careful census of 25,000 people regarding their experience of anomalous events. The census selected people at random from a number of countries, all of whom were asked "whether, when in good health and awake, [they] had ever heard a voice, seen a form, or felt a touch which no material presence could account for."[16] Of the 25,000 people questioned, roughly one in ten reported having had such an experience at least once. Among those experiences, 14 percent corresponded to some distant and identifiable real event. In other words, one person out of every 140 appeared to have experienced what the SPR named a "veridical hallucination," a hallucination that was "true" in the sense that it reflected accurate knowledge of a verifiable event.

The SPR's other staggeringly prodigious piece of work was a 1,300-page volume, *Phantasms of the Living,* published in 1886. *Phantasms* contained hundreds of corroborated reports involving purportedly psychic experiences. Monumental efforts were expended in verifying each case. Witnesses were interviewed, official records obtained, and supporting letters solicited. Thousands of cases were examined and over ten thousand investigative letters written in one year alone. *Phantasms* established a methodology for evaluating testimony concerning psychic experiences that remains unsurpassed today.

Phantasms developed after SPR members had collected a number of reports of apparently psychic experiences. They found that a significant number entailed what the SPR termed "veridical crisis apparitions." They were reports of seeing (or hearing) an apparition of a distant person who was in some form of crisis, experiencing injury, trauma, or death.

Phantasms came up with a fascinating interpretation of those reports (still piled in forty-two large boxes and available for inspection in the SPR archives). Veridical crisis apparitions were not, argued

Phantasms, the product of spirit visitation as claimed by the Spiritualists. Instead, they were frank hallucinations. But not hallucinations in the usual sense. They were hallucinations "generated by some sort of telepathic message from the person in the crisis."[17]

Contemporary research that looks at how nonanomalous capacities develop suggests the SPR might have been on to something. It turns out that it's not uncommon for crisis to precipitate the manifestation of human capacities ordinarily unavailable, even deemed impossible. Although I couldn't find the earliest example, we've all read about mothers who were able to single-handedly lift cars off their children who'd been accidentally pinned underneath them. A quick Internet search will yield dozens of contemporary reports. Such urgent need—*crisis*—seems to permit people access to capacities customarily out of reach.

The SPR suggested that access to anomalous mental capacities might be precipitated by just such an urgent need or crisis, but on the part of a person removed in space or time from the person who then manifested the capacity. One person's crisis was somehow translated into another person's extraordinary knowing. Hence, said the SPR, the appearance of "veridical crisis apparitions." Hence as well an emphatic challenge to our ordinary understanding of how space and time impose fixed boundaries between individuals.

Even after the American society was subsumed by the British, William James remained a powerful spokesman for the combined SPR. In 1892, he was asked to summarize his view of its purpose and its achievements.

> [W]ere I asked to point to a scientific journal where hard-headedness and never-sleeping suspicion of sources of error might be seen in their full bloom, I think I should have to fall back on the *Proceedings* of the "Society for Psychical Research." ... Quality, and not mere quantity, is what has been mainly kept in mind. The most that could be done with every reported case has been done. The witnesses, where possible, have been cross-examined personally, the collateral facts have been looked up, and the narrative appears with its precise coefficient of evidential work stamped on it, so that all may know just what its weight as proof may be. Outside of these *Proceedings,* I

know of no systematic attempt to *weigh* the evidence for the supernatural. This makes the value of the seven volumes already published unique. . . .

Now, it is certain that if the cat ever does jump [in the direction of clairvoyance, thought transference, and ghosts], the cautious methods of the "S.P.R." will give it a position of extraordinary influence. . . . [I]ts efforts at exactitude about evidence and its timidity in speculating would seem supremely virtuous. Sober-headed scientists would look to its temper as a bulwark. . . . In short, the "S.P.R." would be a surprisingly useful mediator between the old order and the new. . . .

Now, the present writer (not wholly insensible to the ill consequences of putting himself on record as a false prophet) must candidly express his own suspicion that sooner or later the cat *must* jump that way. The special means of his conversion have been the trances . . . in the *Proceedings*. . . . Knowing these trances at first hand, he cannot escape the conclusions that in them the medium's knowledge of facts increases enormously, and in a manner impossible of explanation by any principle of which our existing science takes account. Facts are facts. . . . [T]he trances I speak of have broken down for my own mind the limits of the admitted order of nature. Science, so far as science denies such exceptional facts, lies prostrate in the dust for me; and the most urgent intellectual need which I feel at present is that science be built up again in a form in which such facts shall have a positive place. Science, like life, feeds on its own decay. New facts burst old rules; then newly divined conceptions bind old and new together in a reconciling law."[18]

One final aspect of research conducted under the auspices of the SPR was to prove critical for future investigation of anomalous mental capacities. It set the stage for the next major development in such research: tightly controlled objective experiments with simple, measurable outcomes subject to meticulous statistical analysis.

Charles Richet, a professor of physiology at the University of Paris Medical School and a future Nobel Prize winner, laid the foundations for that next phase of research. During the 1880s, he initiated a series of experiments on clairvoyance by testing whether subjects could identify ordinary playing cards that had been sealed in opaque envelopes. He also published a paper on the application of statistical analysis to apparently anomalous phenomena. Most intriguing, he offered a hugely significant observation, one that would have critical implications for subsequent experimental design aimed at assessing anomalous capacities. A notable feature of such capacities was, Richet observed, "the curiously unstable nature of the subject's clairvoyant ability."[19] This was the first formal recognition that when it came to conventional experimental method, anomalous mental capacities just might not submit to playing by ordinary rules—rules of replicability, predictability, and stability.

William James therefore set a revolutionary and overarching scientific agenda for investigating anomalous mental capacities that took into account how such capacities might, in Richet's terms, prove unstable. Along with other SPR founders, he called for a clear and explicit scientific program: "first, to investigate psychic phenomena according to the methods and criteria of science; and second, to enlarge the scope of science to include the study of phenomena that are random, non-repeatable, and dependent on universal personal capacities and dispositions."[20] That issued no small challenge to the science of James's day, a challenge that remains undiminished in our own. Over the next century, the second half of James's program was to prove stunningly prescient, locating precisely the radical edge on which any science of anomalous mental capacities would be required to operate.

William James died in 1910. Following his death, academic interest in anomalous mental capacities continued briefly to sputter along, particularly at Harvard, Stanford, and Clark Universities. But without James at the helm, rising opposition within those institutions soon took over, and research into psychic phenomena receded once again into scientific silence.

Just as interest in Spiritualism and other psychic phenomena was peaking at the close of the nineteenth century, Sigmund Freud was pioneering the field of psychoanalysis. Freud, a neurologist by training, had broken free of his conventional scientific background and begun publishing his radical theory that a vast portion of the human mind functioned unconsciously. He argued that all kinds of physical symptoms and observable behaviors were produced by mental activity outside conscious awareness or conscious control. Psychoanalysis was based on the systematic investigation of these unconscious processes, with the analyst helping the patient draw connections between unconscious thoughts and conscious thoughts and actions. Freud's masterwork, *The Interpretation of Dreams,* published in 1899, claimed that the study of dreams was one path to elucidating such processes.

The idea that we're motivated largely by unconscious thoughts constituted a mighty and unprecedented assault on late-nineteenth-century science, with its mechanistic rejection of the internal, subjective, or mental as appropriate objects for scientific study. Moreover, Freud declared that unconscious aspects of the mind had effects on material reality, starting with the body, far beyond any mental effects science had previously acknowledged. That opened the door to imagining a panoply of new ways that the mind might conceivably influence matter, including potentially anomalous ways.

But when it came to frank acknowledgment of the anomalous, Freud was deeply conflicted. He himself was convinced that anomalous mental capacities were real and hugely significant. He was particularly fascinated by telepathy, which he'd dubbed thought transference. He enthusiastically pursued its investigation with a few close associates, in particular a Hungarian psychoanalyst named Sándor Ferenczi, with whom he'd begun a collegial correspondence in 1908. On August 20, 1910, Freud triumphantly wrote to Ferenczi,

> Your—carefully preserved—observations . . . seem to me finally to shatter the doubts about the existence of thought transference. Now it is a matter of getting used to it in your thoughts and losing respect for its novelty and also preserving the secret long enough in the maternal womb, but that is where the doubt ends.[21]

"Preserving the secret in the maternal womb" turned out to be no small matter for Freud. On the one hand, he believed that the observations he and Ferenczi had collected led to an earthshaking truth—anomalous mental capacities really did exist. But understanding those capacities would take time, slow gestation in the womb of sober scientific consideration. That was Freud the prudent scientist speaking.

But Freud was also a political realist. He was keenly aware that his new science of psychoanalysis was already skating on exceedingly thin ice. Most risky, it had asserted that children—all children, no matter how young and apparently innocent—harbored powerful sexual feelings. That had been enough to inspire moral outrage from every respectable late-nineteenth-century quarter. Freud handled the resulting personal vilification with grace. But when it came to censure that might endanger the future of psychoanalysis itself, that was another matter.

Freud made a decision, one of the most important in his career. Despite his vast courage in confronting the scientific and medical establishments on other counts, he drew the line at anomalous mental capacities. To acknowledge such capacities officially might be to link psychoanalysis permanently to the occult and sever its already tenuous ties to science. His message to colleagues was clear: keep thought transference quiet (never mind that he himself went on to publish six papers acknowledging its reality, unable to resist his fascination).[22]

The real power of thought transference, Freud decided, was to be held sequestered as a psychoanalytic secret, closeted in the minds of several select colleagues who could be trusted to explore it with utmost discretion. Freud wrote letter after letter to the less cautious Ferenczi, urging him to restrain his enthusiasm for public revelation regarding thought transference.

On October 6, 1909, he wrote, "...Keep quiet about it for the time being, we will have to engage in future experiments...."[23] A few days later, concerned that he hadn't been emphatic enough, he added, "...[L]et us keep absolute silence with regard to it. The only one whom I have drawn into the secret is Heller, who also has had experiences with it. We want to initiate Jung at a later date.... Think out some good plans and have your brother formulate experiments.... I am almost afraid that you have begun to recognize something big here, but we will encounter the greatest difficulties in exploiting it."[24]

By 1910, Freud had reluctantly realized there were limits to how long he could enforce collegial silence around thought transference. "I see destiny approaching, inexorably, and I note that it has designated you to bring to light mysticism and the like, and that it would be just as futile as it is hard-hearted to keep you from it. Still, I think we ought to venture to slow it down. I would like to request that you continue to research in secrecy for two full years and don't come out until 1913...."[25]

On May 11, 1911, Freud acknowledged he was beaten and wrote to Ferenczi, "Jung writes that we must also conquer occultism and requests permission to undertake a campaign.... I see that the both of you can't be restrained. You should at least proceed in harmony with each other; these are dangerous expeditions, and I can't go along there."[26]

Despite the warning tone of that letter, Freud signed it on an affectionately teasing note, a concession granting some acceptance if not outright blessing to Ferenczi's pursuit of the mystical.[27]

> Regards to you, uncanny one.
> Cordially,
> Freud

At the end of his long and extraordinary career, Freud made a remarkable statement. If, he said, he had it to do over again, he might devote his life to the study of thought transference. In an unpublished letter to Hereward Carrington, a leading investigator with the Society for Psychical Research, Freud wrote, "I am not one of those who from the outset disapprove of the study of the so-called occult psychological phenomena as unscientific, as unworthy or even as dangerous. If I were at the beginning of a scientific career, instead of as now at its end, I would perhaps choose no other field of work in spite of all difficulties."[28]

In the 1920s, the scientific tide began turning again. This time it was thanks largely to William McDougall, a physician and psychologist from England, who was eager to rekindle the spark that had guttered upon the death of William James in 1910.[29]

McDougall, a cofounder of the British Psychological Society and the *British Journal of Psychology,* taught psychology at Oxford. He also had a deep interest in mental telepathy, and in 1920 was named president of the British Society for Psychical Research. That same year, he was offered the distinguished chair in psychology at Harvard vacated by James's death. He brought with him a resolve, one thoroughly in the spirit of James, his eminent forebear. McDougall was intent on launching the brightest young students on careers that would include serious scientific investigation of anomalous mental capacities.

As a scholar, McDougall was a fascinating paradox. On the one hand, he was a staunch empiricist. That made him entirely at home with academic psychology's growing shift toward emphasizing objective experimental evidence. On the other hand, he was not one bit comfortable with another emerging trend that was sweeping through American universities and being touted as psychology's future: behaviorism. Behaviorists focused the study of human beings on pure behavior, which was observable and therefore real. Thought processes, states of consciousness, feelings, attitudes, values, and personal meaning were considered mere artifacts, unworthy as data.

McDougall believed that humans were more than the sum of their behaviors. But it was a conviction that put him in a steadily diminishing minority at Harvard, where the influence of fellow professor B. F. Skinner, behaviorism's leading proponent, was huge and growing. So when McDougall received what he called a "gilded offer" to leave Harvard and create a psychology department at Duke University in North Carolina, he was delighted. The offer gave him carte blanche to design his own curriculum, choose any faculty he liked, set his own research priorities, and establish a home for his distinctive vision of psychology. It was an easy call. In 1927 McDougall departed New England for the South, where he would oversee the design and implementation of research into anomalous mental capacities, which he dubbed parapsychology.

By the time he left for Duke, McDougall had already pointed a number of young scholars toward this field. Several would make their own distinctive contributions to McDougall's work at Duke. Two would go on to become the next generation's leading figures in the scientific understanding of such capacities: Gardner Murphy and Joseph B. Rhine.

Born in 1895, Murphy was educated at Yale, Harvard, and Columbia. Widely beloved as a man of wit, charm, dignity, and culture, he was an old-fashioned gentleman to the core. For generations of psychologists, Murphy ranked second only to James as the great visionary of American psychology. In fact, an American Psychological Association poll of its membership in the 1940s actually placed Murphy ahead of James, right after Sigmund Freud as the individual who had most influenced the history of Western psychology. The scope of Murphy's work was astounding, from studies on perception and motivation to essays on evolution, philosophy, and social behavior. On top of all that, he undertook a series of pioneering explorations into anomalous mental capacities. (And that, according to some students of his work, may help explain why his name slipped into such relative oblivion following such extraordinary renown.) Elected to the board of the American Society for Psychical Research, he later became its president.

Murphy was also an ardent supporter of his Duke colleague Joseph B. Rhine, who couldn't have been more different from the East Coast intellectual. J. B. Rhine was raised in the hills of Pennsylvania, the son of an itinerant farmer and sometime teacher. He was hard-nosed and irascible, meticulous in attention to detail and quickly impatient with those who weren't. But his impatience shot sky-high when it came to fundamentalism of any kind, whether religious or scientific. As a student of botany at the University of Chicago during the '20s, he saw plenty of both. Battles over evolution versus creationism were raging. To his dismay, Rhine found some of his Darwinist university colleagues no less dogmatic than their Bible-thumping opponents. That, in Rhine's view, betrayed everything essential about the spirit of science.

In 1922, Rhine and his wife, Louisa, attended a lecture in Chicago by Sir Arthur Conan Doyle, who, in addition to his authorship of the Sherlock Holmes stories, was a member of the Society for Psychical Research with an avid interest in Spiritualism. Sir Arthur noted that a number of eminent scientists were keenly interested in psychic phenomena, including the British physicist Sir Oliver Lodge. The skeptical Rhine later tracked down Lodge's book on the possibility of communication with the dead. Then he tackled William McDougall's *Body and Mind,* in which McDougall suggested that psychic capacities were real, important, and deserved serious scientific study. Rhine was shaken by both books. At the very least, these men were presenting evidence he judged worthy of thoughtful scientific consideration. He pronounced it "unpardonable for the scientific world today to overlook evidences of the supernormal in the world—if there are such."[30]

In 1926, Rhine and his wife decided to go to Boston, hoping to meet McDougall there and do research on anomalous mental capacities under his auspices. Neither hope materialized. McDougall was about to leave for a year-long stint in Europe the day they arrived, and the funding they'd hoped to obtain for research wasn't available. McDougall gave the Rhines the names of some SPR members to contact in Boston. As a result, they were soon invited to a séance with a famous Boston medium named Margery. The séance took place in semidarkness and Rhine happened to be seated next to Margery. He became more and more suspicious that physical signals purportedly produced by the spirit of Margery's dead brother were in fact the product of hidden devices she cleverly manipulated. He finally saw her kick a hidden megaphone, and publicly exposed her in an outraged letter addressed to the SPR.

Unlike James and Murphy, who managed to question apparent psychic fraud in ways that won them allies and increased their credibility, Rhine lacked the gift of diplomatic communication. His exposé proved disastrous for his standing in the SPR community. Sir Arthur Conan Doyle himself reacted by paying for a black-bordered ad in a Boston newspaper. It simply read, "J. B. Rhine is a monumental ass."[31]

It was a bad beginning in terms of public relations. But it

couldn't have been a better beginning in terms of drawing William McDougall's attention to the young J. B.'s observational acuity and scientific conscience. When McDougall began to select cohorts for his work at Duke, he initially offered the Rhines funding for a semester's research. Within the year, he had appointed them to become founding faculty of his new psychology department.

The Rhines suggested they should establish a parapsychology lab at Duke dedicated to scientific investigation of anomalous mental capacities. McDougall eagerly offered his support. The lab, they agreed, would be based on three essential principles:

1. the use of experimental subjects claiming no unusual abilities
2. simple, easily controlled restricted-choice procedures
3. rigorous statistical evaluation of results.[32]

The Rhines' focus on those three principles had crucial import for the nature of their research as well as for the long-term future of their lab. (Eighty years later it is still a major center for experimental research on anomalous mental capacities, now independent of Duke and known as the Rhine Research Center.) They were determined to study ordinary people using ordinary, thoroughly conventional scientific methods and procedures. "Simple, easily-controlled restricted-choice procedures" and "rigorous statistical evaluation of results" meant producing data that were readily quantifiable and easily subject to objective measurement as well as formal statistical analysis. The Rhines' central goal was to see whether, by experiments that adhered to every standard of accepted scientific method, anomalous mental capacities could be shown to exist.

They devoted the first few years of their experimental work at Duke to developing procedures that not only fit those criteria but would allow their experiments to be replicated both at Duke and elsewhere. Their early experiments all asked one simple question: could subjects identify a specific card from a series—preselected either by the experimenter or by someone else having no sensory contact with the person identifying the cards—with an accuracy significantly beyond what pure chance would predict?

Initially, the Rhines tested subjects using a standard deck of playing cards. As they improved their experimental designs, they asked a colleague—Karl Zener, an expert in the psychology of perception—to design a deck more efficient for the simple guessing tasks their experiments required. Zener created a deck of twenty-five cards, each card portraying one of five simple geometric designs: a star, a square, wavy lines, a circle, and a plus sign. They were christened Zener cards.

The Rhines performed two kinds of tests with the Zener cards, tests of clairvoyance (asking subjects to name a card when no other person knew which had been turned up) and telepathy (asking subjects to name a card that another person was thinking of).

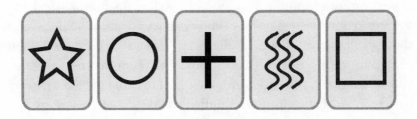

Zener Cards Used in ESP Tests at the Rhine Lab

A correct guess was called a hit. Given a series of twenty-five cards, people would be expected, on the basis of pure chance, to guess an average of five correctly. The Rhines wanted to see whether people could do better than that, and better with enough consistency to suggest there might be something besides chance at work, something potentially anomalous.

After three years of experiments and 100,000 individual tests with ordinary people—from college students to volunteers off the street—the Rhines went public with their findings. They reported results that were both positive and statistically significant, well beyond chance expectation.

Those general results were interesting enough. They suggested that some form of anomalous mental capacity might actually exist in the general population. But even more interesting were the findings from a small subgroup of subjects whose guesses turned out to be extraordinarily accurate—far beyond anything chance would predict. One man's guesses stood out especially: those of a young divinity student named Hubert E. Pearce Jr. It was a series of experiments conducted by J. B. Rhine's assistant, Joseph Pratt, that shot the lab, and Pearce with it, into renown.[33]

Pearce and Pratt started out by synchronizing their watches. Then they went to different buildings, Pearce to the Duke library and Pratt to the physics building, a hundred yards away. At a prearranged time, they set to work. Pratt shuffled a deck of Zener cards. He then picked the top card and, without looking at it, laid it facedown on the table in front of him. During the subsequent minute, Pearce wrote down which card he thought Pratt had laid down. After the minute was up, Pratt picked up another card and Pearce, from his seat in the library, guessed again. They went through all twenty-five cards that way. When they'd finished, Pratt turned his deck of cards faceup, looked at them for the first time, and wrote down the order in which he'd actually picked them off the deck. At that point he reshuffled the deck and they started all over again.

At the end of every run of twenty-five cards, Pearce and Pratt each had a written record sequencing them. Pratt's listed the exact order in which he'd actually picked them up, and Pearce's the order in which he'd guessed them. As soon as a session was completed, each man sealed his report and turned it over to Rhine, who then compared them.

Pearce produced astonishing results. On his first experiment with Pratt, he went through 300 trials with the Zener deck and averaged 9.9 hits per run of 25 cards instead of the expectable 5. He achieved similarly impressive results when he moved from the library to the medical school, 250 yards away from Pratt instead of just 100. Apparently, distance didn't affect Pearce's abilities. Pearce then continued his success rate, but in a series of guesses *before* Pratt had actually shuffled the deck and laid the cards facedown one at a time. Pearce's abilities appeared no more constrained by time than by distance.

By the time the Pearce-Pratt experiments were completed, the two men had conducted 1,850 trials out of which Pearce had achieved 558 hits. Pure chance would have predicted he'd accurately guess 370. The odds of Pearce making 558 correct guesses out of 1,850 were an inconceivable 22 billion to 1.

Rhine pondered how to label the apparently anomalous capacity he believed Pearce was demonstrating. He wanted a name that normalized his findings, distancing them from Spiritualism or the occult. He finally coined the term *extra-sensory perception*. This placed his research firmly within the study of perception, a respected subfield in psychology. In Rhine's view, extrasensory perception—ESP, as it soon came to be known—differed from ordinary perception only in that it was generated by another sensory modality, one beyond the familiar five senses of sight, smell, hearing, taste, and touch.

In 1934, Rhine published a monograph describing the lab's findings. He kept the title simple: *Extra-Sensory Perception*. It's hard these days to imagine how provocative that title was. Despite the fact that it was an academic treatise, Rhine's book was immediately snapped up by the public. The *New York Times,* New York *Herald Tribune, Scientific American,* and just about every other major organ of the American press gave it huge attention. It eventually reached millions of readers.

Rhine's monograph also managed to break into the world of academic science, where it stirred no small amount of controversy. As the first soberly scientific publication of data from systematically conducted experiments on anomalous mental capacities, it was hailed, on the one hand, as "epoch-making."[34] At the same time, it initiated a series of assaults on Rhine and his research that would dog him for the rest of his working life. They ranged from respectful methodological critiques to viciously vituperative attacks on his character. Rhine remained steady in the face of it all, calmly sticking to the credo that had informed his work from the beginning, remarking, "In the history of more than one branch of research, the stone which a hasty science rejected has sometimes become the cornerstone of its later structure."[35]

From those early beginnings at the Rhine lab, further experiments proliferated, both at Duke and elsewhere. Other laboratories at other universities were established. Professional associations, peer-reviewed journals, annual conferences, and a mushrooming literature followed. Occasionally, some research managed to break through the general scientific silence around anomalous mental capacities, though rarely with the drama that accompanied publication of *Extra-Sensory Perception*. But those flurries of public and scientific attention, even the most dramatic, rarely lasted long. For the most part, research on anomalous mental capacities continued to proceed quietly out of the public eye, outside the purview of everyday academic and scientific life. It developed instead as a vast parallel world.[36]

And so it was that at the time I began to explore Rhine's work, I was only vaguely aware that someone named Rhine had once done research on purportedly psychic phenomena at Duke University. Of one thing I was certain, however: that whatever the experiments had been, they'd been discredited as poorly controlled, their results discredited as well. I, like many people, knew enough both to know Rhine's name and to have it solidly associated with pseudoscience—or, in a more generous mood, maybe just not very good science.

But then I'd taken the trouble to look into the actual history. I'd begun with the Rhines' scientific past and the start of their lab. I'd gone on to examine their early experiments. I discovered the rigor surrounding their work, a far cry from what I'd heard. And then I started examining the history of criticism around the Rhine work. I looked into what the criticisms were, how the best of them had been taken into account by the Rhines, and how other attacks were disputed, discredited, and even formally retracted. It amounted to quite a story.

Soon after *Extra-Sensory Perception* was published, several outside researchers identified ways in which the Rhines' experiments could be better controlled in order to rule out nonanomalous explanations for their positive ESP results. Critics also objected to ways the lab employed their statistics. All those critiques were widely publicized.

The Rhines took on every criticism. They found some of the questions about experimental design valid and useful. By the late

1930s, they had redesigned relevant aspects of their experiments to take account of them. Most of the criticisms pointed to possible sensory leakage, ways in which ordinary sensory cues could have "leaked" to subjects. For example, an experimenter might have inadvertently signaled the identity of a card through body movement, a sideways glance, by coughing, or some other sensory cue the subject could have picked up on. In response, the Rhines had a machine instead of a person shuffle the Zener cards. They completely isolated subjects from contact with experimenters. They put in place additional steps for checking and double-checking experimental results. In 1937, the American Institute of Mathematics pronounced the lab's statistical procedures fully valid. With that, furor over the Rhines' use of statistics calmed down.

In 1938, the American Psychological Association devoted a session at its annual convention to a debate entitled "Experimental Methods of ESP Research." Three well-known critics were assigned to challenge three ESP researchers: Rhine, one of the Rhine lab's statisticians, and Gardner Murphy. Rhine was anything but enthused at the prospect, privately referring to the debate as a "heresy trial." Still, he agreed to participate, on the slim chance that productive dialogue might result.

The day of the debate arrived. To Rhine's surprise, the discussion proved lively and respectful. On top of that, he and his colleagues met the critics with rebuttals that the audience repeatedly found convincing. At the debate's conclusion, the three ESP researchers were met with resounding applause from the entire APA membership present.

The first decade of work at the lab was drawing to a close. Rhine decided the time was ripe for another book, one that would offer a definitive and highly detailed report of all the experiments undertaken at the lab since its inception. It would enumerate every major criticism—thirty-two, according to his count—and meet each one with solid argument. Finally, it would demonstrate how positive results achieved by six of the strongest experiments stood up in the face of every criticism raised.

Before going to press, the completed text was shown to each critic cited. All were invited to reply and urged to publish their replies in the book itself. In 1940, *Extra-Sensory Perception After Sixty Years* appeared (a reference to the sixty years that had passed since the founding of the original Society for Psychical Research). *ESP-60,* as it came to be known, right away followed in the astronomically successful trajectory of its predecessor, *Extra-Sensory Perception.* To Rhine's astonishment, it promptly joined classic texts as required reading for introductory psychology classes at Harvard. For a brief moment, it looked as though anomalous mental capacities might finally enter the scientific mainstream as legitimate objects of scientific study.

But the scenario turned out to be all too familiar. Other forces denouncing *ESP-60* as pseudoscience were quickly brought to bear, and it had no more lasting legitimacy than Sir Robert Boyle's endorsement of Valentine Greatrakes. *ESP-60* disappeared from Harvard's assigned reading lists, and silence regarding anomalous mental capacities once again descended at annual meetings of the APA. The lab settled into scientific obscurity, regularly publishing experimental results in the *Journal of Parapsychology,* which was read only by a small group of devoted subscribers.

It was yet another sixty years before I started asking colleagues what they knew about the Rhine research. It turned out most were like me; they'd heard of it, but dismissed it. Also like me, they thought they knew what they were dismissing. The fact was, we were all misinformed. So much for priding ourselves on judging by the evidence.

Once I confronted my own prejudice, I began subscribing to journals I'd never heard of, all concerned with understanding aspects of anomalous phenomena. There were plenty of them, covering a wide range of topics and points of view. I began with the most medically minded. While mind–body medicine made occasional forays into the apparently anomalous, it tended to keep one foot reassuringly grounded in mainstream science.

But those journals rapidly led me to others. From journals such as *Alternative Therapies in Health and Medicine* and *Advances in Mind-Body Medicine,* I moved on to *Frontier Perspectives, The International*

Journal of Parapsychology, IONS Noetic Sciences Review, the *Journal of the American Society for Psychical Research,* the *Journal of Parapsychology,* the *Journal of Scientific Exploration, Network: The Scientific and Medical Network Review,* and *Science and Spirit,* to name just a few.

I also started subscribing to the *Skeptical Inquirer: The Magazine for Science and Reason,* a journal put out by CSICOP, the Committee for the Scientific Investigation of Claims of the Paranormal. CSICOP was started in 1976 by Paul Kurtz, a professor of philosophy at the State University of New York at Buffalo, in collaboration with Carl Sagan, Isaac Asimov, Martin Gardner, and other respected science writers. One of its founders, the former stage magician James Randi, has achieved international fame as a debunker of paranormal claims and even received a MacArthur "genius" award for his work in educating the public on the need for scientific rigor and a healthy sense of skepticism. CSICOP boasted a small but prestigious membership, featuring a list of editors from universities and scientific organizations all over the world. The organization's original purpose was laudable, described by Kurtz as "the critical investigation of paranormal and fringe-science claims from a responsible scientific point of view [making available] factual information about the results of such inquiries to the scientific community and the public."[37]

I had high hopes for what CSICOP'S journal might provide. At the very least it would, I thought, offer useful balance to journals with a clear bent toward belief in the paranormal. I was particularly enthused about the *Skeptical Inquirer's* policy of reviewing research on anomalous mental capacities published elsewhere. I figured that CSICOP would help me come up with useful challenges to articles written from the more credulous side.

But it didn't work that way. Reading the *Skeptical Inquirer* was like reading a fundamentalist religious tract. I found the journal dismayingly snide, regularly punctuated by sarcasm, self-congratulation, and nastiness, all parading as reverence for true science.

After many months of this, I mentioned my reaction to a skeptical colleague who'd never seen the *Skeptical Inquirer.* He was, well, skeptical. Maybe the problem was mine, not the journal's. I challenged him to judge for himself: "Grab an issue, any issue. Pick a page—any page—and read what's on it. Then tell me whether that counts as reasoned scientific skepticism by your standards."

He pulled out the January/February 2002 issue and opened it to the first page, where an editorial commented on the anthrax scare that occurred following the September 11 terrorist attacks on the World Trade Center in New York City. The piece concluded,

> Pseudomedical nonsense is not going to get quite the free ride it has for so long. When the anthrax mail attacks came, people turned to real medicine, not unfounded remedies. As Bob Park of the American Physical Society put it in his *What's New* electronic newsletter: "Fortunately those exposed to anthrax are being diagnosed and treated with the very latest scientific medicine. They are not being treated with homeopathy, acupuncture, touch therapy, magnets, reflexology, crystals, chelation, craniosacral therapy, echinacea, aromatherapy, or yohimbe bark. And no one is complaining."
>
> The September 11 attacks may begin to usher in a new era of no-nonsense. People know they have no choice but to confront the real world directly, on its own terms. There is no escape into a trivial, pretend world of nonexistent woo-woo.

My colleague agreed that that was hardly an example of scientific skepticism. He also agreed that "nonexistent woo-woo" isn't how acupuncture is viewed by the National Institutes of Health or thousands of Western-trained M.D.'s or millions of patients around the world for whom evidence of its benefits appears unequivocal.

But fine, I said to him, it's an editorial. Opinions belong in editorials. He turned the page. Next came an article with the headline "Astrology Teaching May Enter Universities in India." It was a purportedly objective report regarding current changes in India's educational policies. The author began by praising the distinguished intellectual achievements of India's citizens in fields such as computer science, space technology, genetic engineering, marine biology, and microbiology. With some horror, he went on to report that the University Grants Commission in India recently recommended teaching "ancient Vedic Sciences" in university curricula, a decision this author denounced as "defying logic."

Veda comes from the Sanskrit word for "knowledge." The Vedic tradition is as much a part of Indian culture as the intellectual brain power this author was quick to admire. Both are highly valued by most Indians, and the Vedic tradition has had profound influence on every form of knowledge in India, including on the sciences. Many Indian physicians, for example, incorporate Vedic medicine into their practices as Western-trained M.D.'s. To headline teaching the Vedic tradition as teaching astrology is not just blatantly incorrect, it's culturally pejorative as well.

My colleague continued to leaf through the *Skeptical Inquirer.* He smiled at a few of the caustic headlines. But the intention to deflate was so glaring that I found the gibes offensive rather than funny. My friend finally tossed the journal on my desk and said he'd read enough. He was ready to agree. It was hard for either of us to imagine much genuine science taking root in conversation with the *Skeptical Inquirer.*

Just as I discovered a proliferation of journals neither I nor my colleagues had ever heard of, I encountered an array of equally unfamiliar research centers, places where projects investigating anomalous mental capacities appeared to be thriving. They were housed in hundreds of universities all over the world, from the University of Freiburg in Germany to Princeton University in New Jersey; from Shanghai Jiao Tong University in Shanghai, China, to Edinburgh University in Scotland.[38] Some universities even had endowed professorships devoted entirely to pursuing the study of anomalous human capacities.

I had colleagues and friends teaching at several of the places that turned up in my reading. I contacted a few, assuming they might have formed impressions regarding the nature and caliber of the work being done, often just down the hall or across the street from their own offices. With rare exceptions, my associates were astonished to hear that research on anomalous mental capacities was going on right under their noses.

The pervasiveness of the silence was just plain impressive. I'd become strikingly aware of it in our APA discussion group, then in the letters and e-mails I'd been receiving, and it was a chronic undercurrent in the history of research on anomalous mental capacities. Here it was again, as intriguing as the research hiding behind it.

Science is rooted in conversation. And that, I kept realizing, was the point. Science doesn't take root in determined absence of conversation, in resolute commitment to silence. What happened to that conversation after the publication of *ESP-60* in 1940? What other good science was being dismissed or silenced? And why? I decided to take a closer look at more recent research and the culture of silence around it, as well as the researchers living on the boundaries.

7

Tossing Out Meteorites:

Science, Fear, and Anxiety

A PROSPECTIVE PATIENT CALLED to ask for a consultation. She was a statistician contemplating a move to the Bay Area for a new job. She was planning to accept, but wanted to discuss her decision. When she arrived at my office, a tall, elegant woman in her midfifties, she greeted me cordially but moved right to the point: she was in a bind, a familiar one. She'd run away whenever it had arisen in the past. If she made this move, it might mean she was running away again.

On paper, her career looked highly successful. She'd worked all over the world at great universities and top-notch labs. Her résumé read like a travelogue of fabulous places and fascinating projects. It would have been easy to explain her wanderings as a tribute to her competence, but that wasn't the whole story and she was getting too old to keep pretending it was. The fact was, she moved to keep people from getting to know her too well. As a result, she was lonely—professionally but also personally.

She'd called me because a colleague had mentioned I had an interest in odd ways that people know things. For years she'd avoided getting psychological help out of fear that she'd be diagnosed as crazy. "It began with something that happened in graduate school. It traumatized me. I'm scared to think about it even now. Versions of the same thing have been happening ever since. I keep running away, but that's no solution. I want help. I need a different way to live with who I am."

She explained that she knew things in ways that were real—she was defensive as she said it: "real"—but they were real in ways her colleagues called impossible. Could they be right? Was I open to the idea that people might know things in ways that seemed impossible and crazy?

I was cautious but reassuring. I told her that, yes, I was interested in the apparently peculiar ways people knew things, even things that seemed impossible to know. I acknowledged that people did sometimes get dismissed for claiming to know such things. I agreed that it could be deeply disturbing when that happened. She nodded and picked up her story again.

> I know things and it mystifies me how I know them. Sometimes it terrifies me. It starts with getting a good read on things. I'm intuitive. But lots of people are intuitive. It didn't get really scary until I was in graduate school. I was in my third year of Ph.D. work. I had a good fellowship. My professors thought well of me. I had an idea for a dissertation that built on the work of one professor, someone I liked a lot, very smart but very gruff....
>
> He was teaching a seminar. One day he'd given us a problem to work out—very complicated. I took it down like everyone else. Then I said the answer. Just said it—the right answer. To four decimal places. It just came to me. It seemed natural to say it. It was a disaster. The professor swore I must have stolen his notes. That was crazy—there was no way I could have gotten those notes. But it was just as crazy that I came up with the answer.
>
> After that, he wouldn't work with me anymore. The other students

stopped trusting me. It got so bad I had to find another university where I could do my dissertation research. I've been moving ever since. I get afraid people might start attacking me for things they think I shouldn't know. Now I move before things blow up.

What happens is I'll suddenly know something. Like I'll know an experiment won't work. Or I'll know some data analysis is faulty. The more I let on what I know, the more obvious it gets that I don't have any basis for knowing. It's just an idea that comes to me. But I *know*—I can't tell you how powerful the sensation is. Maybe you know what it's like. It's spooky. It scares me. I want to be normal.

My patient—I'll call her Grace—did move to San Francisco and we started meeting regularly. We soon agreed we had two tasks. The first was the question of evidence, establishing the reality of what she actually knew and didn't know. As Grace put it, "If I'm deluded I want to know it. If I'm not, I've got to learn better ways to live with this spooky knowing."

So we set about reconstructing all we could about her previous anomalous experiences. Had she really, back in graduate school, pulled that solution out of thin air—no hints, no cues, but accurate to four decimal places? Were other similarly spooky incidents really as inexplicable as she'd registered them to be?

This reassessment turned out to be the easy part. Much harder was grappling with her terror. Whenever Grace would recall some inexplicable piece of knowing, she'd relive the circumstances, vividly, convincingly. Then abruptly, unexpectedly, she'd be invaded by panic. Her deer-in-the-headlights feeling, we named it. Bringing her back from her terror became our second task. We had to make it safe to keep her engaged with the knowing she wanted to understand.

I gradually became convinced Grace did have unusual and remarkable intuitive capacities. But the depth and extent of her virulent fear impressed me at least as much. As a psychoanalyst, I'm used to seeing fear. But Grace's fear was unusual. She didn't just fear for her mental stability. She feared for the stability of the world around her—the existence of a world she could count on, reliably constrained by boundaries of space, time, and individual identity.

Beneath these terrors lay far more conventional fears of a child raised by an abusive alcoholic father and a blandly unprotective mother. Home was ugly, unstable, and terrifying. In his drinking bouts, Grace's father was uncontrollably violent. He beat up on Grace, her younger sister, and their mother. Grace learned to find safety in a locked closet where she'd sheltered herself and her sister. But what scared Grace the most was how she'd known just when to get the two of them inside that closet:

During the late afternoons, I'd start listening for him. It was a funny kind of listening. It was like listening with my whole body, not my ears. I don't know how to describe it except to say I was tuned in, vigilant with every part of me. Suddenly I'd *know*—know he was fifteen minutes away and driving home drunk. Then I'd hustle me and my sister into the closet. I couldn't afford to wait and hear him at the door. He'd crash in and grab whoever was in sight, then hit. He grabbed my mother a lot—she just stood there. So I had to be the one to protect me and my sister—I had to learn how. Somehow I just started knowing when he was headed home and when he'd be dangerous. I *knew*. It was like the spooky knowing with my professor but it was different because I *had* to know, I had no choice.

My dad didn't drink all the time. So there was no predicting. I had to stay tuned in every day, be ready and never trust any pattern. We'd go for weeks and be safe. But I couldn't get lulled into thinking that's how it would stay because suddenly he'd drink again and we'd have to hide again. I'd have to know way before he pulled up at the house. As soon as I knew, I'd start getting ready—turn off the lights in the bedroom, get water for my sister, bring in her blanket, and settle us with pillows to make it cozy. . . . How did I know when he was on his way and drunk? As a child I accepted it, I thought I just knew because I had to. But now that isn't good enough. . . . I keep wondering, am I crazy? If I'm crazy, how come I kept being right? It scares me to death. . . .

"I knew because I had to." Grace's remarks reminded me of the studies done in the 1880s by the Society for Psychical Research on subjects who claimed to have had "veridical crisis hallucinations."

The people questioned in those studies reported knowing things "through no known sensory means" when people they loved on the other side of the world seemed to contact them by sight, sound, or touch during a moment of crisis. Like Grace, they knew because they had to.

Grace's comment also reminded me of what clinicians had reported at the discussion group I'd led in 1997 with Carol Gilligan at the American Psychoanalytic Association, the group devoted to studying "Intuition, Unconscious Communication and 'Thought Transference.' " One after another, the participants had described patients with extreme intuitive gifts, extreme enough to register as anomalous. Those patients believed that they had developed their gifts in response to trauma, in order to survive circumstances that required knowing more than people can possibly know. Again, those patients said they *had* to know. They couldn't afford not to.

Many of those patients also reported that their apparently anomalous capacities terrified them. I remembered asking my "professional intuitives"—Helen, Deb, John, Ellen, and Harold—whether their unusual abilities ever frightened them. Helen and Deb told me that they'd had to work their way through times of terrific fear. In fact, they said they couldn't start developing their extraordinary intuitive abilities until they'd confronted that fear.

Even though there's plenty we don't know about apparently anomalous cognitive abilities, one thing seems clear. If they happen at all, they happen outside conscious control. For people used to rational mediation of experience, that can be a very frightening prescription. It means living outside the rules we rely on to make much of life safe. It means living in a world unconstrained by ordinary boundaries associated with space, time, and individual identity. Fear stops people dead in life. It distorts how people feel, think, and love. It paralyzes them and stops them from letting themselves know what they know. Long ago, recognizing that turned me into a psychoanalyst.

Much psychoanalytic theory today is outmoded, culture bound, irrelevant, or just plain wrong. But the essential brilliance of Freud's clinical theory survives, and it hinges on how he understood fear. The human psyche, Freud declared, is organized to escape the experience of fear. We use a vast array of defenses to channel, transform, suppress, and regulate fear. When those defenses work best, they operate unconsciously. We don't even know that we're defending, much less what we're defending against. The conscious mind is thereby freed for attention to other things, from problem solving to the pursuit of pleasure.

It's a highly efficient mental organization and one that contemporary neuroscience is now elaborating, once again, in ways remarkably coincident with Freud's early ideas. But what captured me when I initially encountered those ideas was their clinical import. They made a difference.

The face we present to the world, said Freud, is quintessentially patterned by the unconscious defensive strategies we've made our own. These strategies betray themselves right on the surface of who we are. So some people shape themselves around denial: "I never said that." Others project: "I didn't say it, you did." Others intellectualize: "Even though I said it, it's just an idea, so don't hold me to it."

Those are the simple renditions. Then there are our most sophisticated attitudes, solidly reasoned ideas, and carefully chosen values. These are all irrevocably determined by the idiosyncratic ways we erect our defenses, conscious as well as unconscious. And those, in turn, are dictated by what we fear—what we're defending against. So, said Freud, pay exceedingly close attention to how people express themselves. Then you'll learn how they defend themselves. Help them attend to themselves in the same way and together you'll start observing what's underneath, what's motivating their need to defend. Once you start to see that, you liberate choice. People can start consciously choosing whether they need to stay afraid. But they also can start choosing to modify their defenses and make them more adaptive, more consonant with a happy life and being who they want to be.

I decided to listen more closely to what modern scientists were saying about the research into anomalous mental capacities. I wanted to observe what lay underneath those appraisals, whether they were erecting any defenses against what they were finding and, if so, what they might be defending themselves against. I decided to delve more deeply into the last fifty or so years of research into extraordinary knowing.

Science is based on evidence, "that which makes itself seen" (from the Latin *evidens,* meaning "that which is clear or visible to the naked eye"). The question is what we allow ourselves to see. According to philosopher of science Michael Polanyi,

> It is the normal practice of scientists to ignore evidence which appears incompatible or irrelevant.... But there is, unfortunately, no rule by which to avoid the risk of occasionally disregarding thereby true evidence which conflicts (or seems to conflict) with the current teachings of science. During the eighteenth century the French Academy of Science stubbornly denied the evidence for the fall of meteorites, which seemed massively obvious to everybody else.[1]

Such was the awe in which Parisian scientists were held by their foreign associates that curators of public museums in Germany, Denmark, Switzerland, Italy, and Austria, "anxious not to be considered as backward compared with their famous colleagues in Paris...threw away whatever they possessed of these precious meteorites."[2] The museum curators were quick to defend their actions; any lurking notion that meteorites might descend from the sky smacked dangerously of popular superstition about heavenly intervention. That was precisely the kind of superstition that progressive science was working hard to defy. The scientists and museum curators asserted that getting rid of meteorites was actually in the service of science.

Scientists in those days didn't believe in throwing out evidence any more than we do now. But to them, rocks falling from the sky represented a category of event so closely associated with heavenly acts of God that they were prima facie judged nonevidence— judged instead dangerous to science. The question isn't whether that reason has merit. The sincerity of their judgment may be beside the essential point. Drew Westen, a professor of psychology at Emory University who has done extensive research on implicit unconscious processes, writes that people typically cannot report why they carry out much of the behavior that stems from workings of the unconscious mind, even though the behavior appears formed in full consciousness. According to Westen, they do something even more insidious: "When they try, they often make up plausible but incorrect explanations."[3]

Under an umbrella of fear, science acts like a deer in the headlights, just as Grace did. In the face of fear, two versions of bad science proliferate, both rife with "plausible but incorrect explanations." One is credulous science: "I have to prove it so I can prove I'm not crazy." But equally bad is dogmatic science: "This doesn't fit with what I already know, so it can't possibly be true." Both are implicated in the volumes of bad science associated with studies of anomalous cognition. Finding the elements of good science inside these volumes means doing just what Grace did, deconstructing every account of apparently spooky knowing to locate the studies that plow ahead in the face of fear, needing neither to prove that anomalous cognition exists nor that it doesn't.

I did my own share of plowing, reading study after study. They were rare, the studies that managed to sidestep the pitfalls of bad science. Some of them challenged my own fears; what would it do to my world to discover that this kind of anomalous knowing really existed? My skepticism caused me to reject many of the studies I read, easy fodder for the voice in me that refused. *I can't go there,* I told myself. *That stuff's not possible and I won't be taken in.* Certain terrain just made my hackles rise, in particular the issue of "life after death" that consumed so many purported mediums. I had such a problem with all this that I put the whole thing on the shelf. I wanted no part of it.

And then I came across a body of work that blew it all open, pushing me past my incredulity, pushing me into considering how something inconceivable just might enter the realm we call possible. It was evidence I couldn't ignore, although I found out that so many others had done exactly that.

From 1963 to 1972, Harold Puthoff, Ph.D., a theoretical and experimental physicist, had been doing laser research at Stanford

University, then at Stanford Research Institute (SRI) in Menlo Park, California, a think tank spun off from the university. The work was fascinating but conventional. On the side, Puthoff became interested in the question of whether physical theory as we know it could be used to describe life processes. In pursuit of an answer, he'd circulated a small grant proposal addressing some implications of quantum theory for biology. The proposal ended up on the desk of Cleve Backster, an eminent polygrapher who was measuring electrical activity in plants. There it caught the eye of Ingo Swann, a New York artist who happened to be visiting Backster's lab. Swann's interest started a chain of events that would lead Puthoff in some radically unexpected professional directions over the next decade and a half. It began with a letter he received from Swann.

> Swann . . . wrote me suggesting that if I were interested in investigating the boundary between the physics of the animate and inanimate, I should consider experiments of the parapsychological type. Swann then went on to describe some apparently successful experiments . . . in which he had participated at Prof. Gertrude Schmeidler's laboratory at the City College of New York. As a result of this correspondence I invited him to visit SRI for a week in June 1972 to demonstrate such effects, frankly, as much out of personal scientific curiosity as anything else.
>
> Prior to Swann's visit I arranged for access to a well-shielded magnetometer used in a quark-detection experiment in the Physics Department at Stanford University. During our visit to this laboratory, sprung as a surprise to Swann, [we asked him] to perturb the operation of the magnetometer, located in a vault below the floor of the building and shielded by mu-metal shielding, an aluminum container, copper shielding and a superconducting shield. To the astonishment of Stanford physics professor Dr. Arthur Hebard, whose experiments depended heavily on the magnetometer's much vaunted imperturbability to outside influence, Swann doubled the rate at which the magnetic field in the magnetometer was decaying. Then, in response to Hebard's disbelieving subsequent request, Swann stopped the field change altogether for a period of roughly

forty-five seconds. As if to add insult to injury, he then went on to "remote view" the interior of the apparatus . . . by drawing a reasonable facsimile of its rather complex (and heretofore unpublished) construction.[4] It was this latter feat that impressed me perhaps even more than the former, as it also eventually did representatives of the intelligence community. I wrote up these observations and circulated it among my scientific colleagues in draft form of what was eventually published as part of a conference proceedings.

In a few short weeks a pair of visitors showed up at SRI with the above report in hand. Their credentials showed them to be from the CIA. They knew of my previous background as a naval intelligence officer and then civilian employee at the National Security Agency (NSA) several years earlier, and felt they could discuss their concerns with me openly. There was, they told me, increasing concern in the intelligence community about the level of effort in Soviet parapsychology being funded by the Soviet security services; by Western scientific standards the field was considered nonsense by most working scientists. As a result they had been on the lookout for a research laboratory outside academia that could handle a quiet, low-profile classified investigation, and SRI appeared to fit the bill. They asked if I could arrange an opportunity for them to carry out some simple experiments with Swann, and, if the tests proved satisfactory, would I consider a pilot program along these lines? I agreed to consider this, and arranged for the required tests.[5]

That visit with Swann initiated a twenty-four-year, $20 million research project sponsored first by the CIA, then the Defense Intelligence Agency, and eventually transferred from SRI to Science Applications International Corporation (SAIC) in 1991. The project was designed to investigate the phenomenon the scientists decided to call remote viewing, to see whether it was possible for subjects to identify and describe a distant "target" hidden from their view. Puthoff was appointed founder and the first director of the project, a position he retained until 1985 when he moved on to become director of the Institute for Advanced Studies at Austin, in Austin, Texas. At that point he turned the directorship over to a physicist colleague, Edwin May, Ph.D., now director at the Laboratories for Fundamental Research in Palo Alto, California.

From what I knew, this government-sponsored project had been mired in controversy, and contradictory reports on its success abounded after information on the research was declassified in 1995. I decided to get a bird's-eye history of the entire effort from Harold Puthoff himself. He was uniquely suited to describe and appraise phases of the experiments, procedures, and methods as well as politics. He'd been centrally involved through much of the project's existence. Equally to the point, I trusted him as a fine scientist. A theoretical and experimental physicist, he'd graduated from Stanford University and later taught there in the electrical engineering department. Later he was director for the Cognitive Sciences Program at SRI International, the research institute. We were both senior research scholars at the International Consciousness Research Laboratory (ICRL) in Princeton. I'd been consistently impressed by his scientific caution, attention to evidence, experimental brilliance, and the clarity of his thinking. He didn't have an ax to grind.

I told Hal that I wanted to get a really thorough assessment of all the remote-viewing experiments sponsored by the government, now, with the hindsight of thirty years. He was typically gracious. We scheduled a series of conversations. Hal was incredibly forthcoming:

First, you should know that many key documents are still classified—17,700 pages have been denied in full and 20,800 remain in review. That's inevitably tempted people to evaluations that are premature or outright incorrect. On top of that, evaluation of this research has been about as burdened by ideological controversy as it's possible to get. So there are a number of assessments out there which are anything but objective, some in the direction of making wildly exaggerated claims for the accuracy of remote viewing but many doing the opposite, blatantly denying the presence of solid evidence.

With that as background, let's go back to the beginning. You know about my first contact with Ingo Swann. The next step involved month-by-month development of double-blind protocols and refining of our experimental methods. We were attempting to study phenomena we knew nothing about and that posed extraordinary challenges to our experiments. In that sense, much of it was the ordinary plodding work of designing good science on questionable, barely defined phenomena.

But occasionally we got data that was anything but ordinary and it just blew our minds. That renewed any lagging enthusiasm on our parts. Those moments were crucial because, as you can imagine, I had great skepticism. And I had continuing doubts throughout, about whether we really could be seeing what we were apparently seeing. The very last day of the program, I vividly recall walking in to do an experiment and thinking to myself, "I can't be doing this! These data can't be real, it's simply not possible!"

Despite how powerful my doubts were, another part of my mind was forced to take those experiments on. There was no choice. I had to think seriously about them, because the evidence was just too strong. For example, I've got here a seventeen-page bibliography of 266 highly detailed technical papers and reports I worked on, some of which remain classified but all of which were really significant think-pieces about this research. I look at that list now and I'm amazed I wrote all that. The fact was, I could barely stop thinking about it. There was so much good data and it was so damn compelling.

Now, looking back, I think it's fair to say that over the years, the evidence turns out to be there. It's solid. The back-and-forth criticism of protocols, improvement of methods, and successful replication of remote viewing in independent laboratories all added up, by the end, to considerable scientific evidence for the reality of remote viewing as a genuine human capacity. We haven't begun to understand *how* consciousness can interact with the physical world to make remote viewing possible. On that we've barely started. But in the meantime, there's enough data that remain substantial and convincing to require serious scientific consideration.

Hal recommended a few of the best, most carefully documented experimental reports, articles, and books describing the remote-viewing research. All well and good. But I had questions they couldn't answer. He mentioned that he'd encountered evidence that really blew his mind. I wanted him to tell me about that. I also wanted to know how he came to terms with having his mind blown, subjectively as well as scientifically. How did he manage his ongoing doubts? I hoped his experience would help me as I teetered between accepting the evidence for remote viewing and refusing to believe any of it. We continued our talks.

In 1995, after the first round of declassification, I published an account of one episode that occurred in July 1974, drawing heavily on the final report from the CIA records, backed up by verbatim transcripts of the entire event. I'll summarize the whole thing for you.

Our general procedure in the early experiments was straightforward. We'd send someone we called a beacon to a series of locations some distance from SRI, randomly selected from a huge list. The beacon would spend thirty minutes at each site. Meantime, the remote viewer was sitting back at SRI in a locked room, drawing the site and offering verbal impressions of where he imagined the beacon to be. The whole procedure was double-blind—neither the experimenters nor the viewers were given any information about any of the sites where the beacon was—usually a series of six to ten sites in any given trial. Then we gave a list of that trial's target sites to outside blind judges who had nothing to do with the experiment and asked them to go to each site in the series. While there, they were to match up the viewers' drawings and descriptions with the series of sites, pair for pair, based on how closely they resembled each other. At that point, we'd look to see if the resulting matches were more accurate than chance would predict.

After some months, we had enough data to suggest the matches were highly unlikely as a result of chance. There was a small flurry of media coverage at that point, not linked to the CIA but simply naming the fact that SRI was sponsoring experimental work on remote viewing. A retired policeman named Pat Price from Burbank, California, read about it and called us. He told us he'd been using what he called ESP all his life and had relied on it to produce some of his more spectacular successes as a police commissioner.

Later we found out just how spectacular some of those successes were. But when Price first called, I happened to be right in the middle of thinking about something else. We'd been regularly sending our data to the CIA and they had really stepped up their interest. They'd just notified us that they wanted some new experiments, tests in which they themselves chose the targets and no one from the scientific end had any conceivable access to knowledge of the selected sites. They wanted to rule out any form of cheating or [sensory] leakage, intentional or unintentional. We were delighted for a couple of reasons. First, we ourselves routinely worried about whether we might have missed anything at all in our double-blind procedures. The results were just too unbelievable. But even more, the CIA's willingness to manage target selection freed us from having to demonstrate we were in fact doing exactly what our protocols said we were doing. Great, we thought, we'll let them see for themselves.

So the CIA told us they'd give us geographic coordinates—latitude and longitude—of a site they wanted our people to remote view. Nothing more. The idea was that this would be a rigorous long-distance test under external control.

Pat Price happened to call right after I'd gotten those first coordinates from our CIA contact. There they were, sitting on my desk just as I got on the phone with Pat. Why not, I thought—why not test this guy with these? So I said, "Well, we happen to be doing this experiment right now, why don't you try it? I'll give you some geographic coordinates. Give us a remote viewing of the place you think they identify and let us know what you see."

Pat agreed and immediately sent us a five-page report. At first he described a few log cabins and a couple of roads and that was it. But then he'd added, "Oh, over a ridge there's this really interesting place. That must be the place you're interested in." He went on to describe in great detail a military site he named as highly sensitive and surrounded by the heaviest security. He came up with code names that all centered on the game of pool, along with other information about what was going on there and personnel involved. We sent the verbatim transcripts back to the CIA for confirmation.

We asked Ingo Swann to focus on the same coordinates and we sent his report off along with Pat's.[6]

The CIA's first reaction was that the viewings were way off. The coordinates had been provided by an officer from the Office of Scientific Intelligence (OSI) and pinpointed the location of a staff member's vacation cabin in West Virginia. So a high-security military site seemed wildly inaccurate. But the CIA officers noted a striking correlation between the two independent descriptions from Pat and Ingo. That seemed unlikely enough to send the OSI officer out to the site itself. What he discovered was that, unknown to the staff member who owned the cabin, just over the ridge *was* a highly sensitive underground government installation. The guy's vacation cabin was indeed there. But so were other elements of the viewing, and they were top-secret, a total surprise to the officers looking at the data. Some of the details were wrong but a lot were right and they were stunningly precise, like the fact that the labels of each file folder in a locked file drawer inside the underground building were all designated by pool terms: cue ball, cue stick, and so on. Pat had even come up with the actual code name of the site: Haystack. From that point on, it got really serious. There was no question about the government's interest in what we were doing at SRI.

Even that wasn't the end of this particular episode. Pat had been intrigued by the experiment, so, as a personal challenge to himself, he decided to try scanning the other side of the globe for a Communist bloc equivalent to the site he'd just scanned in the U.S. He came up with a site in the Urals. We sent that off to the CIA. That viewing also proved substantially correct, verified by several classified sources within the agency.

What made both the West Virginia and the Urals material so startling was they weren't best-ever viewings culled from a much larger list. These were literally the first two viewings ever carried out in a simulated operational-type scenario. That's what I mean by mind-blowing.

Hal told me that the most accurate information in those early remote viewings often came from viewers asked to draw their impressions, which were consistently more accurate than straight verbal descriptions. He suggested we look at the very first remote viewing of a Soviet site, the result of a CIA request sent to SRI soon after Price's successful viewing of the Urals site.

Pat Price was the viewer. He was given a set of geographic coordinates by the CIA contract monitor and locked into a small electrically shielded room with an experimenter who was blind to all aspects of the experiment. The experimenter turned on a tape recorder and the session began. After a moment's silence, Price reported:

> I am lying on my back on the roof of a two- or three-story brick building. It's a sunny day. The sun feels good. There's the most amazing thing. There's a giant gantry crane moving back and forth over my head. . . . As I drift up in the air and look down, it seems to be riding on a track with one rail on each side of the building. I've never seen anything like that.[7]

Once the viewing was completed, the CIA revealed that the site was the top-secret Soviet test site facility at Semipalatinsk. The CIA had satellite photographs of the site since it had long been regarded as having critical strategic importance. CIA artists had previously rendered details of the satellite photos, including the portrayal of a large crane, a central feature of the photographs.

As I compared the drawings, which were astonishingly similar, Hal remarked,

> That's the kind of data we had to deal with. The correspondences were frankly extraordinary. Note, for example, that both cranes have eight wheels. Then look at the size of the thing. In the CIA rendering there's a man who's only half the height of the rear wheel. Meantime, that's what Pat had to say while describing the crane's scale. There are other drawings that are equally dramatic. We conducted several phases of research on the Semipalatinsk site. They're all available in the CIA contracting officer's technical report, which is now declassified. . . . We haven't begun to mine those data for all they could teach us. . . .

So the data were really impressive, really out there. Like I said, mind-blowing. You're asking me how I came to personal terms with them. You know, they really got me looking inside myself with a depth and honesty that were very challenging. They got me reading people like physicist David Bohm with new and passionate interest. He helped me because he turned the essential question upside down. I'd been asking, since everything in the world looks so separate, how can the connections that would seem to be required by this evidence be possible? Bohm was asking, since everything in the world is interconnected, how come everything looks so separate? I steeped myself in his work.[8] Since my rational mind was rebelling, I needed input from rational thinkers I respected. He was one. There were others—certainly a number of physicists, but there were also people doing research on subliminal perception. Their work had a major impact on me. It turned out their experimental subjects were making exactly the same types and patterns of errors ours were. If you think about it, that's big. It suggested the errors weren't due to chance. For example, the shape of an object might be discerned in a flash presentation, but without recognition of what it was; the presence of a sign might be identified, but the sign couldn't be read. It looked like there was a smooth curve between the apparently anomalous perceptions we were getting and other nonconscious, nonanomalous perception. That encouraged us to think we might be observing something on a continuum with previously established perceptual phenomena.

So all that helped me open some conceivably rational avenues into considering our findings. But as we finished examining the data from Semipalatinsk, I hit what I now view as a real turning point. The evidence we had was rock hard. I saw that. But I also saw that it didn't eradicate my doubt. That made me see my doubts weren't the problem. On the contrary, the problem lay with my beliefs. I was having terrible trouble giving up my beliefs about how the world worked, even in the face of evidence that said my beliefs were wrong. It really brought home what any good scientist knows: doubts aren't what interfere with good science. The trick is to keep looking at evidence in the face of doubt, not letting doubt stop you. It's a scientific truism, but it's one thing to know it and another to keep

practicing it when your ordinary worldview just can't contain your
evidence. It's easier to think there must be something wrong with
your experiments. And that's ironic because it looks like humility but
it isn't. It's privileging your own personal beliefs above the evidence.
That's not science, it's hubris.

Pat Price died of a heart attack in 1975, at the age of fifty-seven.
Hal, fellow physicist Russell Targ, and others engaged in the first
SRI experiments believed that Price had offered critical and tantalizing evidence that anomalous cognition was possible.[9] Those early
experiments led to publication of several papers in mainstream scientific journals, for example, *Nature* and *Proceedings of the Institute of
Electrical and Electronic Engineers (IEEE)*.[10] Each article summarized
experiments to date and raised cautious but far-reaching questions
about their implications. Meantime, Price's death highlighted one
of the many issues facing further investigation of remote viewing.
How would they find other experimental subjects able to do what
Price and Ingo Swann appeared able to do?
    Then Joe McMoneagle came along.

By 1978, the SRI remote-viewing experiments had attracted attention from military intelligence sources outside the CIA.
Frederick Atwater, a first lieutenant and counterintelligence officer
working for the 902nd Military Intelligence Group at Fort Meade,
Maryland, was particularly interested. He saw enormous counterintelligence potential in the experiments. He also recognized the
importance of identifying traits that might distinguish people who
were likely to excel at remote viewing, if it existed. Atwater came
up with a list of such traits, based on characteristics published in an
article on "psi-conducive states" that had appeared in the 1975
Journal of Communications.[11] The author of the article, William
Braud, was at the time an associate professor of psychology at the
University of Houston, Texas. (By then "psi" had become a short-
hand reference to all things parapsychological.)
    Atwater, joined by a significantly skeptical cohort, Major Scotty
Watt, picked over volumes of army records to isolate a few candidates

who fit the profile suggested by Braud, adding an amplified list of traits for military purposes. Joe McMoneagle fit the bill. He was at that time a senior projects officer for the U.S. Army Intelligence and Security Command (INSCOM) and moving rapidly up in the military ranks. A series of interviews was arranged, first with Atwater and Watt, then eventually with Hal and Russell Targ. As he would describe it later, he was mostly questioned regarding his attitude about possibly "paranormal" forms of knowing and their conceivable implications for national security. Repeatedly he replied with meticulous but wary truthfulness that if any such forms of knowing turned out to exist, they could pose a serious threat to the nation's safety. He wasn't a proponent but he wasn't a scoffer. That turned out to be just what the intelligence community was looking for.

Weeks later, Major Watt called McMoneagle with a brief message: he'd given all the right answers. When McMoneagle reported to work the following Monday, he was informed that he was being flown to California for two weeks on a highly confidential visit. His boss, he was told, would be given an appropriate cover story.

Thus began McMoneagle's career as a remote viewer.[12]

McMoneagle passed his first remote-viewing tests with flying colors. At that point, he was asked to volunteer as remote viewer #001 for top-secret Army project Grill Flame, eventually renamed Star Gate. He remained associated with the project for the full eighteen years of the Army-initiated involvement, the only remote viewer to do so. Besides working as an actual viewer, McMoneagle also contributed to protocol design, data assessment, applications evaluations, and the development of conceptual hypotheses that might help explain what remote viewing could be about. In 1984, he was awarded the Legion of Merit by the U.S. government for "distinguishing himself by exceptionally meritorious conduct in the performance of outstanding services during his Army career, culminating in his assignment as Special Project Intelligence Officer with the 902nd Military Intelligence Group.... He was instrumental in developing a new revolutionary intelligence project." In the certificate accompanying the award, McMoneagle is credited with "the execution of missions for the highest echelons of our military and government, including such national level agencies as the Joint

Chiefs of Staff, DIA [Defense Intelligence Agency], NSA [National Security Agency], CIA, and Secret Service, producing critical intelligence unavailable from any other source."[13]

Hal was deeply impressed with Joe McMoneagle's abilities:

> He'd produce masses of data that were really hot and totally inexplicable by ordinary means. One example that had particular impact on me was when Joe identified that the Russians were building a new form of submarine. Not only were the size and design judged by our military to be completely impossible. Worse was the fact that Joe said the Russians were building this huge submarine in the dead of a frozen Russian landscape with no direct access to water, so there would be no way to launch it. The whole thing seemed not just unlikely but crazy.
>
> It was during the fall of 1979 and it was one of the first operational targets we received once Joe was on board. A high-ranking naval officer from the National Security Council (NSC) brought us a photo of a massive, industrial-type building, some distance from a large body of water, located somewhere in Russia. The U. S. government didn't know what the building was, what it was used for, or what its strategic importance was. It was unusual for its size and appeared to house a good deal of activity, so they wanted to know more.
>
> We gave Joe the geographic coordinates, nothing else. His immediate response was that they identified a very cold wasteland with an extremely large industrial-looking building that had enormous smokestacks, not far from a sea covered with a thick cap of ice. Later we found out the location was Severodvinsk on the White Sea.
>
> Since that first quick impression corresponded very closely to the photograph, we showed Joe the picture and asked what might be going on inside it. Here's his own retrospective account of the viewing.
>
> > *I spent some time relaxing and emptying my mind. Then with my eyes closed, I imagined myself drifting down into the building, passing downward through its roof. What I found was mind-*

blowing. The building was easily the size of two or three huge shopping centers, all under a single roof....

In giant bays between the walls were what looked like cigars of different sizes, sitting in gigantic racks.... Thick mazes of scaffolding and interlocking steel pipes were everywhere. Within these were what appeared to be two huge cylinders being welded side to side, and I had an overwhelming sense that this was a submarine, a really big one, with twin hulls....

What I didn't know was that my session was reported back to the NSC and created some dissension. The almost unanimous belief at the time, by all the intelligence-collection agencies operating against the building, was that the Soviets were constructing a brand-new type of assault ship—a troop carrier, and possibly one with helicopter capability. A submarine was out of the question.

On my second visit, I got up very close.... Hovering beside it, I guessed it to be about twice the length of an American football field and nearly seventy feet in width, and at least six or seven floors high (if it were sitting next to a standard apartment building). It was clearly constructed of two huge elongated tubes run side-by-side for almost their entire length. (I didn't think this was possible with submarines.) ... I moved up over the deck and was surprised to see that it had canted missile tubes running side by side. This was critically important because this indicated that it had the capacity to fire while on the move rather than having to stand still in the water, which made it a very dangerous type of submarine....

After the session, I did a very detailed drawing of the submarine, adding dimensions, as well as noting the slanted tubes, indicating eighteen to twenty in all. This material, along with the typed transcript of my session ... was forwarded to ... the NSC....

We soon received a follow-on request ... to return to the target and to try to provide an estimated time of completion....

I revisited the site and, based on the speed of construction and the differences in the condition of the submarine from one session to the next, I guessed that it would be ready for launch about four months later—that would be sometime in the month of

January—a singularly crazy time of year to launch a submarine
from a building not connected to water, near a sea frozen over
with ice yards thick. (I reported that very soon a crew of bulldozers
and other types of heavy equipment would arrive to cut a channel
leading to the sea.)[14]

In mid-January of 1980, satellite photographs showed a new canal running alongside the facility and out to the sea. There was a two-hulled submarine with twenty canted missile tubes clearly evident in the photographs. It turned out subsequently to be the first in an entirely new class of submarine, the largest ever built, and named the Typhoon Class in tribute to the amount of water each sub displaced. The first Typhoon was in fact built in the Severodvinsk Shipyard on the White Sea and moved into the water for sea trials in January of 1980.

Joe's Typhoon viewing had a huge impact on Hal:

In the back of my mind were these astonishing experiences I couldn't argue myself out of, even if on any given day I'd be doubting that remote viewing could possibly be real. Recalling those experiences gave me confidence to go forward when experiments weren't going well or the whole thing just seemed too impossible to be true.

Besides that, I've always had great faith that science is self-correcting. We can count on good science to flush out the signal from the noise—that is, if there's any signal present. That's why the doubts aren't a problem. Remote viewing appears to operate on a very noisy channel. When the noise-to-signal ratio is really high, you spend a lot of time wondering if there's any signal there at all. But then a signal does suddenly cut through and you get viewings like the Typhoon. Most of all you try to figure out how to study it. You register that. Meantime you register the doubts. You can't let moments of doubt cancel out moments of conviction any more than moments of conviction cancel out doubt. When you're experiencing either one, the other seems totally out of reach, even nuts. But both are crucial to staying on track with figuring this kind of stuff out.

The remote-viewing studies continued under various names and auspices, with key players retiring, leaving for new positions, or being reassigned. The program, which ran from 1972 to 1995, essentially ended as the cold war wound down.

Inevitably, I was left with one big question after hearing Hal's account. At the end of the day, what did it all add up to? What did twenty-four years and $20 million of government-sponsored experiments yield in the way of overall evidence for or against remote viewing?

Hal's response plunged me into the murky waters of one of the longest-running controversies in research into anomalous cognition. It had its roots in a report that did not reference Star Gate at all.[15]

In 1984, as part of its mandate to train and maintain a highly skilled fighting force, the Army undertook to evaluate a broad range of current techniques and claims for enhancing performance. It commissioned a report by the National Research Council (NRC) of the National Academy of Sciences, which was published in 1988 under the title *Enhancing Human Performance*.[16]

The Army study set out to assess the effectiveness of a number of "controversial" approaches, including biofeedback, neurolinguistic programming, accelerated learning, mental practice, and—parapsychology.

Right off the bat I was intrigued—*parapsychology*? The label set off a mild alert in me. Even minimal exposure to the literature on anomalous mental capacities reveals that "parapsychology" is a questionable term in the minds of many serious investigators. By definition, it suggests that whatever's included will fall "para," or outside, the real thing. (As biologist Rupert Sheldrake once observed, "Being a biologist, I wouldn't have much use for a field called *para*biology.") It also struck me as notable that the U. S. Army considered parapsychology something that might "enhance human performance." On top of that, they registered it "controversial" in the same breath as other techniques that, while not immune from all questions, were widely accepted in mainstream circles as effective and standard techniques for learning. But most astonishing of all was the sweeping judgment rendered in the press conference that announced the publication of the report: "The Committee finds no scientific justification from research conducted over a period of 130 years for the existence of parapsychological phenomena."[17]

The presumed basis for this conclusion was not the Star Gate material, which was still classified at the time. Rather, it was the NRC's very selective analysis of a category of remote-viewing experiments known as ganzfeld studies. Ganzfeld studies—from the German for "total field"—are remote perception experiments conducted in a setting that minimizes stimulation to a person's total perceptual field, an attempt to quiet the "noisy signals" that might hamper the ability to "receive" purportedly anomalous signals. (I'll discuss these experiments more fully in Chapter 10.) As it happened, the ganzfeld studies had provided some of the strongest positive evidence for anomalous mental capacities, but the NRC report managed to omit all the most recent, best-controlled replications. In addition, the evaluators gave no evidence that they'd examined anything resembling 130 years of other research, which, I discovered, was readily available and filled volumes.

Not surprisingly, several of the most highly regarded researchers in the field issued a formal and carefully argued reply protesting this flatly negative assessment.[18] But it was not clear until several years later how thoroughly the committee had stacked the deck, relying on background papers that were negative about parapsychology while discounting a paper by a leading authority that came to a favorable conclusion.

The NRC had sought out Harvard psychologist Robert Rosenthal to review the experimental evidence for a number of the performance-enhancing techniques. Rosenthal was renowned as a crack experimental psychologist, brilliant in evaluating research strategies as well as spotting methodological flaws or sloppy thinking. He also had very special expertise in evaluating research in performance enhancement—precisely the thing the Army wanted to study. He accepted the commission and brought his associate Monica Harris on board with him.

Rosenthal was not remotely identified with the peculiar world of psychics, fortune-tellers, and all the other hodgepodge elements that sometimes fall under the name of parapsychology. He was an eminent academic and accustomed to being taken seriously. He and Harris gave exceedingly careful consideration to the research the

NRC had commissioned them to evaluate. They duly submitted their report, which concluded that, of all the research in the five areas they examined, "only the ganzfeld ESP studies regularly meet the basic requirements of sound experimental design."[19] They went on to declare that it would be "implausible" to suggest that the positive findings obtained in the studies they evaluated resulted from chance. In other words, the evidence for "parapsychology" was good and deserved further investigation.

The full story of what happened next appeared in 1994 in *Psychological Bulletin,* a journal of the American Psychological Association that applies rigorous standards to anything that appears on its pages. The article was coauthored by Daryl Bem, a social psychologist at Cornell, and Charles Honorton, the man who originally developed the ganzfeld experiments that Harris and Rosenthal had praised.

> In a troubling development, the chair of the NRC Committee phoned Rosenthal and asked him to delete the parapsychology section of the paper (R. Rosenthal, personal communication, September 15, 1992). Although Rosenthal refused to do so, that section of the Harris-Rosenthal paper is nowhere cited in the NRC report.[20]

"Nowhere cited in the NRC report"? That's a remarkable and worrisome absence. When that kind of absence characterizes how the National Academy of Sciences handles a serious report from a serious researcher, there's something seriously wrong with the way science is approaching anomalous mental capacities.[21] Science has stopped acting like science. Instead it's acting a lot more like religion—or politics.

In fact, at the same time the NRC was declaring publicly that there was "no scientific justification" for "parapsychological phenomena," the government was continuing to fund secret research into remote viewing.

In 1985, physicist Edwin May had taken over the Star Gate project after Hal Puthoff left to become director of the Institute for

Advanced Studies at Austin. May subsequently initiated a review of all the research conducted between 1973 and 1988: 154 experiments comprising over 26,000 separate trials. The final report concluded that the odds that the positive data resulted from chance were less than one in a billion. At odds like that, remote viewing emphatically appeared to exist. While the earliest experiments suffered from the inevitable growing pains of brand-new experimental protocols involving baffling, unfamiliar variables, investigative procedures became increasingly clean over time. Meantime and strikingly, levels of remote-viewing performance remained constant over the entire history of the 154 experiments. That suggested that the experiments were tapping the same phenomenon over and over again, even at the beginning. Therefore, the report concluded that early design problems couldn't be invoked to explain the early dramatic successes.[22] But this internal report was never made public.

Finally, thanks to President Clinton's 1995 Executive Order calling for more open government, the CIA declassified a massive number of documents, though not all, describing the remote-viewing research. With Project Star Gate officially shuttered, for the first time Puthoff and May were able to publicly link the CIA, the DIA, and the Department of Defense with their work.

At that point, a welter of accounts describing the history of the project started pouring forth. A few were sober appraisals from people who had been centrally involved, both as scientists and remote viewers. There were also detailed accounts from project managers on the government side.[23] But there were in addition numerous other reports that were highly sensationalistic and bore little relationship to events as they'd actually transpired. All over the country, people started claiming affiliation with the research, frequently suggesting they'd played key roles.

In the midst of all this came the official CIA assessment of the twenty-four-year-long project. To say it produced fireworks is an understatement. The story was J. B. Rhine's *ESP-60* all over again. An ostensibly objective investigation by the American Institutes for Research (AIR) forcefully discredited the government-sponsored remote-viewing research done by SRI International and by Science Applications International Corporation (SAIC). It culminated in a statement to the press that "there was no case in which ESP [remote viewing] had ever been used to guide intelligence operations."[24] That's no small contrast to the effusive text of Joe McMoneagle's Legion of Merit award, in which he was credited with having provided "critical intelligence unavailable from any other source," not just to the CIA but to the Joint Chiefs of Staff, Defense Intelligence Agency, National Security Agency, and the Secret Service.

Rhine was on his deathbed when he heard about the attempt to discredit his research and *ESP-60*; he died without being able to defend his lifework. However, the key players from Project Star Gate were very much alive when the CIA/AIR report went public. They systematically tackled the report as well as the issues themselves. Point by point they showed the report to be methodologically flawed, heavily biased, and reliant on numerous assertions that had little or no basis in fact.

In the spring of 1996, the *Journal of Scientific Exploration* published a series of articles addressing the controversy. The *JSE* issue included two background reports submitted to the CIA from members of the AIR panel—Professors Ray Hyman and Jessica Utts. The overall picture that emerges is not a pretty one. It was soberly summed up by Star Gate director Ed May in the article he contributed.

> In addition to questioning the validity of CIA/AIR's conclusions, I find such serious problems with their evaluation methodology that I have become reluctantly convinced that their conclusions were set before the investigation began and that methodological and administrative choices were made to assure that the results of the investigation would support the CIA's pre-determined perspective.... I will document that as a result of their minimum effort, they have come to the wrong conclusion with regard to the use of anomalous cognition in intelligence operations and greatly underestimated the robustness of the phenomenon.[25]

May offered a blow-by-blow account of scientific failure on the part of the CIA/AIR evaluation. He claimed that there had been instructions to the evaluators to examine radically incomplete data sets; directives to exclude a wide range of experiments and backup reports that might have challenged eventual negative findings; known anti-ESP bias among a significant proportion of the evaluators; deliberate decisions not to interview a number of crucial participants and to ignore previous extensive program reviews, including ones conducted in-house by the Department of Defense; deliberate refusal to control for standard variables widely known to disrupt cognitive performance in experimental settings; and finally, the decision to use the National Research Council's negative review of parapsychology as the basis and starting point for the review.

Reliance on the NRC report was especially startling. Statistician Jessica Utts of the University of California was one of the researchers who had published the 1989 refutation of the report in the *Journal of the American Society for Psychical Research*. As a result, May was puzzled that Utts had not included any critique of the NRC report in her contribution to the AIR evaluation. Her response to his query shocked him.

> The answer is that I was explicitly asked by AIR staff NOT to mention the NRC report in my review! This is very troubling to me for a number of reasons....
>
> When I was explicitly asked by AIR staff NOT to mention the NRC report in my review, I assumed they had realized the problems with it, and, especially given the involvement of the AIR President with the NRC Committee, were happy to let it fade into oblivion.
>
> Given that background, I was quite disappointed to see that AIR made liberal use of the NRC report in their conclusions. Had I known they were going to do that, I certainly would have discussed the multiple problems with it in my report. By not mentioning it, an uninformed reader may assume that I support it, which I certainly do not.
>
> I would also like to explain another omission in my report that occurred for much the same reason.... In a memo dated August 1, 1995, you provided me with phone numbers for [a former DIA project officer, a former senior DIA official, a military general who had program responsibility], and Joseph McMoneagle. You sent a copy of the memo to the AIR staff.

Shortly after you sent me that memo, I was contacted by the AIR staff and told that I was NOT to contact any of those individuals. Thus, I was not able to gain any details about the operational remote viewing work. I thought you should know that in case you were wondering why I requested that information and then did not use it.[26]

The CIA/AIR report purported to have thoroughly evaluated the operational (i.e., nonlaboratory) remote-viewing phase of the Star Gate research and reported there was no evidence for its success. But Utts is more than clear on this point: she was refused access to the operational remote-viewing data and was puzzled by CIA/AIR claims that those data were examined or evaluated.

In addition, Utts's own background report had come to an unequivocal conclusion:

It is clear to this author that anomalous cognition is possible and has been demonstrated. This conclusion is not based on belief, but rather on commonly accepted scientific criteria. The phenomenon has been replicated in a number of forms across laboratories and cultures.

I believe that it would be wasteful of valuable resources to continue to look for proof. No one who has examined all of the data across laboratories, taken as a collective whole, has been able to suggest methodological or statistical problems to explain the ever-increasing and consistent results to date.[27]

Ray Hyman's background report was, if anything, even more striking, because Hyman, a psychology professor at the University of Oregon, was notorious for his dogged refusal to regard anomalous cognition as a genuine or adequately demonstrated phenomenon. Nonetheless, he offered the following summary.

I agree with Jessica Utts that the effect sizes reported in the SAIC experiments and in the recent ganzfeld studies probably cannot be dismissed as due to chance. Nor do they appear to be accounted for by multiple testing, file drawer distortions, inappropriate statistical testing or other misuse of statistical inference....

The SAIC experiments are well-designed and the investigators have taken pains to eliminate the known weaknesses in previous parapsychological research. In addition, I cannot provide suitable candidates for what flaws, if any, might be present. Just the same, it is impossible in principle to say that any particular experiment or experimental series is completely free from possible flaws.[28]

Since the 1995 declassification, government-sponsored remote viewing had become headline news all over the world. The CIA stuck with the AIR report's conclusion: after millions of dollars spent, the CIA officially declared there was no value whatsoever to remote viewing. ABC's *Nightline* and other major media were quick to exploit the controversy. Joe McMoneagle, who recounted his experiences in *The Stargate Chronicles: Memoirs of a Psychic Spy,* was angry, and said so.

It's way beyond a reasonable doubt that the knives were out when it came to a fair and open-minded evaluation of remote viewing—it just didn't happen. [For the CIA/AIR Report] to state that there was absolutely no evidence that it provided materials of value flies in the face of more credible oversight committees on the research side of the House, and enthusiastic end-users of the methodology who walked into Senate and congressional hearings held secretly year after year, presenting highly classified and sealed results of the effectiveness of remote viewing, arguing for its continued existence, use, and funding. . . .

I'll break the ugly silence with the unspoken question that no one ever wants to ask. *Is there a defense* [psychological need to defend] *against remote viewing? Is that the real problem here?*[29]

How to explain these official government assessments, which seem to fly in the face of so much solid evidence? Like McMoneagle, I wondered whether fear had something to do with it—fear of having one's worldview shaken, of being thrust into a scientific realm where the old rules suddenly didn't apply. I told Hal about my patient Grace, and the extreme anxiety I'd observed in her as she described her experiences of apparently anomalous cognition. Had he ever observed anything like that in his work on Project Star Gate? Hal listened attentively, then began to talk more about Joe McMoneagle:

> He was one of our very few subjects whose ability to perceive places thousands of miles away was so reliable we could document it consistently and unequivocally. Soon after we began conducting experiments with him, he started realizing what he was doing. One day he looked at me and said he had to tell me something. He'd done duty in Vietnam and while he was there he'd seen the worst human beings can do to each other. He'd always thought that taught him fear as bad as it gets. But what he wanted to tell me was it was nothing compared to the fear he felt when he really grasped the extent of his remote-viewing abilities. It hit him—what he was seeing didn't amount to watching some kind of movie. Instead he was *there, in* the viewing, immersed in a reality utterly unrelated to his ordinary life. He was terrified.
>
> It shakes the foundations. The fear Joe described and the fear you're seeing in your patient—I think it may be as basic as any fear there is.

Hal was right. That level of fear is elemental. It reaches straight into the most deeply intimate, personal ways we've learned to trust the world and ourselves in it. In the face of fear like that, no wonder rational consideration of apparently anomalous experience is so elusive. No wonder the scientific establishment looks the other way, moves elsewhere as fast as it can.

I asked Hal for a final summing up.

> The evidence is in—solidly in. But our ability to rely on remote viewing as an intelligence tool isn't ready for prime-time TV and that's a very real problem. We don't know enough. The results produced by remote viewing have been truly impressive but they're inconsistent, unpredictable, and we know very little about who's good at it or why. That makes the findings easy to tear apart. I don't doubt we'll get beyond that, and when we do, inadequacies of evaluations like the CIA/AIR report will speak for themselves. In the

meantime, we're dealing with the same thing your patient Grace was confronting. This is scary stuff. The fear is worst among people I'd call middle-management types, people who rely on the status quo for their security. This work upends the status quo. Though there were certainly smart minds appointed to the AIR Commission, the people calling the shots from the government side were, frankly, middle management. The irony is that at the upper echelons, in government but in other venues as well, I find there's solid acceptance of remote viewing and real excitement about its potential. We just need to keep working. We need to work at allaying people's fears, but also at clarifying the underlying processes and mechanisms—the *how*.

Ongoing controversy about remote viewing remains astonishingly active. There are a dazzling number of books, Web sites, and associations dedicated to its exploration. But maybe most intriguing for the future, Hal reminded me about those boxes upon boxes of SRI/SAIC data that remain barely tapped for what they have to teach us. Many are declassified; many are not. Some are still under review for eventual public access. The sum total represents an extraordinary twenty-four-year collaboration between top-flight scientists, major government agencies, and a few people with apparently remarkable intuitive talents. They're a continuing gold mine for scientific exploration of possibly anomalous cognition.

Vast amounts have been written about the fact that science gets in the way of its own most revolutionary ideas. If revolutionary ideas stay silent, established science is able to perpetuate the illusion that its own most valued assumptions are safe from question. Banished to silence, revolutionary ideas don't disrupt the scheme of things. They don't threaten our most treasured, familiar ideas.

And few ideas are as treasured in Western culture as those declaring that space, time, and individual identity impose inviolable boundaries on human experience. Tampering with those ideas is big—big enough to remind me of the night when I turned into my driveway with that harp in the back of my car. *This changes everything.*

Helen Palmer echoed the other professional intuitives when asked about the role fear had played when she first began to recognize and develop her abilities. She also wondered whether this kind of fear and anxiety, which she believes is a universal experience, affects scientists in a particular way:

> When I first became aware of these abilities, I thought that I was deluded, that my profound spiritual experiences were make-believe fantasy or wish-fulfilling dreams. Out of fear I suppressed my inner states for far too long. The universal experience of childhood anxiety closes off our awareness of receptivity. That's why everyone gets anxious when we get anywhere near recognizing reality as it actually is. Freud himself said something to the effect that we prefer our conditioned neurotic reality, which allows us to function well enough, to having to face reality as it actually is. Intuition requires being receptive to reality as it is, not how we'd like it to be, so why go there when cognitive reasoning assures us that reality is predictable? From childhood on, we develop and reinforce an automatic pattern of closing ourselves off from a state of receptivity to protect ourselves from psychological wounding. Why become receptive when it only leads to pain? Receptivity opens you to pain. A lot of my intuitive sessions with clients are focused on strategies for alleviating their emotional pain.
>
> I live and work with scientists all the time, and I respect what they do—after all, I depend on aspirin and antibiotics when I need them—but I find that they can become overly reliant on cognitive reasoning. That means they miss a lot of reality as it is actually unfolding. Why should scientists study intuition if it doesn't serve them? Why proselytize? Reality goes on anyway, regardless of who's noticing. As long as no one actively persecutes me for my own perceptions, I see no reason for science to trouble itself about the "paranormal." But the question of people being afraid of knowing what is so—and polarizing against what is so because of that anxiety—that's a real question.

John Huddleston has also contemplated the role of fear and anxiety in his work:

> In my practice, I work with a broad range of people. Some may have a fear of being overwhelmed by intuition because their logical minds have everything buttoned up. But the logical mind isn't the fount of intuition. Look at it this way: Each of us has two natures; there's the physical body, and the spirit or soul that infuses it. Intuition is a function of the spirit part of a person, not the body part. Now let's make a further discrimination, that it's not the busy, intellectual, rational mind that engages intuition but a more subtle mental faculty: calmer, deeper, smoother. This is an important distinction, because when people hear "nonphysical" they simply assume it means the intellect, because that's their comfort zone. And when a person understands that using his or her intuition means stepping back from analyzing, he or she may become fearful. But a reading is not analyzing. It's not intellectualizing. It's not about figuring things out. It's simpler than that. It's merely being open to what's there. I've taught intuitive development for many years, and that's one of the first things I teach. The fear of what lies outside the bounds of the rational mind is a curiously Western condition. Building on my anthropology major at university, I've visited traditional shamans in the Amazon rain forest, Tibetan lamas in the Himalayas, and Zulu diviners in southern Africa. What we label as intuitive, those cultures consider normal. In approaching intuition, we aren't learning something new but rediscovering something much older than we can imagine. Perhaps if they can appreciate that, people won't be afraid of being overwhelmed by spiritual experience.

In *The Structure of Scientific Revolutions,* the classic work on the nature and culture of science, author Thomas Kuhn defines normal science as everything that occupies science before a scientific revolution, before the moment when everything changes. Normal science doesn't make room for observations that don't fit its own basic assumptions. Normal science is about solving problems that arise inside those assumptions. It is the problems that refuse to fit that lead to scientific revolution. They lead to the thing Kuhn christened a paradigm shift.

Following publication of *The Structure of Scientific Revolutions,* the phrase *paradigm shift* became so overused and misapplied that Kuhn himself finally recommended abandoning it. But by that time, his original concept had done its job; it had permanently affected our understanding of how science develops. Science doesn't change by accommodation. Nor does it change through gradual accretion of new ideas. Instead, science changes when revolutionary ideas gain enough force to turn science upside down. It's neither a smooth process nor a gentle one. As eminent physicist Max Planck remarked, "Science advances funeral by funeral," meaning that it usually takes a new generation of scientists to come to grips with a paradigm shift.

But long before normal science gets disrupted, we're likely to find, on the edges of normal science, a persistent coterie of scientists who have happened across some observation that won't fit, and it nags at them. Their work becomes increasingly concerned with making it make sense. They develop experimental programs. They establish labs and accumulate research. Meanwhile, normal science proceeds as usual, barely noticing what's piling up at its edges.

The challenge for the scientists who work at the edges grows as well. Some pay back their marginalization, starting to ignore the conventions of normal science just as normal science ignores them. Others become fanatics, determined to make normal science notice them, often at the price of measured dialogue. Still others adopt permanently disenfranchised status, quietly pursuing their work as though the normal science establishment had ceased to exist. A few—very few—manage to live creatively inside the world bounded by normal science while investigating observations that threaten to undermine it. They manage to weather both dismissal from their peers and the daily experience of confronting phenomena that don't appear to make scientific sense at all—normal scientific sense, that is.

Kuhn's ideas go a long way toward explaining our resolute silence around research on anomalous mental capacities. If even some of that research proves reliable, we'll have to stop tossing out meteorites and admit that we have a scientific crisis on our hands.

8

Nighttime Eyes:

Learning to Live with Paradox

A COLLEAGUE WHO'S a high-energy physicist sent me an article from the *Proceedings of the Institute of Electrical and Electronics Engineers,* one of the foremost journals in engineering and electronics. As it happened, the article was by Puthoff and Targ and offered an overview of past and recent research into remote perception. What really caught my attention, however, was an introductory note from the journal's editor in chief. He explained why, over objection from his reviewers, he'd decided to publish the article. To make his case, he quoted one reviewer who had assessed the article as methodologically impeccable and could find no substantive basis for rejection. However, that reviewer recommended rejecting it for publication with the following declaration: "This is the kind of thing that I would not believe in even if it existed."[1]

The reviewer's statement was yet another dramatic illustration of the way apparent anomalies challenge our Western scientific worldview. Here was a presumably distinguished scientist—a reviewer for a major scientific journal—who declared that he was dismissing evidence he'd just assessed as solid and good.

As I was discovering, the reviewer's response typified one way in which people committed to rational thinking respond to anomalies. But I was also finding other, more complex and nuanced responses.

My colleague Phyllis Cath is one of the most highly regarded and beloved psychiatrists in San Francisco. Phyllis came out of an unusually intensive medical training in Boston, and along with her clinical gifts she has a vigorously rational mind. One evening, I found myself telling her Patrick Casement's story about thumbing that ride and encountering his grandmother's long-lost friend. Phyllis asked one question after another about its possible implications. Her reflections were both intriguing and illuminating.

> On the one hand, listening to that story, I kept feeling, "Oh, of course!" But on the other, I'm completely amazed and find it unbelievable. How can I think both things at once? It makes no sense! In either mental framework, each is totally true. I'm not used to thinking like that—it's almost dissociative. . . .
>
> Here's what it is. That story entered my mind in two ways at once and two ways that don't add up. It's a very strange thing. . . .
>
> In fact, I know what Patrick was describing—that synchrony with people. I experience it all the time, with people I'm really close to or with patients, the kind of interpersonal synchrony that must have led Patrick to put out his hand the way he did. But the *specificity* of what happened with him is so extraordinary. . . .
>
> What's remarkable about Patrick is how he allows himself to override his rational assessment and conscious determination *not* to take a ride. He must be an unusually open man to respond the way he did.

Part of what was intriguing about Phyllis's response was how ready she was to identify what Patrick did as practically ordinary. Her own experiences might not have what she called the extraordinary specificity of Patrick's, but she put them in the same category.

At the same time, she'd said, "That story entered my mind in two ways at once and two ways that don't add up." With that statement, she was capturing something crucial about how, if we permit them at all, apparently anomalous events enter and register in consciousness, as both expectable and unbelievable. She managed to go back and forth between those two mutually incompatible points of view without rejecting either one or forcing them to "add up."

That's just what the editorial reviewer refused to do. He refused to entertain two apparently incompatible ideas at once. He insisted on resolving their incompatibility as best his customary habits of thought would let him. Believing the good evidence would have meant giving up too much certainty about other things he was sure he knew.

Phyllis took another route. She accepted a paradox. In her words, "In either mental framework, each is totally true." She took on the data exactly as they presented themselves to her. If they didn't add up, that in itself became a feature of the data.

Then I came upon a third solution, a middle way. Judith Butler, a noted feminist scholar and professor of rhetoric at the University of California, exemplified it during an all-day conference we both attended. Judy deals in epistemology, the study of knowledge. I'd told her the story of Harold and the harp; her response was immediate, with an emphatic ring of the academy. "You have just," she remarked, "caused an epistemic crisis."

From Judith Butler, expert in epistemologies, that was no small statement. Unlike the reviewer, her response to the paradoxical data was to name the crisis—acknowledging that it was a crisis, but staying outside it. Unlike Phyllis, her personal experience didn't lead her to assert that two blatantly incompatible ways of knowing might both simultaneously be true.

But to name something is to declare that it exists. Once we grant that it exists, we've at least opened the door to thinking about it.

The reviewer, Phyllis, and Judy represent a spectrum of responses from three highly rational people to apparently anomalous experience. The reviewer dismissed it, much as the National Research Council had dismissed the statistical data supporting parapsychology. Phyllis went straight inside the contradiction, letting herself experience each side without regard for how one measured up against the other. Judy identified a mental category for it, a place-holding solution that invited her to come back to pondering it.

No matter where each of us happens to fall along this spectrum—whether we view the disturbance caused by apparent anomalies as evidence of interpersonal synchrony, or an epistemic crisis, or an invitation into possibilities we wouldn't believe even if they were true—we have to acknowledge that our ordinary ways of adding things up simply refuse to work. Taking serious account of that fact may be the first step into considering anomalies rationally. From there, we might be ready to start looking for a conceptual framework that can accommodate them, a framework that can help us manage suspension of our usual requirements for how things *should* add up.

Back in the late nineteenth and early twentieth centuries, perceptual psychologists began to develop a new field called Gestalt psychology. Derived from the German word for pattern, form, or shape, Gestalt psychology claimed that *experience of every kind gains meaning as a unified whole.* The pattern of the whole makes for more than the sum of its parts. As a result, analysis of individual parts won't ever give full understanding of the whole. Gestalt theorists outlined a series of crucial discoveries about how the mind adds things up, and how it doesn't. As I studied their findings and the conceptual framework that grew out of them, it occurred to me that they might offer us just what we need to grasp the paradoxes of anomalous experience.

Most psychology students learn about gestalt theory by studying drawings that appear to represent different objects depending on how you look at them. In the example below, you might first see a white chalice against a black background. Or you might instead see two profiles in black against a white background. What you see depends on what you perceive as foreground versus background. The gestalt experiments show that we're always dividing up the visual world this way. Whatever we perceive as foreground—commonly named as figure—defines the picture we end up seeing. So, in the example below, when our attention is on the white area as foreground, we see the white chalice against a black background. When we shift to see the black area as foreground, we see the two black profiles against a white background. We spend our lives pulling foreground out of background to create coherent pictures of the world.

What Gestalt psychologists have also demonstrated is that, while we can become adept at changing the picture—at shifting, say, from seeing profiles to chalice and back again—*we can never see both at the same time.* Chalice and profiles can't both be foreground at once. No matter how useful we might find integrating whatever we've learned from seeing one way with whatever we've learned from seeing the other, we simply cannot organize our perceptual field so that we can see both ways simultaneously.

The relevance of the insight is this: *The perceptions that characterize potentially anomalous experience appear to emerge from a state of mind that is, in the moment of perception, radically incompatible with the state of mind in which perceptions characterizing rational thought are possible.* The mode of perception in which Harold says he located that harp is a mode that depends on access to a state of mind in which ordinary linear thought is momentarily impossible, literally suspended.

That's a murderous notion for most of us trained in a Western intellectual and scientific tradition. It's a murderous premise for scientific investigation of purportedly anomalous experience. We're not accustomed to scientific investigation in which the phenomena we're attempting to study are themselves exclusive of the state of mind that lets us study them.

However, that's just where the Gestalt psychologists may offer us some crucial help. They showed us that the way to grasp how profiles and chalice coexist in the same picture is to become adept at moving between one and the other, holding the memory of the chalice even as we see the profile.

But that means allowing an experience of loss. We have to give up one thing in order to see the other. We have to lose what's familiar in order to see what's new. Some losses are easy, like giving up a chalice to see profiles. But some losses aren't easy at all. Giving up our habitual grounding in rational thought to see something else, even just for a moment—that's anything but easy for most of us.

I'd talked to my "professional intuitives," Deb and Helen, about precisely that loss and how it's a requirement for the state of mind in which they worked. It was a familiar process for Deb:

> Over time, as you go in and out of seeing the way I see, you get better at it. When I was a child, it was just natural; it just happened. I didn't work at it. But when you start calling on it in a way that's more disciplined, it's different. You have to begin recognizing what helps get you there and you have to deepen that. But while you can work at it, you can't overthink it. Thinking about it gets in the way. It's a funny balance. I have to let go of thinking while I'm seeing the way I see. Ordinary thinking, that is.
>
> So I actually forget the things I see—I mean, I'll forget in my regular life. In my regular life, I'll even be friends with people I've done sessions for. I'll be with them and I won't remember what I've seen about them. It's like it comes from somewhere else. But then if we have another session—even ten, fifteen years later—what I saw before comes back, vividly. My mind switches back.

In Helen's words:

> The level of intuition we're talking about is a very different variety of knowing than the knowing we call rational. It's different in *kind*. And you cannot, simply cannot, engage in both kinds of knowing at the same time. This degree of intuitive knowing relies on different, subtler signals than rational knowing. Those signals only become

perceptible with a shift in consciousness, a shift out of rational thinking. That's a jolt for intellectually trained people to realize. But as you learn to shift back and forth, you learn to trust it. And the shift gets easier—quicker and more automatic.

Deb's and Helen's remarks reminded me of my first, accidental lesson in gestalt perception, one I received from a date at a college football game. It was late fall. The day was chilly and it was the final, biggest game of the year. People were buttoned to the chin in colorful winter clothing, surrounded by bright banners and other festive football paraphernalia.

My date turned to me. "Try something. Look across at the other side of the stadium, at all those people watching the game. Look for yellow. Just see all the yellow you can. See the pattern? Now switch: look for red. Suddenly it's a totally different pattern, right? A whole new picture. Wild, how that happens. Wild, how one color stands out and makes the other practically disappear. You just have to switch what you look at."

I was impressed. It didn't do much to improve my grasp of football, but it stuck with me as an essential lesson. The lesson wasn't just about how our pictures of the world are organized by what we see as foreground, by the color we name as figure and pull out of a surrounding background. It was also about how switching back and forth changes the pictures we're capable of seeing, how we have to give up some pictures in order to see others.

When I described my memory of the football game to Helen— how I'd had to give up the sense of one color to see the other—she was quick to recognize what I was talking about. But the difference between my experience and what she does is that switching from yellow to red has no cost attached to it. It's easy, like switching from chalice to profiles. Leaving rational thought behind, even momentarily, isn't a loss we easily invite. But if we want access to the state in which anomalous knowing might be possible, a deliberate invitation might be precisely what's required.

And suddenly that brought home why someone like the journal reviewer had such trouble assessing an article on remote perception. It was the same reason that dialogue regularly fails between people who say they've had an anomalous experience and people who do main-stream science. Perhaps it's the same reason that scientists dismissed all the good science in twenty-four years of experiments with remote viewing. There's a basic perceptual problem at the heart of things, and it goes way beyond one color jumping out as foreground across a foot-ball stadium. Instead, it's about the nature of how we review reality, organizing it by two radically different sets of figure-ground configura-tions. Each view defines fundamentally different things as foreground. And seeing the picture outlined by one means not being able to see the other at the same time. To see a view of the world in which anomalous experience happens, we need to temporarily abandon a view of the world in which rational thought happens. Worse, we need to tem-porarily abandon *the state of mind* in which we see what rational thought helps us see. And vice versa. Refusing to undergo either loss means re-fusing the possibility of seeing what the other side sees.

No wonder discussion of anomalous experience frequently has the ring of religious debate. If people on both sides stay lodged in states of mind from which they can't see what the other insists is perfectly visible, why should either side hear the other's truth as re-flecting anything but a matter of faith? Why should either find the other's truth remotely plausible?

Resolution through rational discourse remains unlikely as long as that's where the discussion lives. That's never been the way reli-gious argument gets settled. But the gestalt experiments might show us how to change the terms of the discussion. If we begin by recognizing that the basic figure-ground structures that organize each side's essential premises are, in the moment of perception, frankly and absolutely exclusive of a capacity to see what the other is seeing, we'll start by expecting both camps to do exactly what they do—define the other's truth out of existence. We'll start by ex-pecting that neither will find grounds for talking to the other since, until each side takes the risk of giving up what each customarily sees, neither will see that there's anything to talk about.

Recognizing that in itself might help us move toward rational discussion of apparently anomalous experience and put us in a posi-tion to stake out new and realistic common ground for mutually in-formative discussion.

After I'd explored my gestalt ideas with Deb and Helen, I decided to try them on Hal Puthoff, the former director of the Star Gate remote-viewing project. Hal's response was instantaneous:

Thirty-five years of research on mind-matter anomalies and I simply never *got* it! This is brilliant and it describes a vital truth. I'll use this insight and I'll use it a lot. It just may allow us to start talking to each other differently. There's no question, the incapacity to see both ways at once describes the necessary condition under which we have to work in applying scientific method to mind-matter anomalies. It's obvious, but I'd never seen it before.

Several weeks later, I met with Huston Smith, author of *The World's Religions* and *Why Religion Matters* and perhaps the foremost scholarly authority on religions around the world. In 1996, Bill Moyers had devoted a five-part series on PBS to his work, titled *The Wisdom of Faith with Huston Smith*. Huston and I were discussing the problems he encountered when trying to convey spiritual or mystical experience to scientific audiences. I told him my ideas about applying gestalt perceptual concepts to reframing the issues. They resonated for him as promptly as they did for Puthoff.

How fascinating! It seems utterly right. It makes complete sense and explains a lot. I recognize not just the perceptual incompatibility you're describing but also the requirement that, to see both, we need to switch back and forth. I'm certainly no scientist but I recognize this as where the dialogue fails. The scientific story is a stupendous one but must be recognized for what it is. It's a different way of knowing from the knowing familiar in spiritual traditions, and the knowing we label anomalous. This gestalt perceptual framework may help us understand not just how it's different but why people absorbed in the scientific story have such trouble seeing there are other valid stories as well.

The fervency with which both Puthoff and Smith embraced the gestalt ideas follows from their respective years of frustration in trying to get people to talk to each other about anomalous experience.

Familiar strategies for productive dialogue hadn't worked and both men suddenly saw why: the strategies that depend on adding up two different ways of seeing things will never work when it comes to mutually exclusive percepts. They can't.

The original gestalt findings were limited to findings about visual perception. But the insights of gestalt theory began to exert a remarkable and consistent pull on thinkers in many spheres, leading to influential developments in fields as far-flung as philosophy, neurophysiology, art, education, literary criticism, social psychology, and theories of creativity. Then, during the 1960s, Fritz Perls, a renegade psychoanalyst, launched an approach to psychotherapy called Gestalt therapy, which emphasized awareness of one's thoughts and feelings over analysis or interpretation of their content. It claimed huge popular attention and the word *gestalt* entered common parlance in settings ranging from mental health clinics to the burgeoning encounter group and holistic health circuit.

Ever since the scientific revolution, Western culture has been waging a battle against analytic reductionism and the excesses of atomistic thinking, with its emphasis on breaking things down in order to understand them.

From the beginning, the gestalt findings have provided an answer to this cultural discontent. During the early 1900s, those findings were particularly welcomed by scholars unhappy with the dominance of structuralist, behaviorist, and mechanistic thinking in both the hard and social sciences. At the beginning of the twenty-first century, the gestalt findings exert an appeal no less powerful than they did a hundred years ago.

We're currently hearing calls for a new holism that have unprecedented urgency. They come from every quarter—from those in mainstream science exploring the theoretical realms of chaos theory, quantum theory, and string theory; from those involved with worldwide environmental, biosocial, geopolitical, and health planning; and from those promoting myriad expositions of "new science," with its multiple applications in complementary medicine, alternative energy sources, education, corporate structure, and a host of other arenas. At the heart of those contemporary appeals to holism is a sense that, for all its triumphs, Western science as we know it has missed a critical truth asserted by the Gestalt psychologists: *connections between things make for a pattern and wholeness that can't adequately be located in the sum of component parts.*

Since the era of the gestalt pioneers, however, the world of neuroscience has changed dramatically. If the insights produced by the early gestalt experiments are now critically going to inform our approach to understanding anomalous experience, we need to know not just where those basic insights currently stand but also how contemporary research on gestalt phenomena might inform a new set of questions about how the mind adds perceptions up, and how it doesn't.

The Palmer Lab at the University of California does cutting-edge research on gestalt phenomena. It was established by experimental psychologist Stephen Palmer, whose text on the science of visual perception is foremost in the field. I decided to consult with him and one of his graduate students, Rolf Nelson, now a professor at Wheaton College in Massachussetts, whose special area of study is figure-ground perception. I explained my interest to both of them, particularly my interest in this notion that, when two percepts function as foreground and background to each other, we cannot see both at once. Rolf was immediately responsive.

> You're right, and that finding still holds. It's both basic and critically important to understanding perceptual organization. It's not limited to faces and vases either. Here's a different kind of example. Ask someone, even someone who knows geography well, to identify a picture that contains the shape of the Atlantic Ocean.
>
> People won't recognize it. They won't recognize it because the contour that defines the Atlantic Ocean is a contour that they've assigned to the continents. The continents get identified as shapes. The ocean is ground—it's the land masses that are seen as figure.
>
> And yes, it's also true that you'll never see both simultaneously. However, once you've seen both possibilities—go back to that face-vase picture—you can and do go back and forth. In fact, that's important. People *tend* to go back and forth once they've seen both, because past experience is so influential. Once we've seen

something—meaning we've given it shape and let it emerge as recognizable—we'll tend to keep seeing it, even seeking it.

There's a photograph Palmer has in his book *Vision Science*. When you first look at it, you'll most likely see a pattern of black and white that looks meaningless. But if you look at it again and try to find a Dalmatian, sniffing along a street, you'll suddenly see it. And then you'll keep seeing that Dalmatian, every time you look at the picture.

I promptly went in search of the photograph and experienced exactly what Rolf described. First, I saw a blur of black and white. Then, guided by Rolf's description, the Dalmatian suddenly leaped out at me. From then on, whenever I flipped back to the picture, the Dalmatian jumped out.

Initially, you'll probably see this picture as a nearly random array of black regions on a white background. Once you're able to see it as a Dalmatian with its head down, sniffing along a street, the picture becomes dramatically reorganized with certain of the dots going together because they're part of the dog and others going together because they're part of the street.[2]

Rolf's elaboration broadened the picture of what might be required for rational consideration of potentially anomalous experience. I developed a working definition: something can't emerge as foreground until it achieves *recognizable shape*. If it's true that we're contending with states of mind that are mutually exclusive in the moment of attaining them, *both* states of mind need to achieve recognizable shape before we'll be able to go back and forth between them. We'll have to be able to call up an experience of seeing (or knowing), even just once, out of the state of mind that is unfamiliar to us. With that experience established, percepts enabled by the unfamiliar state of mind might become recognizable, just like the Dalmatian. Until then, they'll stay implacably hidden in the background. Until then, in the conversation between mainstream science and those reporting anomalous experiences, each side will probably, in all good conscience and with all goodwill, reject out of hand the validity of what the other side insists is there to be seen.

Suddenly I remembered the moment of finding my sister's watch. And I realized that *granting recognizable shape to a state of mind with which I'm normally unfamiliar was the crucial thing that experience accomplished.* The point wasn't the feat, bizarre and startling though it was. The point was the profoundly, radically different state of mind. Experiencing that state of mind appeared to enable perception of something as apparently anomalous as what people like Deb and Helen reported being able consistently to see. And neither at the time nor since have I been able to register the state of mind in which I located that watch while I was actually trying to think about it. I could either try to remember what that state of mind felt like or try to reconstruct actually being in that state of mind, but I couldn't do both. I needed to learn to switch back and forth.

After talking with Rolf, I spoke with his colleague Stephen Palmer, who refined my working definition of figure/ground relationships: "Actually, the shape doesn't need to be recognizable to attain figural status. You can draw a completely random closed shape on a piece of paper, and that closed region will be seen as figure and the rest of the page as ground. There are many factors that determine what is seen as figure and what as ground, only one of which is whether the shape is recognizable or not." Steve also added to Rolf's illustration about the Atlantic Ocean.

> In fact, even though people know better when it comes to the way the world really is, people tend to experience maps as though the oceans extend quite literally *behind* the continents. That's another way of thinking about the fact that the oceans aren't assigned a shape—a boundary or contour—which would turn them into recognizable percepts. People tend to perceive only one side of a contour as a thinglike figure. The other side is relegated to background, to the space from which the thinglike figure is seen to emerge.

Steve's comments emphasized a particular aspect of figure-ground configuration: the *contour* where figure and ground meet. He was saying that how we assign the boundaries between percepts will critically determine what we end up seeing. This suggests that it will be crucial to identify *the contours that define whatever mutually exclusive percepts we're confronting.* In particular, we'll need to identify how the contours that turn rational thinking into a thinglike figure—to pick up Palmer's phrase—might be contours that, viewed differently, render anomalous experience visible. We'll need to examine how those contours might constitute literal boundaries between states, boundaries that could turn states of mind that appear mutually exclusive into foreground and background for each other. If we can start to specify how that happens, we might be one step closer to comprehending how a loss that strikes most of us as unimaginable and even dangerous could turn out to be tolerable. We might become more comfortable with the idea of deliberately, temporarily letting go of rational thought in order to see something we wouldn't see otherwise. Even if we can let go of rational thought only at the most rudimentary level, that release might provide the conceptual foothold we need to recognize the state of mind from which people like Deb, Helen, Ellen, and the rest say they do their apparently anomalous knowing. It won't enable us to do what they seem to do. But it might help us conceive of how they do it. It might help extricate us from insisting that such a state of mind is too crazy, frightening, or frankly impossible to be worth even imagining.

Once we've crossed that conceptual divide, experience of the state itself might come unexpectedly, as it did for me when I found myself walking straight into the closet to find my sister's watch. Or accessing that state might suddenly fall into place as the seemingly natural outcome of years honing a skill, as it does for athletes and artists.

How we get to experience of that state is a separate question, and one to be taken up later. But we increase the likelihood that we'll at least be open to getting there if we know that going back and forth is built in. We need to know that getting there doesn't mean giving up our grounding in rational thought for good.

In fact, knowing that might be just what gives the Catfish Hunters of this world such apparently free access to their extraordinary capacities. They've given recognizable shape to the state of mind in which those capacities emerge. But they've also learned to trust going back and forth. They've learned that the contours establishing an ordinary state of mind can be released into contours that delineate a different state. From that different state, they say, their extraordinary abilities simply happen. In that different state, they don't think about what makes those capacities happen. In fact, they say, they can't. "If I'd thought about it," said Catfish Hunter of his extraordinary pitching feat, "I wouldn't have thrown a perfect game—I know I wouldn't."

In that different state, the ordinary thinking that results from adding things up appears to stop. What takes its place is a primary sensation of oneness, of wholeness that doesn't result from breaking things down and adding them up. Perhaps we can understand that shift as a shift in the assignment of contours. Connectedness, not separateness, becomes the new continent.

Until that shift, people asked to consider anomalous experience may be in a position not unlike people asked to draw the shape of the Atlantic Ocean. That quality of connectedness challenges even the experiences of separateness we consider most basic, such as those imposed by the familiar boundaries of space and time.

Once we start becoming interested in something, it has a way of flagging our attention. Whether it's sheer serendipity or an example of the gestalt lesson, the things that interest us suddenly show up at unexpected times, in unexpected places.

In the midst of my gestalt research I took a cross-country flight and found myself seated on the plane next to a young girl. Her father was on her other side. The little girl was reading one of my favorite children's books, and we began chatting about it. Eventually, her father joined in. We introduced ourselves. He was a neurobiologist specializing in visual perception.

Our conversation moved from children's books to his work. At a certain point, I told him I was interested in anomalous cognition and whether research on figure-ground perceptual shifts might teach us anything about how we shift back and forth between mutually exclusive states of mind. He related an intriguing experience.

> I recall one personal experience that made a strong impression on me.
>
> I was at a five-day meditation retreat doing a practice where people were paired up and told to gaze into each other's eyes. At first my partner and I were laughing hysterically, then smiling, then things began to settle down as we really concentrated on the space between us. Then, as we gazed at each other, we just absolutely locked on to each other. I felt the world fade completely away, like it went gray, there was no contrast in my visual field. There was no black, no white. Then the world came back again. That lasted about four seconds and it happened again, that receding. It happened three or four times and then a kind of blue washed over everything. That was all. Just blue.
>
> Later, I started to tell my partner about the weird thing that had happened to my visual field during the exercise. She interrupted me to say that she'd had the same exact experience. And I said, "You did? *You* did? The visual world disappeared and everything went to gray. . . ." And she said, "Yeah, and it went back and forth," and I said, "Yeah, and then everything came back," and she said "Yeah, and the

blue washed over everything," and I said, "*Yeah, exactly. You* saw that, *too?*"

I'm a visual neuroscientist with a Ph.D. and years of rigorous scientific training, and this is certainly beyond my ability to explain away.

I've since had other experiences where I felt my sense of self fall away, and "self" and "other" were no longer meaningful distinctions. Although these weren't visual in nature, I do see how they relate to the figure-ground shift we've been discussing.

The state of mind I experienced is something I can best describe as *not grasping after thinking*. It was a remarkably decisive release of the need to figure things out. It wasn't about *never* thinking—not at all. That's important. For example, that state I was in could be studied. It could be very interesting to think about. Maybe with transcranial magnetic stimulation? I have a number of ideas....

The release of what the neurobiologist called "grasping after thinking" let him see the world with a new connectedness, not broken down into separate component pieces. Connectedness suddenly emerged as foreground.

We might understand what this neurobiologist is describing in terms of how he reassigned the contours of subjective experience. He turned connectedness into continent and let separateness recede to ocean. What he called "grasping after thinking" gave thinglike status and recognizable shape to separateness. The unaccustomed state he achieved with his partner gave thinglike status and recognizable shape to connectedness.

There was a striking similarity in the way this scientist described his experience and the way Deb, Helen, and Ellen described the state in which they gained access to apparently anomalous knowing. In Deb's words: "I know what I know about the other person because I go where they are. I draw on how connected we all are so I really am *seeing with their eyes* when I read them." In Helen's words, "You read the other person accurately because you *are* them; you know them from the inside because you've stopped being separate." In Ellen's words: "It's a state of oneness, really. From that oneness, you get a very profound knowing."

A friend of mine once told her four-year-old daughter a bed-time story, one she'd heard from Sufi folk tradition:

Once upon a time, there was a king with a court full of wise men. The wise men had devoted long hours to considering the question of whether stars actually exist. They finally declared their consensus. The answer was no. If, reasoned the wise men, stars can't be seen in the light of day, they must not be there at all. The entire court went into mourning as everyone gave up believing in stars and yearned for the days when the stars were true.

Inevitably, the king's fool wandered by and offered a cryptic remark: "When the sun is shining, you can't see the stars." The king was puzzled but sensed something hopeful. He offered half his kingdom to anyone who could decipher the meaning of the fool's remark and help bring back the stars.

The next morning, my friend's daughter faithfully repeated that much of the story to her brother. But it wasn't really a story about stars, she told him. It was a story about people's eyes and how many eyes people have. They have nighttime eyes that see stars and day-time eyes that see the sun. And, she went on, "just like it can't be day while it's night, daytime eyes can't see stars and nighttime eyes can't see the sun."

My friend's daughter will someday learn about telescopes and other things that will complicate her view of nighttime eyes and daytime eyes. In the meantime, she may have grasped precisely the wisdom behind the fool's remark. It may be the same wisdom grasped by the meditators and nuns whom Newberg and D'Aquili studied. When the sun is shining, you can't see the stars, and the eyes that help us see by the sun's light aren't eyes that help us see the stars. In the instant we engage the eyes of anomalous experience, the eyes of rational thought are disengaged. And the reverse is true as well. We can't see both at once.

Perhaps the gestalt experiments can help us be more precise about what the four-year-old, the nuns, the professional intuitives, and the meditators all appear to have learned. The eyes that grant thinglike status and recognizable shape to a subjective sense of separateness aren't eyes that give thinglike status and recognizable shape to a distinctive, radical experience of connectedness. That radical connectedness may be the distinguishing feature of a state in which mind-matter anomalies become ordinary, everyday experiences.

The gestalt experiments give us a framework within which we can consider how powerfully our minds fight the notion that, when it comes to certain varieties of perception, *we can't see both ways at once.* They help explicate the experience of paradox. That's in part why Hal Puthoff and Huston Smith responded to the gestalt findings the way they did: "I suddenly *got* it!."

Arthur Koestler, in his book *The Act of Creation,* suggests that the exhilaration of a Eureka experience—I *got* it!—erupts from the sudden juxtaposition of two things usually seen as incompatible. The unexpectedness of the juxtaposition leads, he said, to "a sudden, bisociative surprise which makes reasoning perform a somersault."[3] The gestalt experiments mobilize that somersault. They give us a concrete experience of seeing in two ways—two equally valid ways—that don't add up. They help us recognize that going back and forth between two incompatible worldviews may be precisely the approach we need to examine anomalous experience. And, like Koestler's somersault, they may offer a window on a radically new way of knowing.

Measuring the Power of Prayer:

Is God in the Equation?

ON OCTOBER 2, 2001, The *New York Times* ran the headline "A Study Links Prayer and Pregnancy." The story reported a study conducted under the auspices of the Department of Obstetrics and Gynecology at Columbia University's College of Physicians and Surgeons in New York City. It had just been published in the September issue of the *Journal of Reproductive Medicine* and was titled "Does Prayer Influence the Success of *in Vitro* Fertilization-Embryo Transfer? Report of a Masked, Randomized Trial."[1]

Not the usual fare for the *Journal of Reproductive Medicine*. The concluding paragraph began with an even more unusual sentence: "Our data suggest a benefit of IP (intercessory prayer) on IVF-ET (*in vitro* fertilization-embryo transfer)."

For the flagship journal of Western reproductive medicine, that's an extraordinary claim—*prayer makes a difference*. Editors for the journal apparently decided the evidence in support of that claim was extraordinary enough to warrant its publication, fulfilling Marcello Truzzi's criterion that extraordinary claims be matched by extraordinary evidence. Two of the authors submitting the article were then on the staff at Columbia: Kwang Cha, M.D., from Cha Hospital in Seoul, associate research scientist, and Rogerio Lobo, M.D., chair of obstetrics and gynecology. Joining them was Daniel Wirth, J.D., M.S., a lawyer by profession who had a long history of involvement in alternative and spiritual healing. The Cha-Wirth-Lobo study involved 219 women, aged 26 to 46, who received in vitro fertilization treatment over a four-month period at Cha General Hospital, Seoul, Korea. The women were randomly assigned to one of two groups: a group that would receive intercessory prayer (petitionary prayer or prayer focused on benefiting another) and a group that would receive no dedicated prayer from outside intercessors. The people praying were in the United States, Canada, and Australia, halfway around the world from the women for whom they prayed.

None of the women seeking fertility treatment nor anyone involved with their care was informed that the study was occurring, much less that half the women were being prayed for. An independent Korean statistician, unknown to the authors, was responsible for retrieving and transmitting the data to a second independent statistician in the United States, who randomized the subjects and transmitted pictures of the prayer subjects to the prayer groups in different countries. Randomization codes were not made available to anyone, authors included, until after completion of the study, when the researchers evaluated who had or hadn't become pregnant. There were double and triple security measures imposed to ensure anonymity of the data.

The results of the study were startling. Women who'd been prayed for were almost twice as successful in becoming pregnant as the women who weren't prayed for. The figures were 50 percent versus 26 percent, a highly significant statistical difference, carrying a probability of less than 0.0013. The number of oocytes (eggs) retrieved and the in-vitro fertilization rate were comparable for the two groups. But the prayed-for group had double the implantation rate as the non-prayed-for group. That is, of the multiple preembryos transferred into each mother's uterus, 16.3 percent implanted in the prayed-for women versus 8 percent in the women who didn't receive prayers, a probability of 0.0005.

In nonstatistical language, the odds that pure chance was responsible for 50 percent of women getting pregnant in the prayed-for group but only 26 percent in the non-prayed-for group *were less than thirteen out of ten thousand.* The odds that pure chance explained why 16.3 percent of the embryos successfully implanted in the prayed-for group versus only 8 percent in the non-prayed-for group were *less than five out of ten thousand.*

Those statistics are impressive enough to suggest an impressive claim, maybe even one that qualifies as extraordinary. They suggest the possibility that intention can affect people halfway around the world.

According to Dr. Lobo, the investigators thought long and hard about submitting their results for publication and putting themselves on the academic line with results that appeared to radically challenge ordinary scientific understanding about how things work. In the end, they agreed that, in good scientific conscience, they couldn't *not* publish them. "It was not even something that was borderline significant," Dr. Lobo told the *New York Times.* "It was highly significant."[2]

Once the *JRM* article appeared, Dr. Lobo's receptionist found herself barraged with an unprecedented influx of calls from the press, Christian fundamentalists, disbelieving medical colleagues, and plenty of others. In self-defense, she developed a stock response, patient and to the point. "Dr. Lobo felt it was a proper study, conducted in a proper way, and therefore should be properly reported."[3]

The study was indeed a proper study, but it was also distinguished by several other features. First, the outcome measure was brilliant. I found myself recalling warnings at age sixteen—*you can't be a little bit pregnant.* You are or you aren't. Pregnancy is a thoroughly binary and therefore readily quantifiable, easily digitizable outcome measure. That's great for doing objective research. And it immediately distinguished the Cha-Wirth-Lobo study from the general pool of studies on distant healing—healing induced by intention of someone physically removed from the person to be healed.

Those other studies—and there are hundreds—almost all examine apparent effects of prayer on highly complex diseases such as

AIDS, cardiovascular illness, or cancer.⁴ Many have produced intriguing and impressively positive findings, but even the best designed and best conducted are enormously burdened by the
difficulty of assessing outcome. How do the multiple variables that
constitute a change in condition—need for medication, pain, mental capacity, or longevity—interface with each other? How do you
factor in outcome when one variable improves but another gets
worse? Is a longer but symptom-filled life a positive outcome? How
about feeling more hopeful or happier when there's no physical improvement? Shouldn't we expect that all those outcome variables
would add up very differently for different patients?

As an outcome measure, pregnancy doesn't have all those assessment problems. It's an easy call. You are or you aren't. Another distinguishing feature of the Cha-Wirth-Lobo design was that neither
the women studied nor any of their medical personnel were informed that the study was taking place. Such a departure from
standard informed consent procedures was key to a design that per-
mitted valid testing of the effect in question—the effect of someone
else's intention on the subject, rather than that effect mediated
through the subject's awareness. In other words, Cha, Wirth, and
Lobo wanted to make sure they weren't looking at some version of
the placebo effect: the effect of people's minds on their own bodies.

The placebo effect is one of the most powerful effects in medicine. Its power is increasingly recognized. It's what's at work when,
say, someone joins a study testing a new medication for headaches,
starts taking the pills he's been given, and reports that his headaches
get better even though it turns out that he's been assigned to the
control group and has been taking nothing but sugar pills. His
headaches have gotten better because he believes he's taking a new
and effective medication. That's the placebo effect in action, and it's
potent. The Cha-Wirth-Lobo experimental design eliminated the
chance for the placebo effect.

One final aspect of the Cha-Wirth-Lobo design led to a quirk
in methodology puzzling to those not sophisticated about distant
healing practices. In every tradition devoted to such practices,
whether Hindu, Buddhist, Jewish, Christian, shamanistic, or any
other, there are age-old questions about what form of intention is

most effective in transmitting distant healing. Is it best to intend or pray for a highly specific outcome? Or is nondirected, general intention for someone's overall well-being more effective? What about the most general intention of all, simply aligning oneself with the larger good, God's will, the universal order, or whatever greater scheme of things fits one's own particular worldview?

Investigators in the Cha-Wirth-Lobo study decided not to decide. They took a triple-barreled approach. The people recruited to pray in their study were from Protestant denominations and familiar with intercessory prayer. They were divided into three groups, each assigned to a different form of prayer. The first group was told to pray in a directed manner with specific intent to increase the pregnancy rates of the women in the prayer group. The second group was told to pray in both a directed and nondirected manner. They prayed in a directed manner for all the people praying in the first group, with specific intent to increase the efficacy of that group's prayers. They also prayed in a nondirected manner for the women in the study, that God's will or desire be fulfilled in the lives of those women. The third group prayed only in a nondirected manner, with the intent that God's will or desire be fulfilled for everyone who was praying in both of the first two groups.

The study seemed to have been designed with great meticulousness. The people praying were sent photographs of the women they were to pray for—five each—with no identifying information regarding who they were, where they were from, etc. The photographs were transmitted to the independent statisticians in a format that was log-in and password protected. The password was changed on a regular basis.

I'd asked a research endocrinologist to consult with me about conceivable pathways that might help explicate physiological aspects of the study's results. He knew Lobo and thought highly of him. First we talked about the research itself—design, methods, and analysis of the data. He couldn't find fault with any of it. Then I asked, did he think he'd be taking the results as seriously as if the active agent were a drug instead of prayer? He was quick with his reply: "Not on your life!"

I liked his honesty. I'd contacted him because I knew he had a strong interest in mind-body medicine and in how various mental techniques—visualization, guided imagery, meditation, or relaxation exercises—might enhance hormonal readiness for embryo transfer. Twenty years ago, the effects of the techniques he was studying had seemed as inexplicable as any effects of prayer. It took learning about neuropeptides and lymphocytes—all the incredibly rich two-way communication linking mental states with bodily function—for the field of psychoneuroimmunology to open up. Then research began exploding. Mainstream medicine started recognizing all the dramatic ways the mind affects the body. Use of those techniques remains in its infancy, but their impact has been well established.

My friend was ready to say that the way the mind affects the body is critical in mediating hormonal processes. On the other hand, he was dead set against accepting the Cha–Wirth–Lobo results because now we weren't talking about the same mind and the same body; we were talking about the effects of one person's mind on *an-other* person's body and from very far away. That's another matter. He told me so in no uncertain terms:

> Are you kidding? You want me to take those findings and consider what they do not just to my research but to all the research that makes for good medicine? I told you, not on your life! Not without lots more good evidence, anyway. I'm open-minded but it would take more than that study—and I don't care how good it is—for me to entertain results like those.
>
> There's no mechanism! Science can't explain results like these and data can't be considered in a vacuum. Until somebody comes up with a plausible way to understand what this study claims, we can't do anything with the data.... We've got no way to think about it....
>
> On the other hand, I will go this far—I won't forget the study and I won't laugh at it. And let me tell you, plenty of my colleagues are laughing hard, much as they may respect Lobo and the *Journal of Reproductive Medicine*. I won't laugh because I myself got laughed at plenty in the old days when the mechanisms behind mind-body medicine were still utterly opaque. Most solid scientists thought it was hogwash. Simonton and his early work on mind-body effects with cancer?[5] All his visualizations with armies of white blood cells?

Back then his ideas about how mental imagery could affect tumor growth were treated as a joke by most of my colleagues.

But we're talking apples and oranges when it comes to the study by Cha, Wirth, and Lobo. There's just no mind-body mechanism that could conceivably explain those results.

I told him my story about Harold and the harp and we ended our conversation on a friendly note. But there was a caveat. I asked if he'd mind my quoting him. He hesitated, then said he didn't mind being quoted but he'd prefer I kept his name out of it. Then he looked at me and smiled.

But I've enjoyed our conversation. Besides, it will make my wife and daughter very happy. They're spiritual types. My wife's a midwife. She's got stories that are up there with your harp story. Some are about prayer, wild stories about births going wrong and people praying and the impossible happens, things work out fine. But that doesn't mean God belongs in science. You can't put prayer inside science. The *JRM* article tries to do that. That's wrong. It's a category error.

A category error is an academic way of saying that apples are getting mixed up with oranges. My endocrinologist friend was saying that prayer belongs inside religion and you can't do science on religion, therefore effects of prayer don't belong inside study by science.

"Category error," however, was probably the least of the troubles besetting the Cha–Wirth–Lobo study. The critics had taken out their knives, putting the entire study into question. Their case was summed up by Bruce Flamm, a clinical professor of obstetrics and gynecology at the University of California, Irvine, in the September 2004 issue of *Skeptical Inquirer*[6] and in a follow-up article in March 2005.[7] According to Flamm the study was "flawed and fraud." He reported that the Department of Health and Human Services had investigated the study because of the lack of informed consent, and that Columbia University later acknowledged noncompliance with some of its own policies. Flamm said he'd written Lobo and Cha repeatedly, raising questions about the study, and had received no responses. He also said that *JRM* refused to respond to multiple queries.

He further reported that Rogerio Lobo, listed as lead author, had in fact only learned of the study six to twelve months after its completion, said he participated only in editorial duties, not study design and execution, and asked to have his name taken off the paper.[8] Meanwhile, the third author, Daniel Wirth, had pled guilty to various felony charges involving conspiracy to commit mail and bank fraud. Flamm used this to indict the research results even though the charges were not related to the study. Many critics quibbled with what they considered convoluted methodology, including the multi-layered prayer groups that I had found so meticulous. Since Wirth had recruited the prayer groups, some wondered whether they had ever even occurred. At one point, *JRM* removed the study from its online archives, but then restored it. In November 2004, *JRM* published a letter of "clarification" from Dr. Cha, who had since stepped down from his position at Columbia.[9] As of this writing, the study is available in *JRM*'s online archives. And despite the innuendo, no one has ever disproven its results.

Wherever the dust settles on the Cha–Wirth study, my endocrinologist friend's remark about category errors deserves further scrutiny. What interests me about that statement is how readily a religious context for exerting distant mental intention becomes conflated with the distant mental intention itself. That's what puts us smack in the middle of a category error. But we only end up there if we identify distant mental intention as the property of religion—the property of God and of territory science can't hope to study, much less authenticate. *If we want to study the effects of distant mental intention, in the form of prayer or anything else, we'll need to separate those effects from any religious or specifically theistic context in which the intention is exercised.*

That's crucial. Questions about God's role in distant mental intention, whether God exists, or which religion has a lock on the truth, aren't questions science can ever hope to answer. The Cha–Wirth study was based in science and the methods of science. It wasn't based in religion and the methods of religion. *It used the methods of science to examine an apparent effect that results from employing the methods of religion.* It examined an ability people schooled in religious traditions have worked to train and develop. In learning how to pray, people may be learning how to exercise an apparently anomalous mental capacity that's not included in our culture's general education of minds. As a result, people schooled in religious traditions may be particularly adept at showing us whether distant mental intention is capable of having some anomalous effect. God or no God, that makes those people worth studying. More specifically, it makes it worth studying what happens when they pray.

It happened that the people recruited to exert intention in the Cha-Wirth study were Christians. For them, God was a reality and they called their intention prayer. But the actual effect reported by that study doesn't speak to the role of God, or of prayer, or of practicing distant mental intention in a specifically Christian mode. If we start claiming scientific studies like Cha-Wirth as evidence of God's actions, we plunge headlong into just the category error my endocrinologist friend was worried about.

Several recent studies of prayer's effects in medicine have been purposely designed to incorporate forms of distant mental intention as practiced by people from a variety of spiritual traditions, some of which don't hold to belief in God at all. The results so far shouldn't surprise the ecumenically minded. Effectiveness doesn't appear in any way related to which God is prayed to, whether a God is prayed to, or to which form of prayer is employed. Some studies even include people who declare themselves to be atheist or agnostic but whose form of prayer simply entails directing compassionate intention toward others. These people seem to do just as well in studies of distant mental intention as people whose form of mental intention is addressed to an image of God.

These days, it's the rare university medical center that doesn't host some study related to prayer or distant mental intention. That's a big change. The research is mainstream and the studies overall suggest that one person's prayer or distant mental intention can have documented positive effects on another person's physical condition. On the other hand, there are huge methodological problems in many of the studies. Given the complexity of measuring outcome alone, as I mentioned above, that's hardly surprising. But it does mean it's crucial to proceed with plenty of caution in evaluating the results.

Larry Dossey, M.D., has been a pioneer in studying the effects of prayer in medicine. He practiced internal medicine for twenty-five years, during which time he was chief of staff at Medical City Dallas Hospital. His book *Healing Words* was a *New York Times* best-seller and continues to have major impact in medical centers and medical training worldwide. Its conclusion is unequivocal: distant mental intention can have dramatic effects on disease processes.

Dossey's a man with a mission. He's written ten books, all of which argue a scientific case for taking a scrupulously rigorous look at medical studies on prayer. He's tall and good-looking, with a big head of white hair and plenty of southern charm. He's got charisma to burn. He talks and people listen. I was no exception.

The two of us had been lecturing at a conference in Princeton. Afterward I asked him for an overview of the research. Even if we have to discount Cha-Wirth, Larry told me, the field demands further investigation. As he summed it up: "Lisby, it's simple. If effects half as strong as those apparently produced by prayer were produced by a marketable drug, they'd be announced by banner headlines and front-page coverage in every newspaper across the country. They'd be recognized for what they are—big news."

Larry pointed me in the direction of Mitchell Krucoff, M.D., an interventional cardiologist at Duke University Medical Center. Krucoff is a veteran in the field who had conducted a well-regarded pilot study evaluating the role of prayer and healing touch. The so-called MANTRA (for Monitoring and Actualization of Noetic Trainings) study had suggested an association between noetic—non-surgical—interventions such as prayer and music-imagery-touch therapy (MIT) and healing.[10] The study received a lot of attention and its results were positive enough to warrant further investigation. Krucoff commented that even ten years earlier, "NIH [the National Institutes of Health] wouldn't have reviewed a protocol with the word 'prayer' in the title. When we started in the 1990s, we were afraid of being run out of town for practicing voodoo medicine."[11]

Based on the results of MANTRA, Krucoff then directed one

of the largest randomized studies of prayer ever done in the United States. MANTRA II followed 748 patients with coronary artery disease to see if noetic interventions might play a role in healing patients undergoing either surgery to have stents implanted or to have cardiac catheterization.

The study took place at nine leading academic medical institutions. Patients were randomly assigned to one of four different groups: 189 patients received intercessory prayer (IP) from prayer groups all over the world that included Christian, Jewish, Buddhist, and Muslim participants, along with MIT therapy. A second group of 182 patients received only long-distance prayer. A third group of 185 patients received MIT therapy only, and a fourth group of 192 patients was given standard care, with neither prayer nor MIT therapy. The prayer aspect of the study was double-blinded, meaning that neither the patients nor their health care teams knew which patients were being prayed for. The MIT portion of the study wasn't blinded, since it would have been impossible to give the patients treatment with music, imagery, and touch without their knowledge. A variety of outcomes were measured: whether patients died, experienced symptoms of heart attack, showed rising levels of a certain enzyme that indicated damage to the heart, needed additional stenting or bypass, developed congestive heart failure, or required rehospitalization.

The MANTRA II study was published on July 16, 2005, in the British journal *The Lancet,* one of the most distinguished peer-reviewed medical journals in the world.[12] After six months, the results showed no significant difference among treatment groups in outcomes, which at first glance would seem to disprove a causal relationship between noetic therapies and healing. However, the patients who had received MIT had a lower mortality rate than the control group, and the lowest absolute death rates were in patients who had received *both* prayer and MIT. There was another suggestive finding from the study, which ran from May of 1999 through December of 2002. After the traumatic events of September 11, 2001, MANTRA II experienced sharp drops in enrollment rates for the next three months. The researchers then decided to add a "two-tiered prayer strategy" after they enrolled new patients.

Twelve additional prayer groups were directed to pray for the success of the prayer groups that had been with the study since the beginning. This would presumably "simulate a higher dose of prayer for the remaining patients enrolled in the study," according to the Duke University Medical Center News Office. The result was that patients treated with the "two-tiered" prayer, according to Duke, "had absolute six-month death and re-hospitalization rates that were about 30 percent lower than control patients, statistically characterized as a suggestive trend."[13]

The MANTRA II study has been praised for its scientific rigor, and it's exactly the kind of study we need if we're to figure out what, if anything, is going on with distant mental intention and healing.

Meanwhile, other scientists were taking a closer look at previous healing studies to assess their design and execution. No one has been as systematic in that evaluation as Wayne Jonas, M.D. For some years he was the hugely influential director of the Office of Alternative Medicine for the National Institutes of Health. He now teaches at the Uniformed Services University of the Health Sciences in Bethesda, Maryland. Jonas, with his colleague, Cindy Crawford, directed a team of experts in a critical review of over 2,200 published reports on distant mental intention and spiritual healing. They published the findings in a four-hundred-plus-page volume that categorized all the studies into six areas and then evaluated them by stringent research criteria. The six research areas were:

1. general health correlates of spiritual and religious practices
2. intercessory or healing prayer
3. "energy" healing approaches
4. therapeutic qigong (Chinese energy healing)
5. direct mental interaction with living systems
6. mind–matter interaction.

Each area was assigned a letter grade for "evidence level" ranging from A to F. Certain A-level studies were also selected as models for future research. An A required at least three independent high-quality studies that met an extensive list of standard experimental criteria for excellence: randomized control comparison groups, double-blinding of the data, placebo-control conditions, independent outcome evaluation, power analysis of the data, and so on. Expert opinion not backed up by solid independent research received an F, even if the opinions were from highly regarded clinicians.

There were plenty of F's. There was a smattering of A's and lots of everything in between. Jonas and Crawford drew this cautious conclusion: "There is evidence to suggest that mind and matter interact in a way that is consistent with the assumptions of distant healing. . . . While conclusive evidence that these mental interactions result in healing of specific illnesses is lacking, further quality research should be pursued."[14]

Another major overview published in the *Annals of Internal Medicine* looked at twenty-three studies of intercessory prayer involving 2,774 patients. With circumspection suited to that journal's readership, the authors soberly conclude: "The methodologic limitations of several studies make it difficult to draw definitive conclusions about the efficacy of distant healing. However, given that approximately 57% of trials showed a positive treatment effect, the evidence thus far merits further study."[15]

In other words, there's more than enough good science out there to support further investigation. Yet the more I read, the more I discovered that many of these studies continue to be characterized as experiments designed to prove the existence of God. The more we engage the question of what could conceivably explain effects of distant mental intention, the more emphatically we confront the irrevocable distinction between science and religion. God trumps the question of mechanism. If we choose to name God as the independent variable—God as the cause for any observable effects of prayer—no science in the world is going to spell out the mechanism. Science can't systematically specify God, much less how God operates. If we don't hold that as basic, we're up to our ears in my endocrinologist friend's category error.

Obvious? One might think so. But it's not so obvious in a number of the most apparently thoughtful and influential commentaries on research examining effects of prayer. And that's led to some unexpected critiques from some unexpected quarters.

In November of 2001, an article on intercessory prayer was

published in the prestigious *Archives of Internal Medicine*. It was called "Experiments on Distant Intercessory Prayer: God, Science and the Lesson of Massah." Abstracts of the article billed it as a criticism of medical studies on prayer. Great, I thought, anticipating a solid methodological analysis that would point up weaknesses in the studies I'd been examining. The subtitle was a bit cryptic, but fine, I was ready to hear whatever lesson Massah (a name I dimly associated with Moses) had to offer. I started reading, yellow highlighter in hand. The article began with an emphatic summation.

> We conclude that research on the effects of religion and spirituality on health should avoid attempting to validate God through scientific methods.... [T]he very idea of testing distant prayer scientifically [is] fundamentally unsound.[16]

I read the paragraph again. According to the *Archives of Internal Medicine*, research on prayer's effects in medicine is about *validating God*? I kept reading.

> The epistemology that governs prayer (and all matters of faith) is separate from that which governs nature. Why, then, attempt to explicate it as if it were a controllable, natural phenomenon?... [P]rayer that tests for a response from God...would not be considered prayer at all because it requires no faith, leaves God no options, and is presumptuous regarding God's wisdom.[17]

I'd abandoned my highlighter by then. The article ended with the relevance of Massah.

> And he [Moses] called the name of the place Massah...because they [the Israelites] tempted the Lord, saying, "Is the Lord among us, or not?"...The lesson of Massah is that God cannot be compelled by our research designs, statistics, and hypotheses to answer our demand, "Is the Lord among us or not?"...As a metaphor for the testing of distant prayer through the scientific method, Massah tells us not only that God should not be tested but, more important, that God cannot be tested.[18]

Talk about category errors! For publication in a theistic religious journal, maybe. But in a medical journal? The authors' central assertion is that God's business is God's business and should be treated as such. The problem isn't whether that's a reasonable assertion. It's eminently reasonable. Given belief in God, it's in the nature of God. Given no belief in God, it's equally reasonable, a tautology about something that doesn't exist. But the one thing it *isn't* is a reasonable assertion for a major scientific journal that publishes by accepted scientific standards. It's a religious assertion, not a scientific one.

In a well-reasoned commentary, "Are Prayer Experiments Legitimate? Twenty Criticisms,"[19] published in the March 2005 issue of *Explore,* Larry Dossey and David J. Hufford, Ph.D., of the Doctors Kienle Center for Humanistic Medicine, Penn State College of Medicine, address in turn twenty common objections to critics of research in this field. Taking up criticisms such as "Intercessory prayer has too many variables to be amenable to scientific study," "Prayer shouldn't be researched because of ethical, moral, and theological reasons," "The purported remote effects of intercessory prayer conflict with current science and should be dismissed," and "Prayer experiments test God and are therefore blasphemous," Dossey and Hufford offer compelling, evidence-based scientific arguments to rebut each objection. They conclude, "These developments suggest that researchers may explore prayer without sacrificing the principles of good science and, we submit, without blasphemy. Prayer need not be dishonored or degraded through research.... Prayer will exhaust us before we exhaust it."

There's one more tricky issue that confronts us as we examine studies on prayer. It's a big one. It's about faith. For people who pray, faith is a crucial aspect of prayer. How do we take account of faith while avoiding religious questions about exactly who or what is invested with faith, questions about God and all the things science can't possibly take into account?

Throughout the history of religion, faith healing—healing through prayer—has occupied a place in religious life. During the midtwentieth century, interest in faith healing surged in a number of

Protestant denominations. The interest developed into a powerful movement backed up by sober theological scholarship. Its tenor was anything but Bible-thumping fundamentalism or TV evangelism. The leaders were respectable Methodists, pillars of the Lutheran Church, and a large batch of the most famously polite of all—Episcopalians.[20]

It began as a grass-roots coalition, inspired by a number of apparently gifted individuals who attributed their healing abilities to prayer. Especially influential were two leaders from the Episcopal Church: Agnes Sanford, author of the classic work *The Healing Light,* and John Gaynor Banks, who in 1932 founded the organization now known as the Order of Saint Luke, a professional and lay order dedicated to promoting the central role of healing in the Church's ministry.

One couple, Ambrose and Olga Worrall, became popularly beloved and were eventually regarded as two of the finest faith healers produced by modern Christianity.

As children, both Olga and Ambrose had been aware of their unusual abilities. They cured people's pain through touch. They knew things about people it made no sense for them to know. Later they'd learn to call that knowing clairvoyance. After their marriage, word of their abilities spread. They started receiving requests for help from all over the world. In 1957 they established the New Life Clinic at the Mount Washington Methodist Church in Baltimore where they saw hundreds, sometimes thousands, of people every week. They wrote a book, *The Gift of Healing,* which remains widely read as an account of prayer's healing power. Clergy, nurses, and physicians regularly came to study with them.

The Worralls often worked by laying on of hands (placing hands on the heads or ailing portions of people being prayed for). When someone who was far away asked for healing, they simply visualized that person and prayed from a distance. Never, in their many years of healing work, did they accept money for their services. As they put it, that would be "profiting from the sickness or trouble or need of others."[21] I thought of Harold and the harp, and how he always refused to take money for his services as well.

The Worralls also worked over the phone and prayed for the hundreds of people who sent them letters every week. They held regular gatherings at their New Life Clinic, open to anyone who showed up. (The clinic is still, incidentally, a thriving institution.) Following an article about their work that appeared in *Reader's Digest,* over fourteen thousand letters requesting help appeared on their doorstep.[22] *The Gift of Healing* also includes examples of the thousands of grateful testimonials from patients, family members, physicians, and other caretakers.[23]

Ambrose himself was a devout Christian, but when asked whether the people he healed needed to have faith, he replied, "When I tell people faith matters, here's what I mean by faith—*lack of resistance to what you hope is possible*."[24] What's intriguing about his definition is how it locates faith as a *subjective quality of mental experience.* His answer is about humans, not God.

Maybe his answer gives us new and unexpected insight into a function of faith, a function that doesn't have to do with God and things science can't address, but a function that has instead to do with how faith helps people engage a distinctive state of mind, a state that, perhaps, facilitates the effects of distant mental intention—the effects of prayer.

If that's true, we might expect to find that a similar state facilitates other forms of anomalous mental capacities. Worrall's emphasis on releasing resistance echoes what professional intuitives John Huddleston and Helen Palmer told me about their extraordinary knowing. As John put it, "You stop resisting, that's all. You get yourself out of the way and it's all laid out right in front of you, everything you think you can't possibly know." Said Helen, "Our minds resist intuitive knowing. Once you learn to relax that resistance, you can start to reclaim intuition from its suppression by the rational mind. The more you work with it, the more remarkable your knowing becomes. You free the receptive state from its armoring by the ego. You learn to live closer to receptivity."

I have an old friend, Rob, who's highly educated and passionately curious about whether anomalous mental capacities can possibly be real. He's a thoroughgoing skeptic but remarkably frank about how he's dying not to be.

I yearn for all this to be true! But I need a harp experience. A bridge experience that feels as real as my skepticism. You had that with the

harp. You had it when you found your sister's watch. People who
have faith in the divine get it that way. I can't do faith in the divine—I
don't believe in it. It's a state of mind I'm after. I'm sure you're right
about that. Somehow I can't allow it. Maybe it's because I literally *feel*
the obstacles in me. They're palpable. You got past them. I haven't.
Why not? Why can't I? That's the question I keep coming back to.

I'd once asked Harold to explain how dowsing worked. How
did you hold the rod? Harold told me to let go of all rational explanations: "The rods just show you what your subconscious mind
knows anyway," he'd said.

Most people don't know how to get their subconscious mind talkin'
to 'em. It's just intuition, that's all. . . . Your subconscious mind
knows dowsing's in your body as much as in your brain and maybe
that's what's good about the rods. You're holding 'em and feeling
'em and that puts you real focused on your body. The rods let your
body tell you what your subconscious mind knows. The rods free you
up that way. They give you a way to stop your brain from stopping all
the rest of you from knowing. But master dowsers, they've learned
how to contact the knowing real directly. So for them the rods don't
matter anymore. They don't need 'em.

Maybe faith functions a bit like the rods. Maybe faith gives us a
way we can *stop our brains from stopping all the rest of us from knowing.*
Maybe faith short-circuits the resistance, pushing us past Helen's armoring by the ego, past our inflated valuations of conscious rational
control, past struggling against a knowing our rationality insists we
can't possibly know. Maybe that helps explain why people claiming
faith appear able to participate in effects that show up in utterly bewildering connectedness to people thousands of miles away.

The Worralls freely acknowledged how inconceivable they
themselves found their apparently extraordinary abilities and
were unfailingly respectful in the face of skeptical questions. They
argued the case for science from two points of view. First, they

were quick to condemn "the heartless frauds committed at times in the name of some cults or religions," as well as "supposed mediums [who] fraudulently prey on credulity to extract money from those who can least afford it."[25] Systematic scientific investigation of extraordinary claims was, they felt, the best way to establish the degree to which the claims were genuine. But the Worralls also believed that scientific understanding of their apparently extraordinary abilities might have huge import for improving human lives. Ambrose himself was a professional aeronautical engineer who worked at a division of Martin Marietta throughout his career. He wrote:

> I believe that all areas of human and spiritual activities should be subjected to the most exacting examination, precisely as I expect the stress calculations on the structure of a new aircraft to be examined down to the most exacting requirements. I believe we should employ, in our research into spiritual therapy, the latest and most applicable scientific methods to gather data that cannot be obtained by casual observation.[26]

Over the years, the Worralls pursued many avenues to help further scientific understanding of their work. They made themselves available for study whenever and wherever they could. They showed up in labs all over the United States, ones run by medical schools, physicists, biologists, polygraph experts, horticulturalists, and psychologists, and were soon sending data regarding their healings to the Rhine lab at Duke University for study. Unfortunately, the early experiments in which they participated often relied on methods that were unsophisticated and procedures that were ill controlled. Nonetheless, there were some intriguing findings that helped lay a groundwork for subsequent generations of experimental work.

Both Ambrose and Olga had a genius for describing the subjective mental experience they believed lay at the core of apparently anomalous mental capacities. Ambrose wrote a pamphlet called *Silentium Altum (Deep Silence),* referring to that quality of mind that seemed to open the capacity to heal. He declared:

In the deep silence it is possible to have revelations. These seem to
have no relation to time as we know it. It is as though one suddenly
becomes aware of something that had been buried deep in the
consciousness. As far as the earth is concerned it may belong to the
future, but in the state of deep silence time does not exist. . . .
[S]eeking silence within [is to] gradually but surely . . . withdraw from
the outer world of sensation and enter [the] realm of intuition. . . . [I]t
is a condition outside conscious experience. It is necessary that
one . . . be prepared to experience the silence that can be *felt*. If a
person is afraid to be completely alone and lacks the courage to face
the unknown, he is not prepared to seek silence. . . . In deep silence
there comes . . . an overflowing awareness . . . that all are one. . . .

Silence is vital to our study of spiritual healing. We must try to
understand its reality and its nearness, for out of the silence comes
the power that heals. . . .[27]

It sounds familiar, this *silentium altum*. Many faith traditions have
emphasized the importance, and difficulty, of entering a state of
deep inner silence. Throughout human history, prayer and meditation have been regular vehicles by which people enter that state, as
well as practices by which the state itself is cultivated. Perhaps those
practices are one reason that faith has, over the centuries, offered itself as a persistent avenue into healing and other forms of extraordinary knowing. Perhaps those practices are one way people establish
access to what are fundamental, generic human capacities.

Within faith traditions themselves, the idea that extraordinary
knowing is an expectable by-product of practices like prayer and
meditation is anything but news. In fact, those traditions generally
caution students not to be seduced, not to get distracted from the
practice of deep silence by excitement over whatever anomalous
mental capacities may accompany it.

I thought of those SPECT images that Newberg and D'Aquili
came up with, the pictures of people's brains while they were praying or meditating. Those images, and the reports of the prayers and
meditators, were all about tuning down the noise and the radically
altered quality of perception that emerges in the silence.

Prayer groups praying for women halfway around the world to get pregnant or for patients to recover from cardiovascular disease. Healers defining faith as "releasing resistance to what you hope is possible" and offering their abilities solely to help others. Professional intuitives "getting out of the way" of their own brains to access apparently anomalous capacities. People experiencing a profound sense of universality when praying or meditating. What emerges from all these distinct pathways is the sense of caring and connectedness. It's a perceptual experience that's in striking contrast to the sense of separateness with which we typically define ourselves in space and time. At the same time that scientists are taking God out of the equation in the study of distant mental intention, connection seems to be an important variable to include.

Some of the most remarkable science currently investigating effects of distant mental intention looks at what happens when people who are masters at tuning down the noise focus their intention on cancerous brain cells—not in people, but in petri dishes.

Garret Yount, Ph.D., is a molecular neurobiologist. He became fascinated by the problem of radiation-resistant brain tumors while doing a five-year postdoctoral fellowship at the University of California's Brain Tumor Research Center in San Francisco. He wondered whether genetic pathways might be altered so that the patients suffering with such tumors would become more sensitive to the radiation used in treatment. He began doing research, choosing one of the very toughest cancers to study—glioblastoma multiforme, a highly malignant and rapidly growing brain tumor. Glioblastoma tumors can double in size every ten days. They are notoriously resistant to any form of treatment. Patients almost always die within a year of noticing their first symptoms.

Garret's research led to publication in such prestigious medical journals as *Oncogene* and *Cancer Research,* where he first put forth his finding that the phase of the cell cycle (cell division) in which tumor cells are irradiated makes a big difference in the response of a gene involved in tumor growth and response to radiation. That

same finding led him to characterize two brain tumor clonal lines
that would have notable implications for the development of molecular therapeutics for treatment of cancer.

In 1990, Garret's father was diagnosed with end-stage leukemia
and told he had between six months and two years to live. He began taking Chinese herbs and practicing qigong, a meditation practice that uses movement, breathing, or sheer silent awareness to
encourage the practitioner's attention to the flow of qi (or chi), a life
force believed, in Chinese medicine, to energize the body. It's the
same life force presumed to be affected when acupuncture needles
are placed along the body lines, or meridians, where qi is said to
run. Integrating these traditional Chinese medicines with his
Western treatments, Garret's father "peacefully coexisted with his
cancer" for thirteen years.

The oncologists at UCSF's Medical Center were impressed and
so was Garret. After completing his fellowship, he joined the
Complementary Medicine Research Institute of San Francisco's
California Pacific Medical Center. From studying effects of conventional Western radiosensitizers known for their exceedingly
toxic side effects, Garret started looking at the vast history of traditional Chinese medicine for possible alternatives.

Garret's passion for his research is palpable, as I discovered when
we met to talk about his current projects. A slight and graceful man,
he has a remarkable smile—gentle, easy, luminous. He was thrilled
to report that the National Institutes of Health was underwriting his
study of how certain compounds in ancient Chinese herbs might
make glioblastoma cells more sensitive to radiation without crippling side effects.

What was equally intriguing was that Garret's work on Chinese
herbs had led him to study effects of distant mental intention. The
transition was in some sense inevitable. As his father had discovered,
herbal remedies are only one piece of a much broader approach to
healing in Chinese medicine. The overarching question for
Chinese medical practitioners is the status of a body's life force, its
qi. So behind the study of herbs is the study of qi. And studying qi
doesn't necessarily just mean effects of qi as they operate inside one's

own body. That's internal qigong. There's also external qigong, a practice that entails moving qi in ways purported to have effects on *other* people's bodies. External qigong is what brought Garret to examining effects of distant mental intention. He explained how it happened.

> External qigong therapy looks pretty much like what we in the West call psychic or spiritual healing. The idea is that there are individuals who, after many years of practicing internal qigong, become adepts. They become masters at the inner state developed in qigong, a state in which there's a capacity for deep mental quietness and highly focused attention. These masters develop the ability to direct and manipulate qi, not just inside their own bodies but outside their bodies as well. I'd seen enough evidence—anecdotal evidence, but that's enough to get you thinking—that I'd started wondering if external qigong might really work.... It seemed to me if we were taking Chinese herbs seriously, we needed to take equally seriously whatever herbal practitioners regularly employed along with their herbs....
>
> Our idea for the research was to bring qigong masters into the lab and ask them to focus their healing intention on isolated human brain cells growing in plastic dishes. We chose cultures of brain cells rather than people for two reasons. First, we wanted to eliminate psychological cuing. But we also wanted a way to manage the problem of complex, multifaceted outcome measures, an inevitable issue when you assess healing as it manifests in people who are ill. We talked to the healers about it and, although there's no section in a Chinese medicine textbook on treating isolated pieces of a person, let alone isolated cells, the healers said it wouldn't be a problem. They said they could perceive qualities of qi emitted from the cell cultures and direct their treatments accordingly.
>
> Our most basic question was whether cell growth could actually be influenced by external qigong treatment. We decided to use an assay, a cell culture, that has been a mainstay in cancer research for more than thirty years, used over and over for testing the effectiveness of chemotherapies and radiation.
>
> I was really skeptical. But I couldn't back down once we had set

up the experiments in Beijing. So the first thing I did was give the qigong master we were testing a plastic dish with a cell culture growing in it.

What you have to grasp before I go any further is exactly how we grow brain tissue cultures. Not surprisingly, human cells don't grow well on bare plastic. To get cells to grow at all, you have to coat the dishes with some kind of organic matrix. And since the favorite thing for any cell to attach to is another cell, the best thing for coating the plastic is the stuff cells are made of. You make what you could call a "cell smear." We do that all the time in the lab. We zap roughly ten thousand brain-tumor cells with a lethal dose of X-rays and smear them over the dish in which we'll be growing the experimental cells of interest. Because the DNA in the zapped tumor cells has been obliterated by the X-rays, the cells we've smeared on the dish begin to self-destruct. After several days, the bottom of the plastic dish gets coated with tumor-cell carcasses, a perfect organic matrix for healthy experimental brain cells to grow on. The cells in the cell smear start dying because of what biologists call programmed cell death. If cells with damaged DNA like the ones we zap with X-rays were to multiply, they could create all kinds of trouble. So—very adaptively from the standpoint of living beings—those cells "make a decision" to self-destruct instead. A few die, then more die and they keep on dying. They keep dying even after we've started growing the healthy cell cultures on top of them.

We deal with all this so routinely in the lab, I didn't think to mention it to the qigong master in our first experiment. We simply handed him a dish with cells growing in it, and said, "There are normal cells in the dish. Please give them a healing treatment. We hope to see them grow well, even more than untreated control cells." That was the procedure. Seems straightforward, right? This qigong master had agreed to the task and I figured we'd let him take his time and do his thing with the dish. But after treating the cells he came out of the treatment room shaking his head. "Those cells are not normal," he said. "They are very abnormal, so I didn't try to make them grow. I tried to eliminate them."

I was feeling skeptical about the whole experiment and my first reaction was one of sheer irritation. I tried to be polite but I told the man he was frankly wrong. There was no question. These were normal brain cells. He came right back, just as confident as I'd been. He defied me outright. "No," he said, "they are *not* normal. I sensed an abnormal qi."

Well, at that point, it hit me. I realized there were in fact only one hundred normal healthy brain cells in that dish, and they were growing on top of ten thousand tumor cells in the process of committing cell suicide. So, if this healer could in fact perceive anything about the cell culture as a whole, we might perfectly well expect he'd take notice of the dying tumor cells, not just the much smaller percentage of healthy cells. At that point, I backed up and explained the nature of the culture to him. He nodded and let me know that now everything made sense.

That episode intrigued me. Maybe this man really was able to perceive something quite unknown to me. Our experiments have unfolded from there.[28]

Garret is also conducting experiments with healers from Japan. They're masters in the practice of jorei, a Japanese form of energetic transmission similar to qigong. In both experiments, the healers are flown to San Francisco and carefully introduced to the lab setup. Garret discovered how crucial that introduction was in his very first experiment. He had—quite routinely, he thought—asked the qigong masters to undertake a second trial after each had done his first healing treatment.

Suddenly we encountered huge resistance from the healers. They acted like we'd utterly betrayed them. Then we realized why. They thought we were asking for more trials because we didn't believe anything they'd done the first time. Replication is a tricky concept. It's utterly outside the worldview within which these healers work. They're looking at truth in a very different way. From their point of view they'd already shown us the truth. They'd shown us what external qigong could do and couldn't imagine any reason we'd need to see them do it again. So we realized we had to explain our methods very carefully, not just the need for repeated trials but also things like how the data remain blinded, how we have to wait until after all phases of the experiment are complete before we know anything about what was achieved in the first trial or any other, and so on.

Interestingly, it turns out there's less need for that kind of explanation with the jorei masters. Their great teacher and founder, Mokichi Okada, believed that, sometime in this century, verification of spiritual effects on matter would come from the West to promote a deeper, truer medicine for the whole world. So the jorei organization in Japan, the Sekai Kyusei Kyo, has been enormously helpful in facilitating every phase of our research, from travel arrangements to preparing the healers for our experimental approach. Enabling scientific validation of their work is actually part of the jorei teaching legacy.

Garret was delighted to be conducting the current studies back in his own lab at CPMC, the same lab where he'd done much of his prior work. One big advantage to being there was the extreme care with which many background variables could be controlled. As Garret put it,

> We're testing something apparently unbelievable, so we have to set our standards of scientific rigor above the ones that keep us comfortable in most conventional research. We need to control for every variable we can think of, including ones we'd never consider in ordinary research. . . . It's absolutely necessary if this research is going to measure up as serious, solid work. Because, from a normal Western scientific point of view, neither the hypotheses we're testing nor the results we're getting make ordinary scientific sense. Any evidence we collect is going to have to be very, very strong.

The protocols Garret developed have already received considerable attention for the creativity of their design as well as their scrupulous rigor. Among the 2,200 studies of mental intention's effects critically reviewed by Jonas and Crawford, 202 examined effects of qigong. Of these, 130 were laboratory studies and 72 were clinical. Of them all, Jonas and Crawford singled Garret's out as head and shoulders above the rest, offering "a clear and systematic . . . model for other rigorous investigations of this type."[29]

As an example of the rigor he builds into his experiments, Garret describes the part of his experimental design called systematic negative controls. These control experiments involve mock or sham treatments.

> The cells in our mock treatment group receive every single physical manipulation received by the real treatment groups except that nobody enters the treatment room during the treatment period. The cells just sit there.
>
> Now, there are two useful things our mock groups give us. One is a straightforward control for the fact that the cells being treated are being moved around and are subject to conditions other than the healing treatment itself. The fact is, we don't know whether the handling of the cells might somehow affect cell growth. So, since the mock groups experience the same conditions as the qigong groups, we have a very useful control right there. If we do see a difference between the mock and qigong groups, we have reason to suspect it results from the single thing that's done to one group and not the other: the qigong intervention.
>
> But we learn more than that from the mock groups. We compare the cells in the mock groups not just to the qigong groups *but also to each other, mock group to mock group.* That might seem odd at first. Why compare groups where you don't expect anything to happen in any of them?
>
> Not surprisingly, that's just the point. What's important about the comparison is it allows us to nail down exactly how much variability is in our experimental system. There's natural variability in any system. If we see more cell death in the qigong dishes than in the controls, we need to be sure the difference can't be explained by that kind of natural variability.
>
> So when we compare mock treatment to mock treatment, we look to see whether the magnitude of difference between those groups is significantly different from the difference we get comparing mock and qigong groups. It turns out that this saved us from

misinterpreting some provocative results in our first large qigong study.

The results of the study were published in 2004 in a journal called *BMC Complementary and Alternative Medicine.*[30] They indicated that during a pilot study of eight experiments, cells that had received qigong treatment for twenty minutes from a minimum distance of ten centimeters underwent increased growth. A similar trend was observed in a formal study with twenty-eight such experiments; cells treated with qigong showed on average more colony formation than the mock samples. This suggested that distant healing intention had some effect on the cells. However, when Garret and his colleagues attempted to replicate the studies, they found no significant difference between the qigong-treated and mock samples. The study concluded:

> We observed an apparent increase in the proliferation of cultured cells following external qigong treatment by practitioners under strictly controlled conditions, but we did not observe this effect in a replication study. These results suggest the need for more controlled and thorough investigation of external qigong before scientific validation is claimed.

Garret wasn't fazed when the replications didn't confirm initial results:

> I was surprised that we weren't able to replicate the results from the first experiment. We're trying to set up the right models, and if it doesn't work, we just have to tweak until we get it right. The healers are still as enthusiastic as they were in the beginning to work with us; their enthusiasm hasn't dwindled, and we continue to get financial support.

Garret is now carrying these studies to the next level by looking at three things that have never before been carefully assessed in studies of distant healing: opposing cellular functions (growth as well as death), "dosage" effects, and distance effects. Each of those elements may help address aspects of distant healing, which, at the moment, remain thoroughly mysterious.

In testing opposing cellular functions, Garret is raising the question of how qigong may affect the growth versus death of cells. If external qigong works as expected, qigong treatment should make normal cells grow while making tumorous cells die. In fact, precisely the same single qigong treatment should simultaneously work to have differential effects, making healthy ones grow and sick ones die. Qigong sets out to achieve a right balance in nature as a whole. Right balance would have us expecting that cancerous cells die while healthy cells thrive. So the healers are given both cancerous and normal cells to treat, with the following instruction: "There are cancer cells and healthy cells here. We would like to see what happens to them when you give them a healing treatment. We would like to see the healthy cells thrive and the cancer cells die."

Western medicine commonly assumes that dosage—the amount of treatment administered—will make a difference in effects of a given therapy. By studying dosage, Garret wants to see if increasing the dosage of qigong will reveal an effect that was missed in the previous study.

Garret's third variable is the possible effects of distance between the healer and the object of distant healing. So Garret will be assessing effects of treatments administered by healers at three different distances from the cell cultures: standing next to the target cells, from another room in the same building, and from across the Golden Gate Bridge. Some of the healers believe that increasing the distance will increase the effect: "The longer the distance, the stronger the qi."

In the current studies, all the brain cell cultures are grown in a six-inch-by-four-inch rectangular plastic box made up of six independent compartments or wells. Three of the wells contain live brain tumor cells and three contain normal brain cells. The box sits inside an incubator, which sits on top of a time-lapse microscope. Only one person involved with the experiments knows which wells contain which cells.

Each box of cells is placed in the microscope for twenty-four hours and cell growth during that time is recorded as well as any basal levels of cell death. Then comes the healing treatment. The healer is asked to do whatever he would normally do in treating a patient through external qigong or jorei. The cell cultures remain in the microscope for another twenty-four hours after every treatment, so data on what happens to the cells can be continuously collected.

Part of what's impressive about Garret's work is how sensitively he's been handling the cross-cultural communication required to conduct experiments like his. It goes way beyond the language barrier that first made him nervous in Beijing. It's a worldview barrier. He's as receptive in his response to the healers as he hopes they'll be to him.

> I can't describe how much I've learned from these people. First, they're enchanting—so dear, so kind, so considerate and devoted. It's a good thing all the data are blinded because I don't know how I'd look them in the face if I knew their results were disappointing. It sounds a little odd to say, but their quality as people has actually taught us a lot about the literal setup we're now careful to establish in the lab. For these healers, a friendly atmosphere—I'll go further and say a *loving* atmosphere—appears critical to an environment in which they're able to do what they do. It's not background. It's intrinsic to the thing itself.

Garret has also designed a study to test the effect of qi on cancer stem cells, the cells that actually seed new tumors and tumor recurrence. The last thirty years of study of cancer cells has tended to consider all such cells uniformly, but evidence is emerging that cancer stem cells might behave in a unique and different way—one amenable to unique and different treatments—and a new wave of cancer research is looking exclusively at these cells. Might it be possible that he didn't see replication in the qigong experiments because the weak signal of the cancer stem cells was overshadowed by the bulk of the glioblastoma cells? Garret's planned study on these stem cells is currently under review by the National Institutes of Health.

In 2003, Garret and several collaborators published two articles listing extensive guidelines for conducting laboratory experiments on distant mental intention.[31] The protocols they recommend are stringent. Only a few studies other than Garret's have at this point managed to achieve them. But, as he says, it's a brand-new field. It will take time for investigators to agree even about the nature of that field, not to mention the science required to study it. Meantime, Garret's work is setting a gold standard.

I have a colleague, Michael Salveson, who is widely read in theological as well as scientific literature. I admire his thinking and he also keeps me honest:

> Lisby, you may not want to deal with the question of whether God is real—fine, that's not the business of science—but what about the question of why people who seem effective at distant mental intention almost all claim belief in *something*? Call it God, the Source, whatever. How are you going to deal with that? Is it incidental? Does it mean something? Is elaborating a subjective inner state enough? Can you reduce the effects of spiritual belief to the power of mental capacities engaged by faith-based practices? Can you really leave the beliefs themselves out of it?

Michael's challenge was tough. But it's real. I thought about the people praying in the Cha-Wirth study, the Worralls, and then those qigong masters. And it hit me, what all their beliefs have in common. It also strikes me that what the beliefs have in common just may be the thing that facilitates distant mental intention.

Traditionally, practitioners of external qigong haven't believed in God, at least as most Westerners consider God. But they do believe in qi, in a life force that transcends the individual. Qi extends way beyond what Westerners view as the ordinary breathing in and out required to sustain life. In the context of qi, people live and breathe as part of a larger something—a flow, a wholeness, the Tao or the oneness of all things.

In that sense, belief in qi may not be so different from belief in the all-encompassing transcendence of a Western God. Maybe, when it comes to effects of distant mental intention, that's the crucial part.

From people praying in the Cha-Wirth study to the Worralls to qigong masters, all those people claim belief in a larger something, a belief that renders them active participants in a reality transcending the limits of personal identity. Maybe that's the heart of the matter.

Maybe that explains why, whether through belief in God, in qi, or a larger pattern or some overarching purpose to life, belief in something spiritual appears so regularly associated with capacities for exerting effects of distant mental intention. In the context of those beliefs, distant stops being distant. Separate stops being separate. I and not-I start being perceived as profoundly, inextricably connected. Maybe that paves the way for one person to affect another in apparently impossible ways. Maybe, in Ambrose Worrall's words, it opens "an overflowing awareness...that all are one."

Michael Faraday, perhaps the nineteenth century's greatest experimental physicist, was widely denounced as a charlatan when he declared he'd discovered a new source of energy by moving a magnet in a coil of wire. When told that his resulting observations about electromagnetic energy couldn't possibly be true, Faraday commented, "Nothing is too wonderful to be true if it be consistent with the laws of nature."[32]

The question is, *which* laws of nature?

Listening Harder:

Tuning In to Dreams and Telepathy

I WAS HEARING IT FROM researchers wielding SPECT scans, professional intuitives, faith healers, qigong adepts, and CIA remote viewers. Whatever they or their experimental subjects were doing—if indeed they were doing what they said they did—came from an unusual mental state, one accessed not by flooding the brain with information and effort but by quieting it down.

Over and over, Hal Puthoff had emphasized how remote viewing operates on a "noisy channel," perceptible as a set of weak signals characterized by a notably low signal-to-noise ratio. His prize subject, Joe McMoneagle, had talked about the same thing. Professional intuitives Harold, Deb, Helen, John, and Ellen had all spoken about letting go of their resistance, getting out of their own way, to arrive at that mental state. The distinctive feature of Newberg and D'Aquili's brain images of meditators and nuns deep in prayer was the way the subjects' brains went dark in areas normally lit up by processing life's daily perceptual input.

Maybe the SPECT scans helped explain something about the ubiquity with which people adept at quieting the mind describe anomalous cognitive capacities. Maybe anomalous capacities are a natural result of gaining access to mental quiet—the *silentium altium* or deep silence Ambrose Worrall described as the mental state he sought to enable anomalous healing.

All this pointed to an emphatic bottom line. Creating experimental conditions that effectively "tune down the noise" might be the step we need to enable systematic investigation of anomalous cognition. We need experimental procedures that help people minimize their attention to ordinary sensory input so they can notice other, normally weak perceptual signals, ones that might feed anomalous cognition.

My friend's four-year-old daughter might have had it just right. In explaining the bedtime story about why you can't see stars when the sun is shining, she'd said, "Really, it's not a story about the sun and stars. It's a story instead about people's eyes and how many eyes people have. They have nighttime eyes that see stars and daytime eyes that see the sun. And, just like it can't be day while it's night, daytime eyes can't see stars and nighttime eyes can't see the sun."

If daytime eyes can't see stars, we shouldn't be surprised that stars don't show up when we look through those eyes. My friend's daughter was onto the idea that a noisy channel drowns out weak perceptual signals. The sun, she implied, makes for a noisy channel. Seeing the glow of stars requires a different kind of seeing than we do with eyes adapted to the sun's brightness. We need experimental protocols that help us find the equivalent of nighttime eyes.

In the modern era, Sigmund Freud initiated a monumental exploration of nighttime eyes that would forever change the Western world. It began with dreams. When we dream, he declared, the things we see have meaning. To a world basking in the triumphs of nineteenth-century medical science that rang as heresy, a regressive

retreat from rationality into domination by the occult and dangerously ineffable.

But Freud stood firm. In dreams, he proclaimed, people see differently. They're one step removed from action. In dreams, people
allow experiences they can't permit during waking hours. You let
yourself feel, think, and see things you ward off during the day. You
kill your wife, seduce your best friend's lover, marry your mother—
then you wake up and it's just a dream. You roll over, kiss that same
wife, and thank your lucky stars you married someone who's never
in a million years remotely reminded you of your mother.

It was over a hundred years ago that Freud revolutionized the
world with those ideas. His classic *Interpretation of Dreams* was published in a limited edition of six hundred copies. It took over eight
years for them all to sell out. When it was finally time for a second
edition, Freud had no illusions about the likely reception. "My psy-
chiatric colleagues," he remarked, "do not seem to have taken any
trouble to overcome the initial suspicions which my new concep-
tion of the dream produced in them."[1]

What affronted Freud's colleagues most was his assertion that
nighttime eyes produced visions of things we won't allow ourselves
to see during the day. Worse, said Freud, that's actually *why* we
dream. We *need* a venue for thinking thoughts we fight off during
waking life. Given what people typically dream, his colleagues were
understandably horrified. Freud was opening shocking possibilities
for what the human mind contained. Dream thoughts weren't crazy
and random. They were filled with all the things we spend our
waking lives trying not to know.

In the Europe of Freud's day, as now, sexual and aggressive impulses were among the things people were most determined to
sweep under the rug. But the thoughts showed up anyway, and they
showed up in dreams. Nighttime eyes lifted them from suppression.
Undo the suppression, Freud said, and debilitating symptoms would
be cured. Undo the suppression, and people would be free to love
and work, Freud's felicitous way of describing the aim of his talking
cure. The key was lifting the suppression so the unconscious could
become conscious. Dreams, said Freud, were the royal road to the

unconscious. Get to know your dreams and you get to know your unconscious.

A century later, researchers are discovering just how right Freud was. Daniel M. Wegner, professor of psychology at Harvard and lead author of a major new study on dreams, has found that thoughts we've suppressed during the day are the ones most likely to appear in dreams. "Any kind of thinking about something increases the likelihood it will show up in a dream," he says. "But trying to suppress something increases the chances even more, indicating that the meanings of our dreams involve things we've tried to sweep under the rug."[2]

Freud was willing to take on the world when it came to attributing unconscious meaning to dreams. But he picked his battles. Privately, he believed dreams were a royal road to more than suppressed sexual and aggressive impulses. He considered them a royal road to telepathic capacities—communication between two minds— as well. He went so far as to declare it an "incontestable fact that sleep creates favorable conditions for telepathy."[3] He also stated that any study of the human mind that excluded dream telepathy was incomplete. But he was having enough trouble getting his general theory of dreams accepted. Venturing into telepathic aspects of dreams would, he was sure, land him thoroughly beyond the pale.

Nonetheless, Freud's theory of dreams opened an intriguing possibility for exploring anomalous cognition. Might dreams harbor not just suppressed sexual and aggressive urges but suppressed anomalous content as well? Might capacities for anomalous cognition be assiduously masked in waking life because they disrupt accepted cultural norms and conscious mental activity just as much as sex and aggression? Finally, might permitting anomalous capacities into consciousness prove as liberating for the human psyche as acknowledging forbidden sexual and aggressive impulses had been?

It was fifty years before another psychoanalyst picked up the torch. Over the intervening years, a few analysts had published clinical accounts of telepathic dreams, their own or (more typically) those of their patients. But in 1961, Montague Ullman, M.D., a prominent

New York analyst at Maimonides Medical Center, moved the study of dream telepathy a huge step forward. He decided to marry the new and exciting world of the sleep lab with Freud's idea that sleep might produce "conditions favorable to telepathy."

The time was ripe. In 1953, Eugene Aserinsky, a young physiologist and graduate student at the University of Chicago, had noted that when electrical activity of the brain was continually recorded during sleep, certain periods characterized by rapid eye movements occurred. He further noted that when sleeping subjects were wakened during those periods, they were likely to report dreams. Aserinsky was at the time working with his mentor and Ph.D. advisor, Nathaniel Kleitman, a distinguished authority on sleep. In September of 1953, the two men published a groundbreaking article in *Science*. For the first time they associated dreaming with a physiological state called rapid eye movement or REM sleep. From there, research on dreams took off. Suddenly it was possible, through monitoring sleepers' eye movements with an electroencephalograph (EEG), the standard device used to monitor brainwaves, to determine exactly when they were dreaming. Researchers could now wake sleepers in the middle of a dream, during REM sleep, when they could typically remember and recount what they'd just been dreaming. That made all the difference to dream research, since even though virtually everybody dreams at least four times each night, the vast majority of those dreams are forgotten by morning. Now they could be captured.

Armed with the findings about REM sleep, Montague Ullman decided to set up one of New York's first sleep labs to investigate dream telepathy. Ullman had started out as a medical psychoanalyst steeped in the standard Freudian training about dreams and the unconscious as well as contributions from people such as Karen Horney and Erich Fromm. He was equally steeped in the premise that normally unconscious mental content becomes perceptible in dreams because sleep tunes down the activity of waking life. Ullman hypothesized that the noise of everyday waking life also masked potentially anomalous signals that nighttime eyes and dreaming might render visible.

Ullman established at Maimonides the most thorough and

extensive research on telepathic dreams ever conducted. He set out to investigate a simple question: could someone acting as a "sender" telepathically communicate something to a sleeping "receiver" that would influence the content of the sleeper's dream? Ullman secured funding for psychologist Stanley Krippner, Ph.D., to head up the dream laboratory to investigate this question.

Experimental sessions for the Maimonides studies began in the evening. Subjects showed up just before the start of their normal nightly sleep cycles. Each was placed in a comfortable bed in an isolated room and hooked up to an EEG. (Interestingly, standard though the EEG and its applications are these days, the EEG was invented in 1929 by a German psychiatrist, Hans Berger, for the purpose of studying the relationship between brainwaves and telepathy.)

Once hooked up and settled into their beds, the Maimonides subjects dropped off to sleep. Their brain activity was steadily recorded. When the EEG indicated the end of a REM episode, sleepers were wakened and asked to describe whatever they'd just been dreaming. Their reports were carefully transcribed. Meantime, from a different room in the laboratory area, someone acting as a "sender" had been alerted by a buzzer at the exact moment the sleeper, or "receiver," entered REM sleep. When the buzzer went off, the sender tried to mentally transmit a visual image to the sleeper, one randomly selected from a large pool of pictures beforehand. That image was designated as the "target." Each attempted transmission from a sender to a sleeping receiver represented a single experimental trial.

Three independent judges blind to the study (that is, unaware of which target pictures correlated to the typed records of the dreams on the night of that experiment) were then asked to read each verbatim dream transcript and examine the original pool of images from which a given trial's target had been randomly selected. They then picked the image that corresponded most closely to the imagery in the dream transcript for that trial. Over six years of studies and 450 separate trials, the judges were able to choose the correct target with overall odds that were less than 1 in 75 million.[4]

Those results caused quite a reaction in the world of sleep research. Inevitably, there was plenty of skepticism. The data challenged too many assumptions about dreams, not to mention the accepted limits of human communication. The methodology was reviewed in great detail by Irvin Child, professor of experimental psychology at Yale University. Dr. Child published a report in the *American Psychologist,* the main publication of the American Psychological Association, verifying that the methodology was sound. In the minds of many, the research was simply too good to be ignored. No less a personage than Gardner Murphy, the former president of the American Psychological Association, lauded its importance and helped collect funds for further research. In the introduction to Ullman's book, cowritten with Stanley Krippner and Alan Vaughan, Murphy stated:

> This volume takes a giant step into the unknown ... with a broad, clear, specific, and highly challenging approach to the telepathy of the dream.... Over a hundred published studies have shown the real payoff which follows from a strict experimental method in which normal, genuine, real dreams of ordinary human beings are studied with full attention to the rigorous techniques of electrophysiology.... Enough ... has been done to show that in a span of a half dozen years with over a hundred subjects, there is a significant relation between what is "sent" and what is "received." ... It is difficult to imagine today a study more important.... Dream telepathy, dealing with the individual's efforts to make contact with distant reality and with the social nature of man's unconscious powers, is likely to be among the sparks which will be made into a science within the next century.[5]

As the Maimonides data accumulated, Ullman became increasingly convinced not just that dream telepathy existed but that science and psychoanalysis had drastically underestimated its evolutionary and functional utility. He suggested that when people disengaged from the mental processes associated with their waking life, a vital capacity to transfer information from one person to another was freed to express itself in dreams. This capacity, he claimed, reflected a powerful social cohesiveness indicating how each individual's life was interwoven with others in the community. People could therefore use this capacity to guide their actions to promote the survival of the species, whether they were consciously aware of their dreams or not. However, the more attuned they were to the knowledge imparted in their dreams, the more they could use it to inform their conscious decision making.

Ullman's propositions were radical, but he put his reputation and considerable persuasive powers squarely behind them. In 1976, he resigned his position as director of psychiatry at the Maimonides Medical Center to devote himself full-time to the development of an experiential dream group approach that could be mastered by the general public. (He is currently clinical professor emeritus, Department of Psychiatry, at Albert Einstein College of Medicine, Yeshiva University, and the author and coauthor of several books on dreams, including one on dream research.) Ullman went on to see his ideas about experiential dream group work welcomed all over the globe. From 1974 on, Ullman taught experiential dream group work in Sweden. In these groups, funded in part by the government, people meet to discuss their dreams, exploring Ullman's proposition that dreams have a collective function from which people can benefit when they examine them in a safe and stimulating environment.

By the late '70s, funding for the Maimonides dream lab had dried up. But the work was on record as a major new episode in the study of anomalous cognition. And the Maimonides dream lab spawned something else—the career of a young man named Charles Honorton. Honorton had been interested in extraordinary knowing since his teenage years, when he'd struck up a correspondence with J. B. Rhine and even traveled to his lab at Duke University to observe the work there. Early on, Ullman had hired Honorton to work with him and his collaborator Stanley Krippner on the dream studies. Honorton went on to become a leading investigator of anomalous cognition, helping catapult that research into mainstream scientific dialogue. He eventually earned the title of director of the Division of Parapsychology and Psychophysics at Maimonides. In 1979, he founded the Psychophysical Research Laboratories at Princeton, which remained active until 1989 and specialized in remote-viewing research. Long after the lab closed, I asked Susan Fassberg, a former research assistant and study participant there, about him.

> You're curious about Chuck Honorton? That man was really
> something—*dedicated*. We called him "the mole." He lived for the
> nights because that's when we did all the experiments. I sometimes
> wondered if he ever saw daylight. He was fascinated by the idea that
> people knew weird, inexplicable things they didn't know they knew.
> He made it his job to bring what people knew to the surface so we
> could examine what they did know. I'm not surprised he eventually
> became such a leader in telepathy research. He was smart and
> utterly committed.

Working at Maimonides gave Honorton more than experience running experiments. It also nourished his investigative roots in unique conceptual soil. It got him thinking about how to devise experimental conditions that tuned down life's everyday noise so anomalous mental capacities might become experimentally observable. That turned out to be a very big idea.

Two investigators from independent labs in different parts of the world hit upon the same idea at just about the same time Honorton did. One was William Braud from the University of Houston, the man who had written the article on "psi-conducive states" that had first drawn the army's attention to Joe McMoneagle. The other was Adrian Parker, a Ph.D. in psychology at the University of Edinburgh where, to the considerable embarrassment of that highly respectable establishment, a chair in parapsychology had been generously endowed. Honorton, Braud, and Parker all speculated that anomalous cognition might best be characterized as a set of weak perceptual signals that ordinarily went unnoticed, drowned out by the noise of everyday life. On that basis, each reasoned that the key to studying those signals would be a device that amplified them so they could be heard above the background din. After combing the perceptual and psychological literature, all three men focused on a technique that had been developed during the 1930s. This technique was called ganzfeld, meaning "total field" (*ganz* from the German "total" and *feld* meaning "field").

Ganzfeld had been the focus of a great deal of the criticism in the controversial NRC report that I discussed in Chapter 7, and I recalled that Honorton had been one of the researchers who had written a paper in reply. I decided to take a closer look at the history of ganzfeld research.

The idea behind the ganzfeld technique was to deprive subjects of as much outside sensory stimuli as possible. Researchers induced the ganzfeld state by taping translucent Ping-Pong ball halves over subjects' eyes and placing headphones over their ears. A red floodlight was directed toward the eyes, producing an undifferentiated visual field. White noise was played through the headphones, creating an undifferentiated auditory field. Typically, at the start of every ganzfeld trial, each subject underwent a series of progressive relaxation exercises to help mute bodily sensations and mental chatter. The goal of the ganzfeld state was to create an unchanging sensory field. In the absence of new input, the nervous system gradually became responsive to faint, barely noticeable perceptions that were normally overwhelmed by the constant stimulation of perpetually shifting perceptual environments.

Within months of each other, Braud, Honorton, and Parker developed ganzfeld experiments to examine telepathy. Just as in the Maimonides experiments, two minds were required for each experiment, a sender and a receiver. The receiver was introduced to the ganzfeld state while the sender was taken to a soundproof room and instructed to spend thirty minutes concentrating on the target, a picture or film sequence that had been randomly selected from a pool of options. The sender was to focus on mentally "sending" the target to the receiver. Meantime, the receiver was instructed to spend thirty minutes simply thinking out loud, describing whatever images or thoughts came to mind.

When the session was over, the receiver was shown several pictures or film clips, one of which was the target image on which the sender had been concentrating. Receivers were asked to rank each image in terms of how closely it corresponded to the imagery or

thoughts they'd experienced during the thirty-minute ganzfeld period. If the receiver assigned the very highest ranking to the actual
target, the session was scored as a "hit." If the receiver assigned anything but the top ranking to the actual target, it was scored as a
"miss." Since the judging sets usually included four choices (the target and three decoys), the hit rate expected by chance was one out
of four, or 25 percent.[6]

Correspondences between the targets and receivers' impressions were sometimes quite remarkable. For example, a possible target in one of Honorton's experiments was Salvador Dalí's painting
Christ Crucified. The pool of alternative targets offered strongly
contrasting images, including a collapsing suspension bridge from a
1940s newsreel and one of horses running across a field. During a
session in which the *Christ Crucified* had been randomly selected as
the actual target, the receiver reported the following sequence of
images.

> ... I think of guides, like spirit guides, leading me and I come into
> like a court with a king. It's quite ... It's like heaven. The king is
> something like Jesus. Woman. Now I'm just sort of somersaulting
> through heaven. ... Brooding ... Aztecs, the Sun God ... High
> priest ... Fear ... Graves. Woman. Prayer ... Funeral ... Dark.
> Death ... Souls ... Ten Commandments. Moses ...[7]

The description in the report was strikingly similar to the Dalí
images.

The ganzfeld protocol had several big experimental advantages.
First, the experiments were easy to set up. They were also cheap,
especially compared with sleep labs. Next, they utilized an investigative procedure with a solid history in mainstream studies of perception. Finally, they were readily replicable, no small advantage in
the tricky business of studying anomalous cognition.

But the thing that really stood out about the ganzfeld experiments was their design. They achieved something unprecedented
in the history of research on anomalous cognition: they produced a
step-by-step experimental protocol designed to give subjects the
equivalent of nighttime eyes.

By 1982, ten different experimenters from labs all over the world had published the results of forty-two separate ganzfeld telepathy experiments. Of those, twenty-eight listed the actual hit rates; fourteen others simply described the results as positive or negative. Honorton decided it was time to conduct an overall assessment of the results. He wrote a landmark paper reviewing every study, which he presented before the Parapsychological Association, and concluded that they provided reliable evidence for telepathy.[8] His composite analysis of the twenty-eight studies that reported hit rates showed that twenty-three had success rates greater than chance would predict, on average 35 percent. That's no small margin of success. In a gambling casino, it would lead to getting very rich, very fast. The odds of its being due to chance computed to a staggering 10 billion to 1.

But besides that, data from the experiments were themselves rich and absorbing. Highly detailed, vividly descriptive subjective reports of visual imagery were, I discovered, engaging to read—far more engaging than the endless tallies produced by card-reading experiments. I also couldn't help but imagine they must have been far more engaging for the subjects to produce.

Perhaps that was why the ganzfeld experiments had proven so successful. I recalled reading about a woman named Eileen Garrett, New York's reigning queen of telepathy and clairvoyance in the 1930s. Many considered her one of the finest psychics the world had ever seen. In 1934, J. B. Rhine had tested her on card-reading experiments. She'd initially shown no aptitude whatsoever. She'd been astonished and was determined to figure out why. Her conclusion was simple: she was bored. Without a subjective, vivid sense of personal involvement—what she termed "an active emanation registering between two people or between an individual and an object"—Eileen Garrett couldn't do anything anomalous at all. It wasn't until she'd invested her work with personal connection—"the emotional keys which I felt were necessary to unlock the door of my sensitivities"— that she was able to produce any positive results.[9]

Here was another suggestion that connection matters. Maybe it's that simple. Along with tuning down the noise, maybe a meaningful sense of connection to the object of cognition is a critical factor in rendering anomalous signals perceptible. Maybe it's even required for their emergence.

As I reviewed the voluminous ganzfeld literature, one final ingredient struck me as intriguing. There was a cast of characters. The same names kept popping up, sometimes as principal investigators, sometimes as critics of others' experiments, sometimes as respondents replying back to that first round of critics.

And that, I realized, was the point. This rapid-fire, never-ending volley heralded something truly new in the history of research on anomalous cognition. It represented yet another coup for the ganzfeld work. For the first time, studies were building on each other. People were talking to each other, proponents and skeptics alike. They were taking account of what others brought to the table, often others of starkly opposed beliefs. No wonder it was interesting. This, finally, was starting to look like science.

Except that not everyone thought so. As I'd learned from my investigation into the National Research Council and American Institutes of Research reports, criticism of the ganzfeld studies had been at the heart of a twenty-year drama that erupted in the halls of the academy, Senate Hearing Rooms, the National Academy of Sciences, and page after page of scholarly debate. Its intensity was fueled by the acknowledged excellence of the studies and the resulting strength of reactions they provoked, both from those who found the results credible and those who didn't.

The controversy began in relative tranquillity, with Professor Ray Hyman's response to Honorton's 1982 paper summarizing all the ganzfeld studies conducted prior to that time.

Hyman was a cognitive psychologist at the University of Oregon and a longtime skeptic when it came to purportedly anomalous cognition. He was central among the characters I was starting to recognize. When the storm exploded over the National Research Council's report on parapsychology, he'd been in the middle of it as one of the principal evaluators of psi research, and he'd also been on the expert panel for the CIA/AIR report.

Hyman made no bones about the fact that anomalous cognition was, in his view, a frank impossibility. But he was as dedicated to science as he was to skepticism. So, rather than simply disagreeing with

Honorton, Hyman decided he would independently analyze all the same data. He spoke with Honorton. They reached a consensus—the first of many, it turned out, and a hugely important one. They agreed that the ganzfeld database was ideally suited to the statistical process called meta-analysis. Hyman and Honorton agreed that they would each conduct separate meta-analyses of all previously published ganzfeld data and compare results.[10]

Meta-analysis combines data from different but methodologically similar studies in order to obtain greater certainty about whatever trends are observed. When trends are subtle or show up only marginally (i.e., only once in a while for any given individual or population), anything that increases certainty makes all the difference. Meta-analysis helps you figure out what's random versus what isn't. When the same trend shows up over a larger pool of data points, it's more likely that it's not a random event.

Hyman and Honorton's agreement to use meta-analysis was a milestone decision for more than just the ganzfeld work. From then on, meta-analysis would be recognized as a legitimate technique for research on anomalous cognition.

In 1986, Honorton and Hyman combined their respective meta-analyses in the *Journal of Parapsychology* in an article called "A Joint Communiqué: The Psi Ganzfeld Controversy."[11] Despite differences in how they'd approached the data and added up the statistics, they came up with a single and shared conclusion: the patterns of correspondence between receivers' imagery and images purportedly sent by senders didn't appear random and couldn't be explained by methodological flaws in the studies. They required further explanation. Predictably, the two men disagreed when it came to interpretation—was it or wasn't it telepathy? But in an exemplary articulation of scientific collaboration, they together concluded:

> We agree that there is an overall significant effect in this database that cannot reasonably be explained by selective reporting or multiple analysis. We continue to differ over the degree to which the effect constitutes evidence for psi, but we agree that the final verdict awaits the outcome of future experiments conducted by a broader range of investigators and according to more stringent standards.

From there, Honorton and Hyman went on to spell out the joint communiqué's most powerful contribution, detailed guidelines for further experiments. The "more stringent standards" they called for included rigorous precautions against sensory leakage and possibility of fraud, extensive documentation of every choice regarding selection of targets, equipments, subjects, and procedures, and, finally, complete enumeration in advance of all statistical tests chosen to measure success.[12]

The 1986 Honorton-Hyman communiqué still stands as a unique document. It laid out an exceedingly precise formula by which a committed skeptic and an equally committed believer could agree that a fair test of anomalous cognition had been executed.

A number of investigators promptly produced new experiments adhering to the communiqué's guidelines. Some were autoganzfeld studies—experiments that met the standards of the joint communiqué by relying on computer rather than human controls. The autoganzfeld experiments confirmed the results of earlier, less automated studies and obtained the same overall hit rate of around 35 percent. Honorton was among the first to initiate them and publish his results. Hyman immediately responded with a simple and dramatic bottom line. First, he agreed that the new experiments produced by Honorton's Psychophysical Research Laboratory in Princeton had in fact achieved the joint communiqué's "more stringent standards." From there, he concluded, "Honorton's experiments have produced intriguing results. If independent laboratories can produce similar results with the same relationships and with the same attention to rigorous methodology, then parapsychology may indeed have finally captured its elusive quarry."[13]

From the still staunchly skeptical Hyman, that statement was no small concession.

Over the next several years, more replications were produced at a series of independent labs, with an overall hit rate of 33.2 percent.[14] A gold standard for subsequent studies of anomalous cognition was slowly being established.

As ganzfeld methods became more refined, investigators became more adventurous. Perhaps most interesting, prior studies of anomalous cognition had intermittently hinted that artistically gifted people might have an edge on apparently anomalous cognition. Several autoganzfeld studies set out to test that proposition.

Marilyn Schlitz was a researcher who'd been studying parapsychology since the early 1980s. As a former visiting scientist at Princeton's Psychophysical Research Laboratories and research associate and project director for the Mind Science Foundation, Schlitz was especially interested in the connection between anomalous cognition and creativity. She was, as she puts it, a whippersnapper of a girl scientist ready to try anything in the name of science. She was intrigued by Honorton's ganzfeld work and decided to design an experiment for the students at the Juilliard School in New York City, a world-renowned conservatory for the performing arts. She then approached Honorton to become her collaborator.

The two embarked on a joint experiment in 1992. They recruited twenty Juilliard students to act as receivers in a typical ganzfeld setup. A sender in a separate room looked at a photo or watched a film clip and tried to mentally encourage the receiver to describe the images he or she was viewing. The receiver described aloud whatever images came to mind. Independent judges interpreted the results. Schlitz and Honorton published their results in the *Journal of the American Society for Psychical Research*. Overall, the Juilliard students produced an astonishing 50 percent average hit rate, double the rate expected by chance and one of the highest ever reported in a single ganzfeld study.[15] Even more impressive, the eight students who were musicians, as opposed to others specializing in dance or drama, produced a 75 percent hit rate. Even in a population as small as eight, that yielded a statistical significance level of less than 0.0042, meaning that the odds it was due to chance computed to less than 42 out of 10,000.

It was a small study and Honorton and Schlitz were the first to say it was merely suggestive, no more. But the questions exploded. Students at Juilliard were already an exceptional population. Might apparently exceptional anomalous abilities correlate with other exceptional abilities? Might anomalous cognition be particularly accessible to artists? To those with unusually creative imaginations? The Juilliard students weren't just creatively gifted, they were also extraordinarily disciplined and focused in pursuit of their technical training. Was their capacity for discipline and focus part of their impressive hit rate? And what about those musicians? Might having a musical ear be associated with an ear for the apparently anomalous?

As I examined the Juilliard results, even more intriguing questions presented themselves. What about the distinctive relationship these artists had to what we call the unconscious? Artistically gifted people have long been credited with unusual access to unconscious imagery, along with unusual freedom to bypass the barriers that prevent such imagery from entering everyday consciousness. Might a talent for apparently anomalous cognition, such as the ability to receive vivid, unexpected, dreamlike images from a sender, be one result? Might the royal road stretching between the unconscious and dreams have its parallel in a road linking the unconscious with anomalous cognition? Might that be why something like nighttime eyes—the kind of eyes that, perhaps, artists work to develop during waking life—prove critical to extraordinary knowing? Might that be why anomalous cognition registers with just the same ephemeral, quirky, unpredictable relationship to conscious thought as dreaming?

Sadly, Honorton died of a heart attack in 1992, right after the work with Schlitz. He was only forty-six. But in the meantime, Schlitz had joined the ganzfeld cast of characters. And together, the two had opened intriguing new terrain for the next generation of research.

The next chapter in the ganzfeld story consolidated around Daryl Bem, professor of social psychology at Cornell. Bem was another familiar name from the cast of characters I was coming to know so well. I recognized him as the coauthor with Charles Honorton of the 1994 article published in the *Psychological Bulletin* that had given a fuller backstory to the whole controversy behind the National Research Council report on parapsychology, which I discussed in Chapter 7.

But I also had a personal interest. I'd taken a course with Bem while I was getting my Ph.D. at Stanford. I remembered him vividly, better than any other professor during my graduate career. He'd been a brilliant teacher with a brilliant mind and had a remarkable gift for inspiring curiosity in students.

I wondered how this professor of social psychology had ended up doing research on anomalous mental capacities. He'd gotten an undergraduate degree in physics and had pursued a graduate degree at MIT in physics before switching to psychology. I discovered that while he was paying his way through school, Bem had worked first as a magician, then as a "psychic entertainer." Early on, he'd joined the Psychic Entertainers Association (yet another organization I'd never heard of prior to the peculiar journey initiated by the harp's return). He'd developed a particular acuity for sniffing out all the ways his companions employed the tricks of their trade, things like blindfolds that didn't really blind and other such manipulations, particularly ones that fell into a category called sensory leakage, which involved divining cues, often unconsciously, from ordinary looking, touching, and hearing. Bem became an expert. In the process, he'd developed a rare set of skills, including the ability to unearth flaws of design, method, or procedure in studies that investigated purportedly anomalous mental capacities. He knew all about psychic cheats and psychic cons, the bane of experiments on anomalous cognition. As a result, his first forays into studying anomalous cognition were as a hired hand. When Charles Honorton needed someone to check his ganzfeld experiments for problems like sensory leakage, he brought Bem onboard as the ideal professional skeptic. If anyone could catch flaws that other academics might miss, it was Bem.

Once Bem started rigorously assessing these kinds of studies, he was hooked. Sensory leakage couldn't explain the results he was seeing. He couldn't debunk the experiments he'd been hired to debunk. He decided to put his crack experimental genius to work investigating anomalous cognition.

Bem and Honorton's *Psychological Bulletin* article summarized meta-analyses of twenty-nine ganzfeld studies from ten separate laboratories. It issued a ringing conclusion: there was solid, replicable evidence for apparently anomalous information transfer between people.[16]

Psychological Bulletin was a major peer-reviewed journal, widely read around the world. For five years, the Bem-Honorton paper went essentially unchallenged. Then, in 1999, Richard Wiseman from the University of Hertfordshire, England, gathered results of thirty new ganzfeld studies and published a meta-analysis with Julie Milton from the University of Edinburgh in the *Psychological Bulletin*. Their conclusion rang out as resoundingly as Bem and Honorton's, but in the opposite direction. The authors declared that the ganzfeld technique "does not at present offer a replicable method for producing ESP in the laboratory."[17]

Another skirmish in the ganzfeld battle had begun, with meta-analysis followed by meta-analysis, apparent replications followed by nonreplications. *Psychological Bulletin* published it all.[18]

By that time, Bem was puzzled. (Who could blame him? So was I.) Why so many discrepancies? Bem came up with an answer in a 2001 paper he coauthored with John Palmer and Richard Broughton, two longtime investigators of anomalous cognition. It had the provocative title "Updating the Ganzfeld Database: A Victim of Its Own Success?"[19]

The ganzfeld procedure had, the authors declared, been hoist by its own petard. It had proven so successful in numerous standard replications that studies were starting to take all kinds of liberties with the basic procedures in an effort to learn more about what might explain the demonstrated effect. No wonder the resulting studies produced such inconsistent conclusions; they were no longer true replications. On the other hand, the authors went on to suggest, this might in fact signify the widespread acceptance of the method. Rather than continue with replications, researchers were pushing into unknown territory.

Following the ganzfeld research had me feeling the way I do watching pro tennis—great volleys, lots to admire, much to learn. Intellectually, it was about the most satisfying foray into exploring anomalous cognition I'd encountered. But at a certain point I'd had enough. I was tired of being at one remove from the action.

In fact, it was worse than pro tennis. With tennis, at least I had no problem believing the pros could do what they appeared to do. With ganzfeld, it was different. I was surprised to find myself aligned squarely with the skeptics. No matter how good the experimental evidence, the underlying phenomenon of one person receiving an image from another in a sealed-off room flew in the face of too much I knew and trusted. The thing made no sense.

And while the ganzfeld experiments were intriguing, they inspired in me none of the relentless curiosity that had left me sleepless after Harold told me where to find that harp. Or that had me bemused after Deb said she couldn't get one of those job applicants I interviewed to unclasp her hands. I was missing some personal experience that would push me out of doubt into a subjective sense that there was something potentially real and meaningful in whatever abilities those ganzfeld subjects were supposed to be demonstrating.

I recalled an observation from a mentor of mine, years ago. Harold Sampson was director of research at Mt. Zion Hospital's psychiatry department in San Francisco. I was at the time a postdoctoral fellow. Harold was much beloved, especially for his laconic way of putting the lid on unproductive discussion. In the middle of one morning's deadlocked debate over the credibility of some research, he'd deprecatingly coughed, his usual way of signaling that he was about to say something we'd want to hear. We all turned to listen. "We say we'll believe it when we see it. But maybe what we do is see it when we believe it."

With the ganzfeld experiments, I had no compelling hook on which to hang believing, while my doubts felt thoroughly real and personal. I wanted to see if the ganzfeld state really tuned down the noise, and if it put me in a state from which I'd know something I usually didn't know. I wanted to put my doubts to the test, and an opportunity soon arose.

I'd met Paul Devereux, a writer and consciousness researcher with a focus on archaeology, acoustics, and anthropology,[20] at an interdisciplinary group called the International Consciousness Research

Laboratories, which held periodic think-tank gatherings in Princeton, New Jersey. (I write more about the work of ICRL in Chapter 12.) Devereux had participated in an experiment with a ganzfeld-type setup at a lab at Laurentian University in Sudbury, Ontario. He'd been sufficiently impressed by the results to tell the ICRL group, "I really think we should take this thing very seriously." When Devereux discovered that I was going to a conference in Toronto, he encouraged me to make the additional trek north to the Laurentian lab. Devereux promised to arrange my visit with the director, professor of neuroscience Michael A. Persinger, Ph.D., whom he'd known for many years.

In all, I spent six hours at the lab. I was settled into a very comfortable armchair inside an acoustic chamber, which greatly reduced the sound level. A student put a helmet, in which small magnetic solenoids were embedded, over my head and neatly halved Ping-Pong balls over my eyes, then retreated from the room. The magnetic fields generated by the solenoids were created by batches of software that imitated certain natural patterns of brain activity. I learned that the strength of the fields was quite weak, less than those created by a blow-dryer. The acoustic dampening, white noise, and filtered light made it easy to relax and the time passed quickly. Grad students ran one experiment after another on me, each lasting fifteen minutes. For each experiment, I was asked to do the same thing—say whatever came to mind, including physical sensations, visual images, feelings, or anything else. That would be easy, I told myself. After all, as a psychoanalyst, free-associating is my bread and butter.

What I hadn't anticipated was that, since I was in a ganzfeld-type state for every experiment, I wouldn't know when we were doing the one testing telepathy—the reason I was there. It wasn't until a student showed up with some colored postcards and asked me to rank them in order of how closely they corresponded to my recent imagery that I realized we'd just done it. Now I was supposed to see if I could pick which postcard some sender in another room had just been trying to mentally transmit to me.

I looked at all the cards. There were six, all very different. There was a merry-go-round, a bright red sunset, an old-fashioned steam engine, and three scenes of the university campus. I laid them out in front of me. I tried to recapture all the images that had crossed my mind during the previous fifteen minutes. Not one bore any resemblance to any of the cards. I picked up the cards and re-ordered them. I tried focusing on one at a time. Then I tried looking away, then looking back at them. Nothing. I reviewed every other image that had flitted across my mind. Maybe there was something I hadn't caught before, something more subtle. I came up blank. I simply couldn't find a single memory that remotely resembled any of the cards.

Finally I shrugged up at the graduate student who'd been patiently waiting and told him I couldn't do it. Privately, I told myself I wasn't surprised. I knew I'd be a dead loss—at telepathy, remote perception, or anything else like that.

I tried to give the graduate student the cards, but he handed them back and instructed me to rank them even if I had to resort to sheer random order; the experimental protocol required me to come up with rankings and I'd agreed to participate.

I rifled through the cards again. By now I didn't much care what I came up with. The student simply needed his data. I'd been a grad student myself; I didn't want to screw up his experiment through lack of compliance. I glanced one last time at the cards and chose one at random to rank first. It was the red sunset. The graduate student asked me why I'd chosen it. I was aware of a fleeting sensation—maybe. One minuscule fraction of a second that had me somehow landing on the sunset instead of any of the other cards. I told the student that it was something about the redness—maybe. But even as I said it, I was sure it wasn't true. I was just trying to please, offering us both the illusion that I was operating outside pure chance. I flipped through the remaining cards, put them in some arbitrary order, and handed them over.

The graduate student went into another room to retrieve a sealed envelope containing the target image the sender was trying to transmit. He opened the envelope and took out a postcard. It was the red sunset.

And at that moment the world turned weird. I felt the tiniest instant of overwhelming fear. It was gone in a flash but it was stunningly real. It was unlike any fear I've ever felt. My mind split. I re-

alized that I knew something I was simultaneously certain I didn't
know. And I got it. This is what my patients meant when they said,
"My mind's not my own." Or "I'm losing my mind." The feeling
was terrifying. My mind had slipped out from under me and the
world felt out of control.

I recovered quickly and launched in on logical explanations.
First and most compelling, it must have been pure coincidence.
The odds I'd picked the right card were, after all, one in six. And
that uncanny feeling—I knew perfectly well that coincidence does
that to people. We all want to feel magical and omnipotent and
we'll grasp for that feeling wherever we can. Uncanny feelings are
one result and psychologists ever since Freud have been coming up
with reasons why.

But I knew it wasn't that simple and my arguments with myself
didn't carry the day. Once again, I was remembering my sister's
watch. Walking straight to that box in back of my husband's closet
had taught me a feeling, a full-bodied, single-minded, wholehearted
feeling I'd described as being "walked by the experience." It was as
if the experience knew me. It brought a thoroughly unaccustomed
sensation to the surface, a feeling that was categorically unlike ordinary knowing. The fraction of a second that had me landing on the
red sunset—so brief and so ephemeral it barely registered—was an
echo of the sensation I'd had when I'd walked straight to my sister's
watch. This time I'd walked not across a room but across my mind,
walked straight out of my ordinary knowing into an inchoate, uncertain mental state that—maybe—deserves to be called knowing,
too. It took the graduate student jolting me into the realization that
I'd picked the correct card for me to consider—maybe—letting it in.

After I left the lab, I realized that I'd gotten what I'd come for:
some feeling for a quality of knowing that gave me that hook for
believing. I wondered if I'd see the ganzfeld experiments differently,
in the sense that I'd now see that there was something there worth
seeing. Part of me still insisted that picking the red sunset was
merely coincidence, no more than a lucky guess and nothing to do
with the ganzfeld state or tuning down the noise.

But believing in that extraordinary tuning in wasn't what I
came for. I'd come for something different. Not the jolt I'd felt

when that graduate student handed me the sunset card, or when the young man gave me back the harp, or when I'd found my sister's watch. The jolt was a signal after the fact. I'd come to find the feeling *before* the jolt. That's what counted.

The problem is, I couldn't find words to name it. I'd spent hours, months, searching for words to label the feeling that came before. None of them worked. They were all too definitive. The closest I came was to say I was "drawn." Drawn to the watch and drawn to that red sunset. But even that sounded too delineated, too conclusive. To begin with, it sounded as if I were conscious of what I did. I wasn't. Even more, it smacked of separation—me in one place, the watch in another, and me being drawn across the space between. That was all wrong. Weird as it sounded, there wasn't any space between.

Whatever that sensation was, that's what I'd come for.

I wrote Paul Devereux about my ganzfeld work. He responded with an account of his own experience, which differed in significant ways from mine. While he'd likewise had his sensory input dampened with Ping-Pong balls placed over his eyes and the helmet with embedded solenoids placed over his head, he'd also donned a kind of headband that Dr. Persinger called a "circumcerebral device" or "the octopus," because it had eight solenoids arranged around the head like a crown. Leads from the solenoids were connected to a computer. When switched on, it created an electromagnetic field that rotated like a vortex around the brain.

Devereux's task was to keep a running commentary on whatever images sprang to mind for the forty-five minutes that the solenoids were activated. During this time, Devereux had noted two recurring images: the first was a kind of colorful fairground object dominated by bright neon green. The other image was of two telegraph poles highlighted against a sunset sky.

At the end of the experiment, the researchers laid out eight or so photos, asking Devereux if he'd seen any of those images during the time the solenoids had been switched on. He immediately recognized the two images he'd reported. What he'd described as two telegraph poles silhouetted against a sunset sky were in fact two smokestacks that dominated the campus where the laboratory was located. What he'd seen as a fairground object was in fact a photo of an old steam locomotive painted in variegated colors with a bright green cowcatcher on the front. Devereux was astonished.

Then Devereux learned of an even more astonishing facet to the experiment. Unbeknownst to him, while he was performing his task, his wife had been taken to a different room where she'd been told to select one from the same stack of photos Devereux would later see and describe it as she thought her husband would. The photo his wife had selected was the one of the locomotive. No one had ever taken the smokestack picture out of the envelope, although that image had come to Devereux's mind. Devereux found the whole experience remarkable:

> Fascinating, fascinating stuff. It was the "experience" of "receiving" the psi-information that caught my attention, too. . . . Even now I couldn't tell you what it was I knew; all I can tell about is what my "left brain" conjured out of the "right brain," if you see what I mean. I'm remembering the remembering, rather than whatever the knowing was that allowed me to identify the pic. That knowing had neither linguistic nor conceptual qualities; it was primarily colour-based, and it was the specific "assembly" of those colours that led me to put enough together conceptually to organize the identification of the picture card. That sounds laborious but it was instantaneous. No effort . . .

The next day, he added a P.S.:

> Let me ratchet this up one more notch. The "assembly" of colour I "saw" was so itsy bitsy that I thought it was some kind of crazily painted fairground piece of machinery. But above all a "neon green" shone out so much that I mentioned it in my stream-of-consciousness report. As soon as I saw the pic of the multi-coloured old steam engine with its brilliant green cow-catcher, I knew what had actually been in my "mind's eye." The decoding process is just that, I think: approximating in a sort of on-board Rorschach mode, I reckon. (This could explain the lack of precision in many "normal" psi accounts.)

Our exchange opened an intriguing set of questions. What did it mean that Devereux and I both were so focused on color? And what about our emphatic agreement that the experience lacked any familiar linguistic and conceptual form? Or my friend's throw-away line about feeling as though his "left brain" conjured something out of his "right brain"? Or his Rorschach reference? That one fascinated me particularly. I thought of those famous inkblots and how patients are asked to describe what they see in them. No two people respond the same way. Might anomalous perceptions arise the same way responses to Rorschach cards do, as highly subjective interpretations that, though triggered by an objective stimulus, manifest in a form that's heavily filtered through each individual's personal unconscious?

I was grateful for the dialogue. It was reassuring that Devereux's experience resonated so strongly with my own—reassuring in a realm where doubt continued to be the order of the day. I couldn't decide whether I'd reported my perceptions out of anything other than a lucky guess, while the two images had persisted for Devereux during his entire forty-minute session, and later when he'd seen the photos, he'd recognized them immediately. Neither of us knew what to make of the whole thing, but we each had a subjective sense of another possibility and we agreed on that much. In response to the task, our usual ways of knowing didn't work. Another way—maybe—snuck in under the radar. While the images had come to Devereux without prodding, I'd needed the graduate student's push to complete the task I'd decided I couldn't do. In the end, Devereux and I both encountered the jolt and the mystifying feeling behind it, the sense that we just might have known something we didn't know we knew.

It made me wonder how often this happens. Might we regularly fail to notice conceivably anomalous knowing because it's not flagged by the usual signals? The signs that help us recognize that we know?

There's one thing my friend tells me he didn't experience. He didn't feel the fear. He speculates about why.

> It didn't fill me with fear at all, but it did amaze me. And excite me. I felt here was the potential for there to be a machine, the "octopus,"

that might be able to make the experience of remote perception available to anyone, especially to researchers. I saw that for the first time it might be possible to study psi phenomena from the inside, so to speak. I found the way I had received the information regarding the pictures to be fascinating—one part of the brain trying to "read out" what another part had received or in some way intuited. It wasn't simply the psi transmission of an image but of raw information that had to be interpreted. I learned more in this one session than in years of earlier research. The other thing was, of course, that such a device, if it could offer repeatability and be used by pretty much anyone, would remove the question of the actuality of psi experience. It would no longer be *if* but *how*. The only time I got a bit scared was in the days afterwards. When I fell asleep, I experienced a torrent of dream imagery unlike anything I had ever experienced. Another "octopus" subject I spoke with had the same experience and for a while we wondered if the device had damaged our brains! It had certainly stimulated the parts of our brains that dealt with dreaming. But, eventually, things returned to normal. I didn't have the sort of researchers' fear, the cognitive dissonance, you refer to because in my life I have had a handful of parapsychological experiences that convinced me that psi phenomena were actual. My frustration had been, and still is, that mainstream thinking simply dismisses or derides these aspects of human experience.

Three Seconds into the Future:

The New Science of the Unconscious

O N NOVEMBER 11, 2003, the *New York Times* published the twenty-fifth anniversary issue of its weekly
Science Times. In celebration, the editors assigned their top
science reporters to cover "twenty-five of the most provocative
questions facing science." Included were big stories on big topics:
"How Did Life Begin?" "Is War Our Biological Destiny?" "Should
the Genome Be Improved?" "How Does the Brain Work?" "What
Came Before the Big Bang?" "Can Robots Become Conscious?"
and "What Is the Next Plague?" Along with these heavy hitters was
a piece by Kenneth Chang: "Do Paranormal Phenomena Exist?"

Chang's article included an interview with Brian D. Josephson,
professor of physics at Cambridge University, who shared the 1973
Nobel Prize in physics for a fundamental discovery in superconduc-
tivity. Josephson made no bones about his view that science at large
brings a less than open-minded attitude to examining anomalous

phenomena: "There's really strong pressure not to allow these things to be talked about in a positive way."

Chang's piece in the *Times* offered the following conclusion: "Perhaps the biggest reason most scientists dismiss paranormal research is that no one has a good suggestion for how the mind could interact with the physical world." And even Dr. Josephson conceded, "It would have to be something we haven't identified in physical experiments. I think if we can get some sort of model, then people may start to look at it."

Models help us think. Without a conceptual home, observations that don't fit our existing models may be intriguing and entertaining, but they have the ultimate impact of writing on water. Without a model to contain them, we have no place to put new and unfamiliar things while we try to figure them out.

The situation with paranormal phenomena is even more dire. The conceptual frameworks we do have tell us they will *never* find a home. And we have real trouble thinking clearly, creatively, or for more than five minutes about things our models inform us are permanently homeless. As long as we're stuck there, we can steep ourselves in impressive data and remarkable anecdotes, but we'll be hard-pressed to get very far in assessing what they mean.

Part of the problem with creating a new model, I think, is that it has to account for data we're not used to considering data: feelings. My experience with anomalous events had begun with the story of Harold and the harp, that unmistakable jolt to the system I've been coming to recognize ever since. My single, conscious thought at the time—*This changes everything*—was inextricably married to a gut feeling, a personal and irrefutable feeling that made me know something had happened. It was the kind of feeling that cognitive neuroscientist Antonio Damasio captured in the title for his hugely influential book on consciousness, *The Feeling of What Happens.* I had to doubt my existing models of reality or I had to doubt myself, the core sense of self that comes, Damasio tells us, when body, emotion, and idea merge to make consciousness.[1]

A model that aims to contain anomalous cognition has to take into account the feeling of what happens. It has to make room for that unique dissociative jolt, the shock of body, emotion, and idea erupting into consciousness with knowing that feels utterly different from ordinary knowing. The feeling of what happens is part of the data. That doesn't mean that the knowing that enabled Harold to find the harp or that led me to find my sister's watch is necessarily anomalous. The fact that a stick seen underwater suddenly *looks* bent doesn't mean it *is* bent. But a stick in water does produce a feeling of what happens that's different from a stick not in water.[2] That's a fact, and an important one. Any useful model of perception will have to account for the difference.

I was back to Freud and nighttime eyes. Models that explain the feeling of what happens when we see with daytime eyes won't explain seeing with nighttime eyes. If we don't recognize that, we end up like the king's wise men, the ones who proclaimed that stars didn't exist. It was only when the king's fool offered a different model for seeing—that when the sun is shining, you can't see the stars—that the people who'd obediently given up their belief in the stars discovered that the stars once again existed.

I was visiting with my friend whose daughter had explained the story about nighttime eyes to her little brother. By now she'd turned nine. She was an entrancing child, with a luminous smile and a delicate, grave way of considering ideas. I asked her if she remembered the story about the people who stopped believing in stars. She lit up. "*Yes,*" she said, "I *love* that story!" I asked if she remembered telling her little brother five years earlier that it wasn't really a story about stars but about people having daytime eyes and nighttime eyes. She hadn't remembered, but it made sense to her. She wondered what it must have been like when all those people suddenly returned to believing in stars. First, she said, they must have been very happy to get the stars back. But, she added, she bet that most people never really ever lost them— they probably knew the stars were real all along, even if they weren't supposed to think so. It must have felt really good when they stopped pretending. She imagined that they were surprised at what a relief it was when they stopped thinking they thought the wrong thing.

Once again, I thought, my friend's daughter might have it nailed. Maybe the jolt doesn't result only from the thought, *This changes everything.* Maybe, against all odds and against all our models, that jolt comes from the inchoate recognition, *I knew it all along.*

This is the feeling of what happens in psychoanalysis at its best. Suddenly there's a moment when insight hits with a jolt and it does change everything. But it's lodged in paradox as well. Even while it's changing everything, it's nothing new to the patient experiencing the jolt. It comes with a sense that *I* knew *this—it's deeply familiar—I knew it all along.*

And it's true. It's new but not new. What's changed is that something has percolated out of unconscious knowing into conscious awareness. We know it in a new way when it joins consciousness. That was Freud's great insight more than a century ago. Consciousness changes things. But at the same time, it's the tip of the iceberg and that was the other half of Freud's revolutionary theory of mind. The vast preponderance of our mental life proceeds outside conscious awareness. We're perpetually and pervasively influenced by the prodigious force of unconscious mental processes. However, the distinction between conscious and unconscious is by no means absolute.

Bit by bit, that insight has become so basic to Western thought that it's lost its radical edge. Over time, we've begun to mistake the content of the Freudian unconscious—repression of forbidden sexual impulses—for the insight itself. These days, it's hardly news that people have sexual drives that precipitate psychological conflict and manifest in symptomatic ways. By retaining that focus as the central truth of psychoanalysis, we've trivialized analysis as a clinical method but also as a theory of mind. That's fueled our domestication of what remains a profoundly disconcerting truth: we can't *ever* know as consciously and fully as we like to think we do. However, we do all we can to resist that fact, preferring instead to exalt our capacities for being conscious.

However, in recent years, a corrective has been emerging. It's come from a surprising quarter, one that spent most of its history declaring Freud dead and his focus on the unconscious passé. Over the past two decades, experiments in cognitive neuroscience have repeatedly demonstrated that the overwhelming proportion of human mental activity occurs unconsciously. While those experiments don't let us directly observe mental activity that isn't conscious, they let us infer its presence and observe its fruits.

We now have experimental confirmation that much of what

we perceive, react to, assess, and decide remains entirely outside our conscious awareness, whether we're driving a car or forming preferences or deciding what works to our advantage. This has caused a humbling reappraisal of consciousness. Damasio sums it up: "The unconscious, in the narrow meaning in which the word has been etched in our culture, is only a part of the vast amount of processes and contents that remain nonconscious ... not known. . . . Amazing, indeed, how little we ever know."[3]

But maybe, if we give their real due to those "processes and contents that remain nonconscious," we'll find it equally amazing how much it turns out we do know—unconsciously. And perhaps one key to understanding anomalous mental capacities is to shift our focus from consciousness to what lies beneath.

Drew Westen, Ph.D., professor of psychology, psychiatry, and behavioral sciences at Emory University, has been in the forefront of scholars who've recognized that the overwhelming trend of contemporary cognitive science takes us directly back to Freud's theory of mind. His seminal review article, "The Scientific Status of Unconscious Processes: Is Freud Really Dead?" opens,

> Probably no one's death has ever been heralded as many times, over as many years, as Sigmund Freud's. . . . At regular intervals for over half a century, critiques of Freud and psychoanalysis have emerged in the popular media and intellectual circles, usually declaring that Freud has died some new and agonizing death, and that the enterprise he created should be buried along with him like artifacts in the tomb of an Egyptian king. Although the critiques take many forms, one of the central claims has long been that unconscious processes ... lack any basis in scientific research. In recent years, however, a large body of experimental research has emerged in a number of independent literatures ... documenting the most fundamental tenet of psychoanalysis, that much of mental life is unconscious, and that this extends to cognitive, affective, and motivational processes. Examination of this body of research points ... to the conclusion that *based on controlled scientific*

investigations alone ... Freud was right about a series of
propositions. ... [4]

Drew Westen is an unusual man. Years ago, he managed to
make himself equally at home in the worlds of cognitive science
and psychoanalysis at a time when that was a highly unlikely thing
to do. Since then, thanks in no small part to his work, the marriage
he helped inaugurate has become practically trendy. Over the past
decade, new journals and professional societies dedicated to its pro-
motion have sprung into existence. Neuropsychoanalysis has become an acknowledged and cutting-edge specialty.

One of Westen's major contributions has been to take current
experimental evidence about unconscious mental processes and explore specific ways in which that evidence illuminates and expands
a psychoanalytic model of mind. He starts with unconscious memory, often designated as *implicit* memory in the cognitive science
vocabulary. He describes first how it can be broken down into two
categories, *procedural* and *associative* memory, both lodged in vast
neural networks whose physical structures are continuously altered
by the day-to-day uses we put them to. Procedural memory involves the how-to's of life—driving a car or throwing a ball or playing a well-rehearsed piece of music. Associative memory pertains to
how our minds form relational networks entirely outside our conscious awareness. As Westen describes them, these networks extend
way beyond the realm of ideas. They include sense perceptions,
emotions, motivations, attitudes, and values as well.

A key feature of procedural memory is, as he puts it, that

> people typically cannot report how they carry out these procedures,
> and when they try, they often make up plausible but incorrect
> explanations of how they did what they did. ... Conscious reflection
> can actually disrupt these processes; the surest way for a pianist to
> make a mistake on a complex piece is to think about what she is
> doing. Procedural memory, like much of implicit memory, is often
> much faster than conscious retrieval, which is why people can play
> several measures of music far faster than they can explicitly interpret
> them.[5]

Westen's summary statement that "conscious reflection can actually disrupt those processes" rang a bell. It was just what professional intuitives like Deb, Harold, and Joe McMoneagle reported when they described their apparently anomalous capacities.

So models that explain procedural memory's peculiar relationship to conscious knowing might give us hints about elements of a model for anomalous cognition. They might also help to define the experimental conditions we need in order to study anomalous mental processes. We might need data that result from bypassing precisely that conscious reflection that, in Westen's terms, "can actually disrupt" knowing rooted in unconscious processes.

Associative memory, the other half of implicit memory, also guides our conscious behavior without our ever being aware of its powerful influence. Many so-called priming experiments have demonstrated how associative memory operates. For example, in one common experiment, subjects are shown a series of words and then asked to press a button as soon as they know whether a subsequent set of letters flashed on a screen forms a real word. People who are shown the word *dog* in the original series—*dog* being the "prime"—press the button faster when later shown the word *terrier* or *poodle* than people not primed with *dog* beforehand. *Dog* is part of an associational network that includes *poodle* and *terrier*. When that associational network is activated by seeing the word *dog, poodle* and *terrier* also end up in a heightened state of activation. So they, along with *dog,* gain increased access to consciousness.[6]

There have been many elaborations of the basic priming methodology, all demonstrating the power of unconscious associative networks. Some of the most interesting involve a phenomenon well known to the advertising world, subliminal priming. In subliminal priming, the prime is presented in such a way that it is never consciously registered by the person being primed. For example, a word is flashed for one hundred milliseconds and immediately followed by a longer exposure to a neutral "masking" stimulus such as a series of numbers. The neutral stimulus draws the conscious attention of the person being primed, effectively blocking conscious recognition of the prime. In one well-known study, subjects were subliminally exposed to a long list of words that included the word *assassin.* When asked one week later to fill in the missing letters of the word fragment A--A--IN, subjects who'd been exposed to the word *assassin* a week earlier were more likely to respond with "assassin" than people not exposed to the subliminal prime, *even though they had no conscious memory* of having seen that word a week earlier.[7]

Subliminal priming experiments have repeatedly demonstrated that we can find perfectly rational explanations for thoughts, feelings, and perceptions that manifest in our conscious awareness as utterly inexplicable. That raises the question, might those same experiments have something to teach us about the inexplicable experience of apparently anomalous cognition? Might unconscious associative networks operate as a motive force in anomalous cognition just as they do in nonanomalous cognition, linking those thoughts, feelings, or perceptions in ways that appear thoroughly surprising on a conscious level? If so, might that help explain the jolt, the feeling of what happens when apparently anomalous knowing hits? Might the jolt signal the surprise with which we habitually greet conscious manifestations of unconscious associative networks, such as moments of déjà vu, or having a name suddenly pop into our heads even when we can't recall learning it? Of course, we'll also need to ask whether there's anything different about apparently anomalous cognition. Does the jolt that can accompany it reflect something beyond the surprise likely to signal *any* conscious knowing activated by unconscious associative networks?

If the jolt of apparently anomalous cognition is distinctive, it will be due not to the surprise alone but to the *actual nature of the associative networks activated.* The anomalous might reside in unconscious associative links that defy our ordinary definitions of what's possible, *not just in the realm of conscious mental processing but in the realm of what we name unconscious as well.* The jolt might come from recognizing unconscious associations between things that don't fit inside associative networks we've learned to identify. It might signal a human capacity to perceive connections that we don't believe exist.

We're already used to bending the rules when it comes to unconscious associative networks. In dreams, for example, we don't expect the norms of consciousness to apply. We can dream of blue people or pregnant two-year-olds or snakes that fly without seeing them as anomalies; they're just dreams. On the other hand, we're shaken when we have dreams that turn out to accurately describe events we couldn't possibly know about. Suppose I dream that my brother is in a car crash on the other side of the world. Then suppose I wake up and discover that this has actually happened. My first recourse will be to explain away the dream as nothing more than coincidence. But if the detail is exquisite enough, the unlikelihood dramatic enough, and its accuracy unequivocal enough, that dream will stay with me, pull at me. The feeling of what happened will nag most of all. Just *how* did I hit on an image of my brother struck by a car in India when he was supposed to be in London but was, as I later found out, actually in Benares, being knocked down as he crossed a street?[8] How can I believe in unconscious associative networks that let me know what's happening to a loved one thousands of miles away? They're not supposed to exist.

A particularly groundbreaking application of priming methodology offers intriguing implications for modeling anomalous cognition. Lloyd Silverman, a psychologist and psychoanalyst at New York University, devised an innovative series of experiments that took associative memory way beyond simple cognitive tasks such as identifying words.

Silverman wanted to test the idea that subliminal priming with the phrase "Mommy and I are one" would lead to measurable shifts in people's adaptive functioning and sense of well-being, improving things like self-esteem, self-assertion, and contentment. In over forty experiments in his lab, plus dozens more in other labs, subjects received a brief exposure—in Silverman's labs, for a mere four milliseconds—to the subliminal prime "Mommy and I are one." The results were dramatic and caused no small degree of controversy.[9] The extremely brief exposure to this prime did indeed help many different kinds of subjects, from schizophrenics and neurotics to normal students, improve their adaptive functioning. The scientific merit of his work was widely accepted. However, its import was hotly contested.

First, the apparent power of the prime itself was surprising, especially given the climate in which Silverman's experiments were conducted. He began his work during the early 1960s. Mainstream psychology was just emerging from its heavy domination by behaviorism. American psychoanalysis was in its conservative heyday, adhering to strict guidelines of medical membership for the American Psychoanalytic Association. Ironically, those guidelines excluded not just psychologists but also many associates of Freud's whose immigration to the United States had planted analysis on U.S. soil. The two worlds—psychology rooted in the behavioral lab and psychoanalysis grounded in unconscious mental processes—had never been further apart.

Meantime, Silverman was proposing that data from the psychology lab could inform both worlds about the powerful effects of unconscious mental processes. Even more challenging, he was suggesting that we needed to look beyond the vaunted sense of personal individuality, held as key to mature adaptation by both psychology and psychoanalysis. He proposed instead "... that there are powerful unconscious wishes for a state of oneness... and that gratification of these wishes can enhance adaptation."[10]

Silverman's thesis held up for experiments in widely different settings conducted by many other researchers. In one study of smoking cessation, smokers looking to kick the habit were taught behavior modification techniques for twelve sessions. Half also received subliminal stimulation with the prime "Mommy and I are one," while the other half were exposed to a prime judged as neutral, "People are walking." While all subjects became abstainers after the twelve sessions, at one month's follow-up, 67 percent of the group exposed to "Mommy and I are one" were still abstaining from smoking versus only 13 percent of the control group.[11]

Similarly positive results were obtained in studies with adolescents suffering from personality disorders, with adults who had insect phobias, alcoholics, schizophrenics, and people complaining of problems ranging from depression to obesity to low self-esteem to difficulties with self-assertion. Israeli high school students who were exposed to "Mommy and I are one" achieved marks in mathematics over a full grade higher than students exposed to a subliminal control stimulus.[12] Other studies showed similar cognitive improvement with other populations and in areas outside mathematics.

The "Mommy and I are one" experiments suggested that unexpected new capacities could be liberated by stimulating an unconscious associative network based in a subjective sense of oneness or connection. Those capacities ranged from frank cognitive skills to capacities for more subtle and complex competencies such as self-esteem, self-discipline, or optimism.

Meantime, it's intriguing to note that the subjective sense of oneness pinpointed by Silverman repeatedly turns up in reports of anomalous cognition, not to mention in the meditators and nuns described by brain researchers Newberg and D'Aquili.

It's tempting to wonder if there's a link. Might elements of a model elucidating anomalous mental capacities be found in the workings of unconscious associative networks? More specifically, might they lie in grasping how an unconscious experience of oneness enables access to adaptive and unexpected capacities? Might the operative ingredient be more than oneness with Mommy? From there, myriad conceptual as well as experimental questions unfold.

Priming research is just one field in a new generation of experiments investigating the unconscious roots of extraordinary knowing. In some of the best recent experiments, the evidence rests on easily quantifiable responses such as heart rate or electrical activity manifested by the skin and the brain, measures that are now routinely used in cognitive science labs to measure unconscious mental activity.

Just as the ganzfeld technique moved the study of anomalous cognition forever beyond card-guessing experiments, these studies may herald another major advance. They avoid the notorious unreliability of subjective evidence; they don't rely on what subjects report of their experiences. In fact, they don't look to any form of consciously mediated knowing at all. They suggest instead that conscious awareness of anomalous cognition is mere artifact—sometimes present, sometimes not, sometimes even getting in the way. What counts instead are measures of the so-called autonomic nervous system, the part of our nervous system that controls "involuntary" functions such as digestion, metabolism, respiration, and perspiration, as well as blood pressure and heart rate; while we're not usually conscious of these functions, they're definitely influenced by our mental state. The genius of the current experiments lies in their reliance on methods that, over countless experiments on *non*anomalous cognition, have offered irrefutable evidence of unconscious mental processes at work.

Ironically, some of the most impressive experiments test precisely the capacity that carnival fortune-tellers have rendered most dismissible: presentiment, or the ability to predict the future. Under highly controlled, double-blind conditions, these experiments suggest that human beings have a nervous system wired to perceive events three to five seconds into the future.

Work in this field began in 1978, when Zoltán Vassy, a Hungarian physicist and later visiting scientist at the Psychophysical Research Laboratories in Princeton, published an article with tantalizing implications for anomalous cognition. He set up a classical conditioning experiment to test whether subjects could register a feeling of what happens *before* an event stimulating the feeling had in fact been initiated.[13]

In Vassy's experiment, the "viewer" was trained so that when he or she saw a randomly timed light flash, he or she would wait five seconds, then press a button. That would give the other subject an electrical shock. The conditioning was carried out with the viewer and shockee together, so the shockee quickly came to understand that when the viewer got the signal, the shock would follow in five seconds. It would take only a few trials for the subjects to be conditioned, because the shock produced a very strong learning effect. As soon as the light appeared, the shockee's nervous system became aroused in anticipation, and this would be reflected in a dramatic rise in his or her skin conductance, a standard indicator of emotional arousal.

After conditioning, the viewer and shockee were isolated so they couldn't see each other. The same experiment was repeated. Would the shockee telepathically know (or more precisely, sense) when the viewer was about to press the shock button?

As Vassy's article reported, subjects' skin conductance was significantly higher prior to being shocked than prior to receiving the neutral control stimulus. In other words, subjects provided physical evidence that they correctly anticipated (or telepathically perceived) that they'd be getting an unpleasant shock far more often than chance would predict.

For some years, Vassy's work went largely unnoticed in the scientific community. Meantime, the momentum generated by dialogue around the ganzfeld experiments was building. Reputable investigators were starting to lay their careers on the line, giving serious attention to anomalous cognition, and looking in every conceivable direction for bullet-proof experimental designs.

One of them was Dean Radin, Ph.D., currently senior scientist and laboratory director at the Institute for Noetic Sciences. He was born in New York City in 1952 and began his full-time research career as a member of the technical staff at AT&T Bell Labs in 1979. While he and his colleagues were primarily focused on research and development into telecommunications, they were given a fair degree of latitude on how they could spend their "free" time at work. This gave Radin an opportunity to explore some odd and interesting tangents.

But Radin's penchant for investigating the odd and unusual began long before Bell Labs. As a young boy, he'd repeatedly gotten the message from his parents that creativity counts. " 'Do something creative!' When I was a kid, I must have heard that a hundred thousand times," he told me. For Radin, being creative meant pursuing the prodigy track on his violin as well as exploring the unexpected through science. At age nine, he'd built an abacus-like computer out of jelly beans. At thirteen, he'd come across C. E. M. Hansel's book *ESP: A Scientific Evaluation*. From then on, applying science to the study of the human mind joined his general passion for experiments exploring the potentially anomalous.

After reading Radin's research, I arranged a meeting with him to discuss his work. Dean is small, wiry, and boyish. I commented on his youthfulness. His reply was quick and deadpan. Actually, he told me, he was only thirteen. Like Gilbert and Sullivan's hapless young Frederic, doomed to an eighty-four-year apprenticeship before his twenty-first birthday could release him from the Pirates of Penzance, Dean was born on February 29. So he had recently celebrated turning fifty by throwing a bash as quirky as some of his experiments. He invited his vast network of scientific colleagues to the ultimate thirteen-year-old's birthday party—hot dogs, soda pop, and gooey chocolate cake at a local roller-skating rink.

Dean might call himself only thirteen, but his lengthy résumé does credit to a lifetime love affair with science. In 1985, he moved from Bell Labs to the Stanford Research Institute. There he joined up with the team doing government-sponsored remote-viewing experiments with Harold Puthoff. In 1996, the *New York Times* ran a story on his career, titled "They Laughed at Galileo Too." He told the *Times* reporter how working at SRI influenced him:

> I was blown away. I had no idea that remote viewing could be that good, for real, on real-life targets. Mainly, I was surprised to see a long list of Department of Defense and intelligence agencies that had been funding the program for decades, with the highest level of support in the Government, and most importantly, the fact that within the agencies there was no question anymore that the basic phenomena were real. They weren't funding for the hell of it—they found the stuff pragmatically useful.[14]

Dean left SRI in 1986. Over the next several years, he conducted one of the most thorough and scrupulous reviews of research on mind-matter anomalies ever done. He took an academic post at the University of Nevada, which he summed up in his 1997 book *The Conscious Universe: The Scientific Truth of Psychic Phenomena.* Meantime, his own experiments had made him an expert in just about every methodology ever applied to the study of anomalous cognition.

Part of Dean's appeal is the wry, puckish way he talks about his work. The thirteen-year-old comes out full force, perpetually excited about some zany, impossible thing he's just decided to try. At the same time, even as he's going whole-hog after an experimental problem, he stays happily detached about outcome. He flatly declares he's simply never had one of those personal conversion experiences that send others into conviction about anomalous mental capacities: "The thing that gets me hooked is the data, that's all. When the data are good enough—and a lot of the data on anomalies are really something, really puzzling—that's when you get the buzz, the urge to find a scientific answer, the fun of seeing if you can get any of it to make sense."

In 2001, Dean joined up with another veteran researcher, Marilyn Schlitz, coinvestigator on the early Juilliard ganzfeld study with Charles Honorton. Schlitz had recently been appointed director of research and education at California's Institute of Noetic Sciences, an institution founded in 1973 by former astronaut Edgar Mitchell to "further the explorations of conventional science by rigorous inquiry into aspects of reality—such as mind, consciousness, spirit—that go beyond physical phenomena." Perhaps as much as anyone, Schlitz had assumed the Honorton-Hyman mantle of pursuing experimental collaboration with declared skeptics. Since 1995, she'd been conducting ongoing experiments with psychologist Richard Wiseman, Ph.D., on the problem of "experimenter effect," the question of how an investigator's beliefs might affect the results obtained.

Marilyn hired Dean to come onboard as senior scientist. Dean continued to explore the question Vassy had posed: might autonomic indicators be a way to determine whether presentiment—an apparently anomalous response to a future event—is really possible?

Vassy had used electroshock as an experimental stimulus to measure galvanic skin response. Dean planned to use emotionally arousing pictures. As he described his work to me:

The design is simple. An investigator attaches electrodes to a participant's left hand to continuously measure the electrical resistance of the skin, which in turn reflects the activity of the sweat glands. The participant then sits in front of a computer monitor displaying a blank screen, and he or she is instructed to press a button at will. After the button press, the computer waits five seconds. It then selects a photo at random from a large pool of photos (some calm and some emotional), displays it for three seconds, and then the screen goes blank again for ten seconds. After a short "cool-down" period, the computer instructs the participant to press the button again at will. A typical session may last thirty minutes, during which time some forty trials may be repeated, each involving a new, randomly selected photo.

What I've observed in these experiments, conducted with a total of 131 participants so far, is that on average people sweat slightly more (that is, their autonomic nervous system becomes activated) before they see emotional photos than before they see calm photos.

The observed overall difference in autonomic arousal is associated
with a probability of p = 0.00003, so there is good reason to believe
that this result is not due to chance. My colleagues and I have
considered numerous conventional explanations for this effect,
including sensory cues, inferences, nonrandom target selection, and
physiological anticipatory effects, but none have been found to be
adequate. It appears that our nervous systems can indeed perceive
about five seconds into the future.[15]

Dean's aren't the only presentiment studies currently under
way. Some of the most interesting ones come from physicist and
former Parapsychological Association president Edwin May, Ph.D.,
who'd directed the SRI/SAIC remote-viewing experiments following Harold Puthoff's departure to Austin. May decided to design a stimulus that avoided conscious mental processing as much as
possible. So instead of showing people pictures they had to register
consciously—Dean's approach—May settled on noise. Subjects
outfitted with headphones and equipment to measure their galvanic
skin responses would unexpectedly be blasted with one-second, 97-
decibel acoustic "startle stimuli," randomly interspersed with an
equivalent number of moments of silence as controls. The experiment used a true random-number generator circuit, not a computer
algorithm, to determine when to blast the subjects with the loud
noise; this would negate any unconscious influence that might result from a human being deciding when to trigger the stimulus.

With a physicist consultant, James Spottiswoode, May collected
twenty-five minutes of continuous skin conductance data on each
of one hundred experimental subjects. In a paper published in 2003,
the researchers reported that participants displayed more agitation—
i.e., they sweated more—three seconds *before* they heard loud blasts
of sound as opposed to silence during control periods. The probability statistics were impressive, with odds that the association was
due to chance of less than 5.5 million to 1.[16]

May next teamed up with Vassy in a collaborative replication in
Hungary. In a carefully double-blinded, randomized series of trials, the
findings were strongly positive. Roughly three seconds *before* a
random-number generator selected a loud noise, people started sweat-

ing more than before a silent control. Remarkably, subjects not only responded before they actually heard the noise, they responded *before the stimulus had even been selected by the computer's random number generator.*[17]

Norman Don, codirector of the brain function lab at the School of Public Health of the University of Illinois at Chicago, has also been studying presentiment. Instead of galvanic skin response, however, he measured event-related brain potentials as recorded by an EEG, or electroencephalogram. In four studies published in peer-reviewed journals, he found that the brains of subjects responded *in advance* to one of four visual images that the computer would *later* randomly select as the target for that trial. Interestingly, the subjects didn't know at the time that they were engaged in an ESP experiment.[18]

Reacting in advance to a loud noise? To a calming versus emotionally stimulating picture? Seeing three seconds into the future, maybe five? Such a response may not seem like much. But if it's true, it changes everything. And it takes us back to the feeling of what happens as a portal for understanding extraordinary knowing.

I was sorting through the recent precognition experiments when I came across Daryl Bem's name again. In late 2003, Bem had posted an article online with the title "Precognitive Habituation: Replicable Evidence for a Process of Anomalous Cognition," adapted from a presentation he'd given at the forty-sixth annual convention of the Parapsychological Association.[19] Bem had also developed a user-friendly, laboratory-free, no-expenditure opportunity for anyone with a computer to conduct his or her own anomalous cognition experiments at home, replicating one that Bem had conducted in his Cornell Lab.[20]

I decided it was time to get back in touch with my former grad school professor. He and his wife, Sandra Bem, also a noted social psychologist, were now on the faculty at Cornell. I contacted Bem and it turned out he had a lecture coming up in San Francisco. We agreed to exchange papers and scheduled a morning to meet.

Daryl—by that time I'd moved past grad-student awe to a first-name basis—started by tossing off a few punchy statistics. In a survey of more than 1,100 college professors in the United States, 55 percent of natural scientists, 66 percent of social scientists (psychologists excluded) and 77 percent of academics in the arts, humanities, and education, reported believing that ESP is either an established fact or a likely possibility. By contrast, the comparable figure for psychologists was only 34 percent. On top of that, the same percentage of psychologists—34 percent—declared ESP to be a frank impossibility, a view expressed by only 2 percent of all other respondents.[21] "Those numbers mean I live among the sharks," Daryl told me. "I'm an academic psychologist. My colleagues down the hall are the people who eat you alive for putting out an idea about anomalous mental capacities not backed up in every detail by a glaringly replicable experiment."

But Daryl wasn't looking remotely perturbed. In fact, he was grinning. He said that those same colleagues had inspired him to come up with the elusive holy grail in experimental research on anomalous cognition: "a straightforward laboratory demonstration that can be replicated by any competent experimenter no matter how skeptical, using participants drawn from the general population."

Daryl's computer-based experiment differed in one hugely important way from those that look at physiologic indicators of unconscious mental processing. He wanted to find an experiment anybody could do using only the measurement tools found on a home computer. That meant galvanic skin response, EKG, and EEG measurements were out. But he was determined to rely on an outcome measure with an equally solid, sanctioned history in measuring nonanomalous cognition. He settled on a well-known psychological phenomenon known as habituation.

When we are exposed to an emotionally arousing stimulus, our internal physiology responds strongly the first time, but after repeated exposures that response diminishes; we become "habituated" to it. For example, in one recent habituation experiment participants subliminally exposed to extremely positive and extremely negative words subsequently rated those words as less extreme than words to which they had not been exposed: negative words were rated less negatively and positive words were rated less positively. The subliminal exposures had caused participants to habituate to those particular words.

Daryl decided to employ the habituation effect in an experiment that turned time upside down. Instead of habituating a participant to a stimulus and later assessing his or her response to it, he reversed the sequence. On each trial of the procedure, the participant was first shown a pair of negatively arousing or positively arousing (erotic) photographs on a computer screen and asked to indicate which picture of the pair he or she preferred. The computer then randomly selected one of the two pictures to serve as the "habituation target" and displayed it subliminally several times. If the subject preferred the picture subsequently designated as the target, the trial was defined as a hit. Accordingly, the hit rate expected by chance was 50 percent.

Daryl's "precognition hypothesis" was that the subliminal exposures to the target would reach back in time to habituate the participant's *first* response to it, that is, to diminish the arousal it would otherwise produce. Under this hypothesis, participants would prefer the target picture on negative picture pairs (the one producing less arousal) and prefer the nontarget on erotic picture pairs (the one producing more arousal).

Bem's results were positive: more than three hundred men and women participated in several variations of the experiment. Across six studies, the hit rate was significantly above 50 percent on negative trials (52.6 percent, $p = .0008$) and significantly below 50 percent on erotic trials (48.0 percent, $p = .031$). Other laboratories have now successfully replicated the effect. Meanwhile Daryl is currently developing and testing other variations of these experiments in "feeling the future."[22]

Studies like those of Vassy and Bem all point to one thing: whether measured by galvanic skin response or habituation-produced preferences, unconscious mental processing might be the place to look for reliable and replicable evidence of anomalous cognition. If that's the case, it's no wonder researchers who look to conscious mental activity haven't satisfactorily located anomalous capacities. They've adopted a position reminiscent of the Sufi sage Mulla Nasrudin, who kept looking under a streetlamp for his keys, not because he lost them there but because there was more light.

As Bem and I were getting ready to end our talk, he remarked, "By the way, I don't think my experiment is terribly interesting in terms of teaching us anything. It won't answer the really important questions—questions about how anomalous capacities may work, what conditions facilitate them, and all that. We'll never get answers to the big questions out of an experiment like this."

And those big questions? I asked. Aren't they questions we'll need to address if we're going to achieve a model that furthers our understanding of anomalous cognition? Isn't he curious about that? Yes, he said. He's curious. But he's not going there. "For now, I want only one thing. I want that simple, replicable experiment that demonstrates these capacities exist—if it turns out they do. I live with hardheaded skeptics and I want an experiment I can hand over, and say, Here, you try it. See for yourself. I want an experiment so simple they can't in good scientific conscience say no."

I have my doubts. Resistance to new ideas is powerful. Resistance to ideas that change everything is even more powerful. Resistance rooted in unconscious associative networks is the most powerful of all. It's outside conscious choice and conscious regulation. And that's another reason we need to consider unconscious mental processes if we want to achieve viable scientific status for anomalous cognition. We need to understand the source of our deep resistance to changing the most basic ways we comprehend the world and ourselves in it.

Perhaps psychoanalysis offers a way in. One of Freud's greatest contributions was a concept called *Angstsignal,* or signal anxiety, which anticipated some of the most sophisticated contemporary work on implicit memory and unconscious associative networks. Freud's development of the concept grew directly from his groundbreaking understanding of fear and the pervasive ways fear organizes human existence.

Signal anxiety, Freud said, describes an unconscious mental function that operates as a kind of early warning system for the psyche. It's what, after you've been burned once, stops you from having to consider consciously the merits of grasping a red-hot poker every time you want to pull it out of a blazing fire. Seeing a red-hot poker leads to an experience of signal anxiety. It's a straightforward danger signal of the distress that would follow were you to keep grabbing red-hot pokers.

Signal anxiety results from the perception of danger. But it's also about *learning to associate one thing with another, often unconsciously.* To that extent, it's about how we create memory out of unconscious associative networks. Once we recognize danger, signal anxiety operates *as an attenuated form of the original anxiety reaction stimulated by the original danger.*[23] We don't, for example, keep picking up the hot end of a poker, scream with pain, and then drop it. We've learned not to do that. We develop instead a straightforward set of defensive strategies stimulated by a fear of getting burned again. We pick up the cool end or we use an insulated glove or we wait until the hot end is no longer hot. We do this so instantaneously that we avoid any conscious experience of anxiety. But that's not because we aren't actively processing anxiety in order to achieve our newly adaptive strategies for avoiding the experience of getting burned. It's because the anxiety is being processed without our being consciously aware of it.

Signal anxiety is also the thing that leads a child to go promptly back to class when he hears the end-of-recess bell after repeated scoldings for staying on the playground. The boy associates the bell with scolding and the memory of scolding is part of an associative network that connects fear of being scolded with staying outside. Eventually, the bell mobilizes a flash of signal anxiety that is fast enough to become automatic and unconscious.

But when associative networks triggered by signal anxiety are more complex, it gets more interesting. Suppose the child leaving the playground keeps catching sight of his pathologically depressed mother, who's lingering outside in hopes of a friendly wave from her son. The child's response to the signal anxiety that sends him inside becomes more complicated, now and later in life.

Years down the road, that same child will be likely to turn into the adult who, against all apparent reason, finds himself insisting to his wife that they shouldn't buy a house that perfectly suits their needs but requires that he commute to work. He offers his wife a series of beautifully logical rationales that no one, he least of all, recognizes as completely irrelevant to what's actually driving his resistance to buying the house: he's worried about commuting because he has an anxious expectation that his wife might become depressed

like his mother if he's out of waving distance. Unconscious associative networks are hard at work, mobilizing that man's signal anxiety
and drastically interfering with his good intentions. He has no idea
that his wife couldn't be further from depression or that she couldn't
care less about his remaining within constant waving distance.

That husband isn't so far from the museum curators who firmly
believed they were rescuing science from religion by throwing out
meteorites. He believes he's rescuing his wife from depression. He's
no more able to recognize the signal anxiety that leads him to do
what he does than the museum curators recognized theirs. Had
those curators been able to understand how signal anxiety led them
to judge meteorites as meaningful evidence for religion and meaningless evidence for science, they probably would have thought
twice before throwing them out.

A friend of mine who's tried Bem's experiment subjected me to
a long, patient monologue about why the evidence he'd obtained
wasn't extraordinary enough to warrant extraordinary claims. He
thought he was rescuing me from my distressing credulity. I, however, felt like the wife arguing with her husband about the house. I
thought my friend, just like the man scared to be out of waving distance from his wife, was worried about himself, not me—worried
about not being within waving distance of his own tried-and-true
models of nature. Like the married couple, we were operating out
of utterly different associative networks that led us to judge different evidence as meaningful. My friend's associative networks had
led him to throw out evidence I found intriguing.

In addition to experiments that aim to defy time, there have also
been a series of recent experiments that challenge the dimension
of space. Especially provocative are those that look at entrainment,
the process by which two people's physiologic functioning develops
synchronized patterns, each with the other.

"Entrainment" is a buzzword in many areas of mainstream research these days. Entrainment shows up when two people watching the same movie start sweating together or develop similar heart
rates or similar evidence of brain fluctuation. Entrainment shows up

between couples, players on a sports team, members of an orchestra. It appears directly related to social bonding and the way emotional bonds produce resonant responses in people.

Daniel Goleman reports on this development in neuroscience in *Social Intelligence: The New Science of Human Relationships*. One of the most astonishing discoveries is that our brains contain mirror neurons, which reflect what we observe in others:

> Our mirror neurons fire as we watch someone else, for example, scratch their head or wipe away a tear, so that a portion of the pattern of neuronal firing in our brain mimics theirs. This maps the identical information from what we are seeing onto our own motor neurons, letting us participate in the other person's actions as if we were executing that action. . . . Mirror neurons make emotions contagious, letting the feelings we witness flow through us, helping us get in synch and follow what's going on. We "feel" the other in the broadest sense of the word.[24]

Our brains appear to be wired for deeper connection to one another.

But while conventional studies of entrainment give dramatic evidence that the bonding of relationship has big unconscious effects on us, there's nothing anomalous there. We may be surprised to hear science driving it home, but it's been common knowledge since humans first started feeling connected to each other.

The new studies add one key element to traditional entrainment experiments. They separate people in space and expose only one of them to a stimulus, and then look for evidence of entrainment. It turns out measures that indicate fluctuations in unconscious mental state continue to correlate, but with no identifiable means of communication between the people.[25]

Consider an experiment in which John, the "sender," and Jane, the "receiver," are sitting in separate, shielded rooms. John is told that his job is to send mental instructions to calm or arouse Jane by picturing serene or arousing scenes. Such experiments have concluded that if the partners are entrained, Jane's pattern of physiologic response is correlated with John's in a presumably anomalous way.

But that's not all. If Jane is asked whether she's *consciously aware of feeling aroused versus calm* at any given moment, her self-reports are *less* correlated with John's self-reports than their physiologic patterns are correlated with each other. If anything anomalous is going on, conscious self-report doesn't capture it as well as unconscious measures, although conscious measures do work beyond chance levels.

Once again, it seems that generations of telepathy experiments may have been based on an essentially invalid premise that inevitably provoked wildly fluctuating, hard-to-replicate results. If there's anything real about telepathy, the current experiments suggest that it's unlikely to be reliably captured by measures relying on consciously processed mental information. While *some* people, *sometimes,* have *some* comparatively clear access to *some* pieces of unconscious information, access to that information is notoriously unpredictable and always incomplete. (The ganzfeld experiments, however, rely on conscious reports and overall they provide strong evidence for telepathy.)

On the other hand, those same current experiments help explain why the dream telepathy data looked so remarkably good. Even though dream reports contain only those elements that reach consciousness, the very nature of dream memory is that it comes closer to unconscious mental processes than any other thoughts we're aware of. We allow dream reports to contain mental connections we'd regularly filter out of ordinary waking ideas.

The data from studies of anomalous cognition that look to physiologic indicators of unconscious mental processes appear quite remarkable. But we're still left with a big question. What do we *do* with them? How do they work? If unconscious mental processing is where we need to look, what does that show us for scientific modeling of those capacities? These questions took me into a world stranger than any psychic phenomena I'd encountered: the world of contemporary physics.

Quantum Uncertainty:

A Working Model of Reality

ON MARCH 25, 2004, the *New York Review of Books* published a review of the recently translated book *Debunked: ESP, Telekinesis, and Other Pseudoscience* by two French physicists, Georges Charpak and Henri Broch.[1] The review came from eminent theoretical physicist Freeman Dyson, who has also reached a wide general audience through books such as *Infinite in All Directions* and *From Eros to Gaia*. It's a cautious, sober think-piece, giving no small credit to Charpak and Broch for their systematic debunking of one parapsychological fraud after another. "Charpak and Broch have done a fine job," wrote Dyson, "sweeping out the money-changers from the temple of science and exposing their tricks." Barely into the review, it was pretty clear that anomalous cognition would find no happy home here.

But Dyson's a master of surprise. He built an inarguable case against parapsychological fraud. But then he suddenly shifted gears:

I claim that paranormal phenomena may really exist.... The hypothesis that paranormal phenomena are real but lie outside the limits of science is supported by a great mass of evidence.... I find it plausible that a world of mental phenomena should exist, too fluid and evanescent to be grasped with the cumbersome tools of science.... One of my grandmothers was a notorious and successful faith healer. One of my cousins was for many years the editor of the *Journal of the Society for Psychical Research*. Both these ladies were well educated, highly intelligent, and fervent believers in paranormal phenomena. They may have been deluded, but neither of them was a fool. Their beliefs were based on personal experience and careful scrutiny of evidence. Nothing that they believed was incompatible with science.

Whether paranormal phenomena exist or not, the evidence for their existence is corrupted by a vast amount of nonsense and outright fraud. Before we can begin to evaluate the evidence, we must get rid of the hucksters and charlatans who have turned unsolved mysteries into a profitable business.

It was a stunning statement. Here was one of the world's great physicists issuing a plea for the plausibility of myriad anomalous mental capacities. Among the most compelling evidence invoked by Dyson was the vast material collected by the Society for Psychical Research. He wrote:

The members of the society took great trouble to interview first-hand witnesses as soon as possible after the events, and to document the stories carefully. One fact that emerges clearly from the stories is that paranormal events occur, if they occur at all, only when people are under stress and experiencing strong emotion. This fact would immediately explain why paranormal phenomena are not observable under the conditions of a well-controlled scientific experiment. Strong emotion and stress are inherently incompatible with controlled scientific procedures. In a typical card-guessing experiment, the participants may begin the session in a high state of excitement and record a few high scores, but as the hours pass, and boredom replaces excitement, the scores decline to the 20 percent expected from random chance.

Dyson also gives us his understanding of why the studies with which he's familiar have failed:

> I am suggesting that paranormal mental abilities and scientific method may be complementary. The word "complementary" is a technical term introduced into physics by Niels Bohr. It means that two descriptions of nature may both be valid but cannot be observed simultaneously. The classic example of complementarity is the dual nature of light. In one experiment light is seen to behave as a continuous wave, in another experiment it behaves as a swarm of particles, but we cannot see the wave and the particles in the same experiment. Complementarity in physics is an established fact. The extension of the idea of complementarity to mental phenomena is pure speculation. But I find it plausible. . . .

Complementarity: we're back to daytime eyes and nighttime eyes, to the figure and ground of the gestalt imagery. Complementarity applies to how the observer sees, not to the phenomena seen. It's still the same sky, a star-filled sky by night and a blazing daytime sky, even if we can't see both at the same time. It's still the same picture, whether we see the profiles or the chalice. We simply can't see both at once.

And if we've spent our lives seeing only one part of the picture, we'll have to work hard to construct the shape of the other. It's hard, if not impossible, to draw the shape of the Atlantic Ocean when we've grown up seeing the globe in terms of continents. We have to reason our way there, reassigning the contours we've assigned to continents. Then we can start going back and forth. Then we can start seeing both percepts, and re-creating them at will.

But we'll have a hard time reasoning our way to nighttime eyes if we've never seen the sky at night. With humility, we might be able to honor the research into extraordinary knowing as Dyson honored his grandmother and cousin even if he'd never seen what they'd seen. But it helps if we've been there ourselves. It helps if we've had even one experience of knowing what it's like, that feeling of what happens when an apparently anomalous experience comes our way.

One final insight from Dyson's review: he pointed out that Charpak and Broch's original French title, *Devenez Sorciers, Devenez*

Savants, would literally translate as *Become Magicians, Become Experts.* As Dyson put it, translating the title as *Debunked!* missed the point. The brilliance of the original title lies in its underlying idea—*learn to do magic and learn to see through it.* In other words, the best way to avoid being deceived by magic tricks is to become expert at doing them yourself. You have to know the feeling of what happens when you're doing staged magic versus experiencing something possibly anomalous.

I recalled that when I'd met with Daryl Bem to discuss anomalous cognition, he'd started our conversation by citing statistics about which percentages of which professions believed that telepathy or ESP might exist. He hadn't mentioned magicians, but I decided that they'd be an interesting category to examine.

It turns out they are. Knowing all they know about the tricks of their trade, between 72 percent and 84 percent of magicians believe ESP to be a genuine phenomenon.[2] Given that only 34 percent of psychologists believe in ESP, the contrast is striking. Magicians are far more certain than people *in any other profession* that psychic phenomena really do exist.

I t was late summer 1995, and I was driving my sixteen-year-old daughter around New England for her college interviews. On one stretch of the highway, she fell asleep. I pulled out a large packet of audiotapes I'd ordered some weeks earlier. They were lectures given at the Center for Frontier Sciences at Temple University. The center had been founded in 1987 in response to concerns expressed by a number of distinguished scientists who wanted more opportunities for collaborative discussion of research that might radically challenge mainstream scientific ideas. The center's explicit agenda was to promote "open and unbiased examination of any theories, hypotheses, or models that challenge prevailing scientific views using sound scientific methods and reasoning...critical review and healthy skepticism....Recognizing the frontier scientific issues of today are often the mainstream science of tomorrow."[3]

Eyes still on the road, I grabbed one of the tapes and glanced at the label. I didn't recognize the name: Robert G. Jahn, Ph.D., of Princeton University. I inserted it into the tape deck and prepared to half listen as I drove, my attention mostly on the pleasures of watching fall come to New England.

Twenty minutes later, I'd forgotten all about fall as well as my daughter's interviews. I was listening to Jahn, professor of aerospace sciences, describe the work he and his colleagues had been doing at the Princeton Engineering Anomalies Research (PEAR) Lab since he founded it in 1979. Jahn turned out to be an eminent physicist, widely recognized as a patriarch in the field of advanced space propulsion. According to its mission statement, Jahn, then dean of the School of Engineering and Applied Science at Princeton, founded PEAR "to pursue rigorous scientific study of the interaction of human consciousness with sensitive physical devices, systems, and processes common to contemporary engineering practice." Since its founding, "an interdisciplinary staff of engineers, physicists, psychologists, and humanists has been conducting a comprehensive agenda of experiments and developing complementary theoretical models to enable better understanding of the role of consciousness in the establishment of physical reality."[4]

Jahn's lecture was about the large body of research on anomalous mental capacities and anomalous mind–matter interaction that had been conducted at the PEAR Lab over the previous fifteen years. It was riveting, both for its clarity and sober scientific reasoning, but also for the thoroughly startling nature of its substance.

As soon as the tape finished, I headed for a phone to request all available reprints of the lab's publications. Forty articles arrived on my doorstep the following week. The experiments they reported were intriguing. Even more so was the sudden glimpse they gave me of colleagues pursuing scientific avenues that had a direct bearing on all the questions I'd been asking ever since the harp came back.

The PEAR lab actually got its start in 1977, when a Princeton undergraduate approached Jahn with an idea for an experiment involving anomalous mind–matter interaction. As Jahn would later describe, because the student was highly motivated and committed to scientific rigor, he found himself "torn between a personal intellectual skepticism and the potential pedagogical benefit of such a project."[5] Initially, he went so far as to sponsor the student only for a thorough bibliographic review. He eventually agreed to the experiment, unaware that he was opening a Pandora's box that would have huge implications for his own subsequent research.

The results of the student's experiment left him uneasy. They suggested that through sheer mental intention, people were literally able to affect matter. Jahn was far from convinced that the results were valid, but he found himself "progressively more concerned about the potential vulnerability of certain technological systems to effects suggested by these pilot experiments."[6] At the time, Jahn was a highly regarded consultant to major governmental organizations as well as to the aerospace industry. He was all too aware of the possible ways that those vulnerabilities might manifest themselves, crazy as it seemed even to consider them. After some months, unable to set his mind at ease, he decided he had only one alternative: he would instigate a program of further research.

Thus was born the Princeton Engineering Anomalies Research Laboratory. One of the first things Jahn did was find Brenda Dunne, a developmental psychologist who was to become his long-time collaborator, inspiration for many of his ideas, and the PEAR Lab's manager. Together, the two of them have spent more than a quarter of a century navigating the lab through painstaking experimental research on mind–matter anomalies.

As I got to know them, I appreciated their power as a team. Bob is small, wiry, and understated. He's an academic with a systematic intellect, a passion for science, and a remarkable facility for explaining complex ideas. Then there's Brenda, with her fast-paced mind and searing wit, both housed in the body of an effusive, intuitive Jewish grandmother, her regular self-description. She galvanizes many of PEAR's projects, but also acts as the eagle eye overseeing their meticulous execution.

The PEAR Lab's experimental work has fallen into two main categories: investigation of mind–machine interactions and remote perception. In the first category, human operators attempt to influence by anomalous means the output of various simple machines, each of which involves some measurable random physical process.

The operators typically sit in front of machines that each produce thousands of binary random signals per second, the equivalent of tossing thousands of coins per second. Using whatever personal strategies they wish but no physical contact, the operators try to get their machines to produce predetermined output values that differ from what would be expected randomly. In other words, the operators state an intention to produce more heads, more tails, or an equal distribution of both, as if the machines were actually going to be tossing coins. Then, through nothing but an exercise of mental intention over two hundred virtual coin tosses, the operators try to produce exactly the result they say they're aiming for. By 1996, the accumulated results were as follows:

> ... some fifty million experimental trials have been performed to this date, containing more than three billion bits of binary information.... Anomalous correlations of the machine outputs with pre-stated operator intentions are clearly evident ... [and] statistically replicable. Over the total data base, the composite anomaly is unlikely by chance to about one part in a billion.... From this huge array of empirical indications, it seems unavoidable to conclude that operator consciousness is capable of inserting information, in its most rudimentary "objective" form, namely, binary bits, into these random physical systems, by some anomalous means.[7]

When you accumulate the results of such a large number of people, the effect is highly, highly statistically significant. It appears that mind affects matter in thoroughly unexpected ways. And what I found truly fascinating was that the PEAR results were obtained with ordinary people—college students, people off the street, and the occasional visitor to the PEAR Lab with an interest in anomalous events. If the PEAR Lab is right, ordinary people have the capacity to alter what machines do.

Those findings certainly don't mean that anybody's individual attempts to affect a machine will, taken alone, look statistically significant. Far from it, which is why most of us don't walk around convinced that we can affect the operation of a machine by simply willing it. But according to the PEAR results, all of us—or just about all of us—do share a marginal, barely noticeable capacity to exert just such an effect once in a while. And some people, maybe people like Harold, appear to be capable of more than merely that marginal effect.

The second category of PEAR experiment involves remote

perception—telepathy, clairvoyance, or ESP. PEAR guidelines specify the typical experimental methodology:

> ... in the usual protocol, two participants are involved in any given experiment. One, the "agent," is physically present at the target location, which has been selected by some random process, and there immerses himself emotionally and cognitively in the scene, records its characteristics on a standard check sheet, and takes photographs of it. The other, the "percipient," located many miles from the scene and with no prior knowledge of it, attempts to perceive aspects of its ambience and detail, and then records those impressions on the same standard check sheet, and in some less structured narrative or sketch. The agent and percipient check sheets are subsequently digitized and their degree of consonance scored numerically by a variety of algorithms.[8]

The degree to which percipient-agent pairs of check sheets correspond to each other is then computed and compared with what would be expected on a random basis—that is, what would be expected if there were indeed no connection between agent-percipient pairs, and agents were merely describing their literal physical surroundings, while percipients were describing whatever imagined physical environments randomly came to mind.

The anomalous effect sizes obtained in PEAR's remote perception experiments are even larger than those obtained for their mind-machine interactions. The likelihood of their being due to chance computes out at 10^{11}, or 1 out of 100 billion. Given the results of remote perception experiments conducted over more than twenty-five years, PEAR Lab drew the following conclusion: "[H]uman consciousness is able to extract information from physical aspects of its environment, by some anomalous means that is independent of space and time."[9]

I pored over the skeptics' challenges to the PEAR research; not one presented a serious examination that might debunk it. Some were angry; others simply cautious. But none came up with plausible arguments criticizing either the overall data or methods of analysis. They argued instead with small statistical details or general philosophical implications. As with the vast bodies of research from the Rhine Lab and the National Research Council/CIA studies, it looked as though the PEAR data had to be reckoned with.

At the same time that I was steeping myself in the PEAR research, I was asked to contribute a paper to the *International Journal of Psychoanalysis* in honor of that journal's seventy-fifth anniversary. I decided to write about the relation of unconscious communication to clinical fact, the process by which analyst and patient arrive at an interpretation of the patient's psychic reality, a time-honored subject in psychoanalysis.

It didn't take me long to realize I could no longer approach the subject the way I once did. I couldn't avoid the question of how clinical facts that resulted from unconscious communication might turn out to prove anomalous. I'd been rethinking too many things. Besides, as an invited contribution, the paper brought a certain carte blanche with it. I could say whatever I wanted, as long as it passed peer review as a solid contribution.

I called my paper "Subjectivity and Intersubjectivity of Clinical Facts."[10] Since I referred to the PEAR Lab's research, I sent a copy off to the lab. Several weeks went by. One morning the phone rang. It was Bob Jahn. He said my article had floated to the top of hundreds waiting on his desk and he'd read it the night before. He thought an exchange of ideas might be mutually informative.

Soon Bob was giving me lessons in elementary post-Newtonian, post-Einsteinian physics. In return, I began telling him about current research on unconscious mental processes.

Bob Jahn and Brenda Dunne soon issued me an invitation to present my ideas at an upcoming meeting of the International Consciousness Research Labs (ICRL), an interdisciplinary group they'd launched back in 1990. (This was where I would later meet Paul Devereux, whom I discussed in Chapter 10.)

There were twelve other people gathered that weekend: eleven men and Brenda, spanning a variety of fields and from Europe, the United States, and Canada, each of them as eager to come up with a model for anomalous cognition as I was. They were bringing all kinds of expertise to the table—biochemistry, cell biology, anthropology, archaeology, philosophy, environmental science, and, most heavily represented of all, physics. By Sunday afternoon, they'd invited me, the lone psychoanalyst, to join them on a permanent basis.

ICRL met every six months for three days running. We would gather over breakfast, then meet. We'd break for lunch, then meet. We'd take an afternoon hike, then meet. We'd have dinner, then meet, usually by that time fortified with Irish whiskey brought by one of our British compatriots.

After I'd been attending for several years, I was surprised when Bob led off the first morning of our meeting in 2001. In his typically understated style, he usually insisted that others go first. But this time he announced that he and Brenda had been thinking about the overarching issue with which we'd all been grappling: could we imagine a model for mind-matter interaction that includes the normal as well as the anomalous? Might such a model start with a very simple four-quadrant box that looks like this?

To the left of the vertical axis, Bob explained, imagine the world of mind, divided horizontally along a familiar dimension—the dynamics

MIND	MATTER
CONSCIOUS DYNAMICS	TANGIBLE DYNAMICS
UNCONSCIOUS DYNAMICS	INTANGIBLE DYNAMICS

of conscious versus unconscious mental processes. To the right of the vertical axis is the world of matter. It's divided into domains established by contemporary physics—the realm of tangible dynamics versus dynamics we'll call intangible. The upper right quadrant represents the science most of us grew up learning. Its mechanics are physical or biological, and its information comes in objective, quantifiable form.

The lower right quadrant falls largely into the domain of quantum physics. It's a realm in which the relevant mechanics are only dimly understood, identified by the evocative coinages of contemporary theoretical science: "quantum wholeness," "string theory," "implicate order," "Einstein-Podolsky-Rosen paradox," "quantum entanglement," "vacuum physics," or "ontic description." The information in this realm isn't conventionally quantitative, defying our usual notions of measurability, reliability, and predictability.

It's heady stuff, the physics inside that quadrant. Bob helped us nonphysicists recognize that its very nature is elusive. But as a psychoanalyst, one thing really caught my interest. That mysterious quadrant of intangible dynamics partakes of a logic just about as inchoate, unspeakable, and ungraspable by ordinary logic as what's represented in the unconscious dynamics quadrant. It's a strikingly similar nonlogic. Space and time don't play by ordinary rules in either of those quadrants. Impossible connections between things become bizarrely possible. Normal associative links that are immutable in both realms above the horizontal axis— the conscious and tangible realms—don't apply at all below. And the relationship between realms—between conscious and unconscious as well as tangible and intangible—looks remarkably parallel.

I was fascinated. Bob explained that the world as we mostly observe it lives above the horizontal axis of the model. That's the world we see with ordinary daytime eyes. However, we all accept the premise that the two quadrants below the axis have an essential role in determining what manifests above. So there's something crucial about what happens in transactions *between* quadrants, at each interface. Three of the possible transactions—between conscious and tangible dynamics, between tangible and intangible dynamics, and between conscious and unconscious dynamics—fall under the purview of what we call normal science. They range from significantly overt and specifiable (across the top, between conscious and tangible dynamics) to subtle, fuzzy, and amorphous (from top to bottom, between conscious and unconscious dynamics, and between tangible and intangible dynamics).

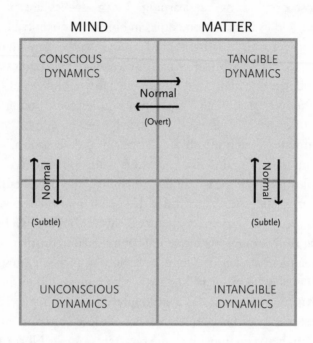

The easiest interface to grasp is the familiar conscious-tangible boundary. We know a good deal about the interaction of conscious minds with tangible matter. For example, we decide to pick up a book and we do (conscious dynamic leads to tangible dynamic). Or a book falls on the floor and we mobilize ourselves to figure out why it fell (tangible dynamic leads to conscious dynamic).

Less easy but still familiar is the interface between conscious and unconscious mental domains. This was my territory and I spoke to the group about it. Contemporary neuroscience and cognitive science are teaching us a great deal about this interface, so that we now realize Freud had identified only the tip of the iceberg when he relegated vast amounts of our mental life to a realm that's perpetually and immutably unconscious. It's the territory of dreams, implicit memory, and unconscious associative networks.

Third, we tackled the interface between tangible versus intangible physical dynamics. Our physicist members took over and together we realized that it's arbitrary to make a hard and fast distinction between what's above and below the axis there, just as in the world of mind. While, say, a vibrating violin string is tangible and produces tangible effects, the propagation of sound waves (or light, for that matter) involves intrinsically less tangible properties. By the time we get to the quantum mechanics of atomic-scale phenomena, Bob told us that we'd lost almost all claim to tangibility.[11]

In other words, on neither the mental nor the material side of the axis are we looking at a sharp divide. We're looking instead at a distinction that proves useful in practice, but is by nature fuzzy. CUNY professor of psychology Matthew Erdelyi once drew an analogy between the conscious-unconscious boundary and the line between childhood and adulthood. He pointed out that, while we consider childhood and adulthood as meaningful concepts and the distinction between them likewise as meaningful, we don't consider there to be a clear and precise threshold over which one is suddenly not the other. Bob explained that the same principle applies to the material side of things at the tangible-intangible interface.

Finally, we arrived at the last interface, the one characterized by unconscious dynamics on the mental side of the vertical axis and intangible physical dynamics on the material side. Bob and Brenda suggested that *this is where we might locate channels through which something like information passes that could eventually manifest above the horizontal axis as anomalous.* In the logic of conscious or tangible dynamics, those manifestations make no sense. In the logic that lives below the horizontal axis, they might make sense, but not the sense of normal science as we know it.

What's key to this model is that we tend to hold certain rules inviolable in our ordinary thinking, rules that simply don't apply in the realms characterized either by unconscious dynamics or intangible physical ones. Could there be something that manifests when these logics connect, something that then manifests in the logic of everyday life as anomalous? Anomalous in the sphere of mind—the conscious sphere—as telepathy, ESP, clairvoyance, or precognition? Anomalous in the sphere of matter—the tangible sphere—as distant healing or effects on computer output like those the PEAR Lab seems to have demonstrated?

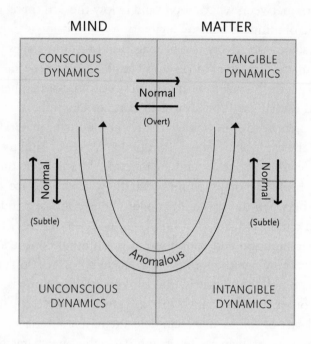

I returned to my own home ground, psychoanalysis. The essential psychoanalytic insight is that all kinds of things can appear in the upper two quadrants that make no sense if we limit ourselves to understanding them in terms of how the upper two interact. They do, however, start making sense once we understand how the upper, conscious quadrant on the mind side interfaces with the peculiar, nonlinear, irrational logic of unconscious mentation.

Why, for example, does the name Dave pop repeatedly into your mind while you're raking leaves one day? A few days later, you're talking to your mother and she recalls how you used to love jumping into big piles of leaves when you were two years old. She tells you that there was a handyman named Dave who raked up the leaves. You rack your brain and can't come up with a single conscious memory either of Dave or of jumping into leaves at age two. But suddenly that irrational preoccupation with the name Dave makes sense. You've unconsciously associated raking leaves with the handyman you think you've forgotten.

That's how things outside apparent logic show up in the quadrant characterized by conscious dynamics. Next door, in the tangible dynamics quadrant, you observe apparently illogical behaviors motivated by unconscious mental processes as well. Let's say that for years there's been a stop sign at a particular intersection on your street. Over all that time you've dutifully slowed down to stop when you've approached it. Suddenly traffic patterns change and city officials remove the sign. But you keep slowing down to stop. Drivers behind you honk and every time your children see you slow down they squeal at your stupidity and ask why on earth you're doing it again. Your visible behavior appears, in the moment, thoroughly irrational. You're still unconsciously associating that particular intersection with the stop sign you obeyed for years.

These are easy examples that allow us to reconstruct a logic that makes sense of apparently illogical thoughts or behaviors. But when it comes to dream thoughts or dream behavior that reaches conscious awareness, the blatantly illogical often remains illogical. It's not and never will be the sense of everyday life as we know it in the realms characterized by conscious and tangible dynamics.

Meantime, in the strange world of quantum phenomena, string theory, and so on, investigators spend their time studying a set of things characterized by a logic at least as foreign to ordinary everyday thinking. Their realm is intangible physical dynamics rather than the unconscious. These investigators are concerned with grasping how a causality so nonordinary as to appear nonexistent might expand our understanding of what appears above the axis, either in the world of what's tangible or in our conscious efforts to understand that world. These scientists are dealing with quantum principles with applications to the lasers or DVD players on which we routinely rely.

This is in part why I've so enjoyed my dialogue with Bob Jahn and the other physicists from ICRL. The physicists and I are doing something remarkably similar, trying to understand what happens when things cross over from below to above that horizontal axis. But we're doing that in relation to only three of the four quadrants portrayed in the model under consideration. Each discipline omits the lower quadrant with which the other is primarily concerned. Yet we're all centrally preoccupied with keeping one foot firmly rooted in the logic that dominates above the horizontal axis, while allowing the other foot to splash around in the logic that lives below, either on the mind side or on the material.

At the least, this four-quadrant model, alliteratively named "A Modular Model of Mind/Matter Manifestations (M5)," will help us talk to each other. Maybe what we've each learned about thinking below the axis could help the other as we try to exercise the mental flexibility that considering the lower half of things seems to require, meanwhile holding on to our capacities for above-the-axis thinking. Maybe it comes down to helping each other think with daytime eyes about how phenomena that demand nighttime eyes might work.

That kind of help is no small service. I'll never be a quantum physicist. Bob will never be a psychoanalyst. We're each deeply steeped in our own spheres of thinking, so deeply that we're barely aware of how they color everything we see. We're like fish unable to recognize water. But that means we each bring something unique and different to the other, something that geneticist Barbara McClintock called a "feeling for the organism."[12] That kind of feeling, said McClintock, was what enabled her to win a Nobel Prize for her stunningly unexpected insights into the genetics of corn. As she explained to the flocks of reporters who asked how she'd done it, she knew corn so well that she could predict how each of her individual plants would differentially respond to a slight change in nighttime temperature. She had a profound feeling for her organism. To put it another way, she had a profound feeling for what happens with corn.

I'll never have that kind of feeling for what happens in quantum physics. Nor will Bob Jahn for psychoanalysis. But because we do each have a feeling for our own particular organism, we also have a feeling for what it *is* as opposed to what it *isn't*. And that matters. New insight comes from knowing what something isn't at least as much as knowing what it is.

———————

I was talking with my skeptical friend, the physicist who had tried Daryl Bem's computer-based precognition experiment. He was vehement in his abhorrence for what he called "New Age physics."

"I'm sick of it! Quantum this, quantum that, quantum everything. Do people have any idea what they're talking about? I don't think so. Do they get it that a quantum leap is a very, very, very *small* leap? People say 'quantum leap' and they think they mean bigger than big—stupendously, enormously big. Do they get it that the quantum realm is the realm of the very *small*? I don't think so. This New Age stuff is literary metaphor at best, not—I repeat *not*—physics."

Psychoanalysis has its equivalent. Freud called it "wild analysis." It's the kind of pronouncement one gets at a cocktail party, or worse, even in certain analysts' offices. "You're fighting with your boss? It's undoubtedly your Oedipus complex and deep-seated envy of your father." Wild analysis drives me just about as crazy as my friend's New Age physics drives him. They're both about surface understanding and nothing more.

We empathized pleasantly over all that and it helped us move past our disagreement about Bem's experiment. Then I told my friend about the model Bob Jahn presented at ICRL. He was fascinated. No quantum anything. And—this is big—he conceded that there might be a provocative parallel in the way upper and lower quadrants relate to each other on the mind and matter sides of things.

For the two of us, the mere fact of conversation was a big step. We were each sticking to our own business, the feeling of what happens in the spheres we each knew best. But he wasn't calling me New Age credulous, and I wasn't calling him scientifically closed-minded. I remembered Heisenberg's declaration: "Science is rooted in conversation." This new model was helping at least one conversation along. That's a certain kind of progress.

My friend and I also agreed that the ability to observe above the axis doesn't work the way it does below, on either the mental or material side. And I wondered whether that might indicate one area where physicists and psychoanalysts could be most helpful to each other. We each work with a key concept about observability. Psychoanalysts work with the concept of unconscious associative networks, how things connect in invisible, apparently inexplicable, ways. Physicists work with the concept of complementarity, the idea that we can't see two ways at once. Both principles are about what we can't see as much as about what we can. Both may be key to understanding what Freeman Dyson called the "fluid, evanescent nature" of potentially anomalous phenomena.

The more I thought about this model, the more subsidiary reflections emerged, in particular the New Age physics problem. We've fallen prey to a peculiar prejudice in the culture at large, one that has us idealizing physics as the ultimate science. That's led to widespread physics envy. Everything gets physicized. Physicists don't like that. They especially don't like it when it's nonphysicists doing the physicizing.

But physics envy aside, quantum theory has managed to offer an extraordinarily evocative series of metaphors for grasping what's inconceivable about apparently anomalous experience. Quantum theory is thoroughly sanctioned to break one ordinary rule after another—rules about space and time, linear causality, even what's considered possible versus impossible. That alone offers a very welcome sense of permission to anyone grappling with an apparently anomalous experience. *Established* science says it can happen. No wonder quantum theory has captured the popular imagination.

Allow me, a nonphysicist trying not to be guilty of physics envy, a dramatic oversimplification. In the macroscopic world in which we live, we're used to defining things using classic Newtonian physics: I'm over here, you're over there; we can observe and measure our separate locations and the distance between us, plot them precisely in space, and describe the relationship between us using a vocabulary of known forces of attraction and repulsion. In the subatomic world, however, quantum physics holds sway, and the familiar rules of Newtonian physics don't apply. In this world of the very, very small, in the realm characterized by what the four-quadrant model calls intangible physical dynamics, the mere act of observing a subatomic particle changes the system. According to the Heisenberg uncertainty principle, for example, when it comes to measuring subatomic particles, the more we know about a particle's location, the less we can

and others who experience the state of mind that might facilitate extraordinary knowing. However, the translation of nonlocality to something that applies in other quadrants, especially to human beings when they function in the realm of tangible matter, has raised exceedingly skeptical eyebrows on the foreheads of most mainstream physicists, and therein lies the New Age physics trap. The probability that subatomic particles behave in certain ways doesn't mean that people do. Nor does it mean that what might look bizarrely analogous between the behavior of people and particles can be explained by invoking the same causal principles for both.

Consider, for example, experiments testing what are known as Bell's theorem and the EPR (Einstein-Podolsky-Rosen) paradox. These experiments have definitively demonstrated that, under certain conditions, *particles that have been in close association with each other as a two-particle system will defy familiar constraints of time and space in relation to each other.* They'll each instantly compensate for a change in the state of the other, no matter how distant they happen to be and without any identifiable channel for communication between them.[14]

This quantum physics equivalent of human entrainment is called entanglement. In "Entanglement: The Weirdest Link," scientist reporter Michael Brooks discusses the latest developments concerning what Einstein once dubbed *spukhafte Fernwirkungen*, "spooky action at a distance."

> Thomas Durt of Vrije University in Brussels also believes entanglement is everywhere. He has recently shown, from the basic equations that Schrödinger considered, that almost all quantum interactions produce entanglement, whatever the conditions. "When you see light coming from a faraway star, the photon is almost certainly entangled with the atoms of the star and the atoms encountered along the way," he says. And the constant interactions between electrons in the atoms that make up your body are no exception. According to Durt, we are a mass of entanglements.[15]

Entanglement may end up playing a large role in how quantum physicists reconcile the roles of relativity and quantum theory in their search for a "grand unified theory of everything." In the meantime, there's an obvious temptation for analogies to ESP or telepathy in human beings, as though the equivalence might be absolute or literal.

Undoubtedly, it isn't. Nonetheless, as molecular biologist (and Buddhist monk) Matthieu Ricard has suggested, "[t]he biggest problem for realists is to reconcile the discoveries of quantum physics with daily reality in the macrocosm. . . . Why should there be a line in the sand between the macrocosm and the microcosm that constitutes it? The former is simply an extension of the latter. What emerges when the microcosm becomes the macrocosm?"[16]

And Ricard quotes quantum physicist Henry Stapp from the University of California: "The important thing about Bell's theorem is that it puts the dilemma posed by quantum phenomena clearly into the realm of macroscopic phenomena. . . . [It] shows that our ordinary ideas about the world are somehow profoundly deficient even on the macroscopic level."[17]

Just because an electron in Tokyo that was once related to an electron now in London appears to compensate instantaneously for a change in spin of the London electron doesn't mean we now know why a person in Tokyo knows what someone in London is thinking. But we at least need to wonder whether principles operating in the intangible dynamics sphere extend in any way to the world of everyday life, the macrosphere. If so, they might help us understand how anomalous mental capacities might defy physical barriers. It's another reason to find the four-quadrant model intriguing.

I discovered that PEAR had also addressed an especially puzzling, ubiquitous set of observations about anomalous cognition. In study after study, the experimental subject's conscious intention appears to interfere with the subject's capacity to produce predictably anomalous results. Over and over, the following happens: The subject sets out to produce positive results, produces them, and then tries again. No luck. In fact, on the second attempt, the subject often does *worse* than chance would predict. That, of course, wreaks havoc with replicability. This phenomenon of subjects "bombing out" in repeated efforts at anomalous cognition is so common that

Jahn, Dunne, and their PEAR colleagues have identified what they call a "series position effect" over large banks of data.[18]

Pyschoanalysts recognize this pattern all too well. It unfolds something like this: Your patient comes in one day and surprises you by the ease with which she gains some powerful insight about an associative link that had been previously unavailable to either of you and apparently unconscious for her. The experience is stunning for both of you. Neither of you is sure how it happened but the whole thing flowed like a hot knife through butter. Suddenly her life looks different and she's discovered some startling new capacity to alter something that's made her unhappy. Glowing with expectation, you settle yourselves in for the next psychoanalytic session. You're both determined to replicate what happened last time.

But that's not how it works. She tries, you try. You can't get beyond the trying. She leaves and you're both disappointed. Next time she comes in, you don't have much in the way of expectations. You're not sure what's likely to happen. You've done your best to think about both sessions, but you've also recognized, probably for the millionth time if you've been in practice long, you're not in control of the ship. You recall what Freud said about letting your attention float free so that you can gain mental access to the unexpected, the unconscious. You stop trying to duplicate that wonderful session and you help your patient do the same. You both let go.

And that gets you back on track. The work stumbles along— sometimes remarkable, sometimes unremarkable—and your meetings approach a baseline pace that heads in a positive direction. You're perpetually reminded that trying hard doesn't get you there, and that you both get there best when you somehow manage a state of trying and not trying, knowing and not knowing, certainty and uncertainty all at once. Every time you think you've hit on a less paradoxical formula, you're humbled again.

You're following precisely the same pattern the anomalous experiments follow. You're dipping into the state of mind that my poker-playing physician friend described, when he said the key to knowing the other guy's cards was "knowing and knowing he didn't know at the same time." The one thing we do know about that kind of state is that it's not one we find ourselves able to produce by pure conscious intention. We're stuck with that series position effect, along with rudimentary indications that, when we find ways to bypass conscious intention, people become more able to produce anomalous results.

I was talking once again with Harold Puthoff, the theoretical physicist who was the founder and first director of the government-sponsored remote-viewing project. Hal was part of our ICRL group and he was as fascinated by the four-quadrant model as I was. I asked him what he thought about the central hypothesis, the suggestion that there's an actual exchange of information between the unconscious and intangible spheres that somehow facilitates extraordinary knowing. Hal weighed the idea:

> I'll tell you what's tricky. The overarching principle makes sense to me and may help clarify what we can't currently explain about the pathway by which anomalous phenomena might manifest in the visible or tangible spheres. But we have to be careful about that word *exchange*. It so readily falls into the notion that something moves from one place to another, something is literally *exchanged* between spheres.
>
> It makes me think of our best remote viewers. They were very explicit about their experience. They made it clear they didn't feel they *went* anywhere to engage an internal image of what was physically present at a site thousands of miles away. It sounds wildly improbable, but what they all said was they went *inside*, not *outside*. They gained access to a sense of profound connection to the place they were viewing which rendered it no longer other. The spaceless, timeless dimension—it's something real. It means, hard as it is to get our minds around it, taking seriously the idea that we're in a realm operating beyond limits of space and time. We just can't manage thinking outside those limits in what you're calling ordinary conscious mentation. That's what so compelling about finding the avenue for the mentation itself via an unconscious mental sphere. Everything you've said about unconscious mental processes helps make sense of the subjective experience reported by our remote

viewers. They knew in a way that emphatically required release of conscious mental control. Conscious control, they said, got in the way of any perception which ranked as anomalous.

Nearly one hundred years ago, William James published an essay called "The Confidences of a 'Psychical Researcher.'" Its imagery evokes both the "inside" world of Hal Puthoff's remote viewers and the intangible, unconscious realms of Bob Jahn's model. It also raises many questions that still lack definitive answers. But today we can begin to glimpse the outlines of the "science of the future" that James so eloquently defends:

> Out of my experience ... one fixed conclusion dogmatically emerges, and that is this, that we with our lives are like islands in the sea, or like trees in the forest. The maple and the pine may whisper to each other with their leaves, and Conanicut and Newport hear each other's foghorns. But the trees also commingle their roots in the darkness underground, and the islands also hang together through the ocean's bottom. Just so there is a continuum ... against which our individuality builds but accidental fences, and into which our several minds plunge as into a mother-sea or reservoir. Our "normal" consciousness is circumscribed for adaptation to our external earthly environment, but the fence is weak in spots, and fitful influences from beyond leak in, showing the otherwise unverifiable common connexion.... Assuming this common reservoir of consciousness to exist, this bank upon which we all draw, and in which so many of earth's memories must in some way be stored ... the question is, What is its own structure? What is its inner topography? ... Are there subtler forms of matter which upon occasion may enter into functional connexion with the individuations in the psychic sea, and then, and then only, show themselves?—So that our ordinary human experience, on its material as well as on its mental side, would appear to be only an extract from the larger psycho-physical world?
>
> Vast indeed, and difficult is the inquirer's prospect here.... But when was not the science of the future stirred to its conquering activities by the little rebellious exceptions to the science of the present?[19]

In 1968, Gardner Murphy, president of the American Psychological Association and later the American Society for Psychical Research, brought James's remarks into the twenty-first century in a paper called "Psychology in the Year 2000." Like William James's commentary, it was remarkably predictive. Gardner's essay astutely foretold developments over the next thirty-five years in fields as far-flung as neuroscience, psychopharmacology, genetics, environmental sciences, and cross-cultural studies. But it also predicted that a critical development for psychology's future would be a recognition that "parapsychology" belonged thoroughly incorporated inside mainstream psychology.

> ...the data [of parapsychological experiences] when closely observed, are like the perceptual and affective data already known, but appear to occur under conditions in which the time and space parameters are unfamiliar....In other words, the difficulty is at the level of physics, not at the level of psychology. Psychologists may be a little bewildered when they encounter modern physicists who take these phenomena in stride, in fact, take them very much more seriously than psychologists do, saying, as physicists, that they are no longer bound by the types of Newtonian energy distribution, inverse square laws, etc., with which scientists used to regard themselves as tightly bound. In the same way, new physical conceptions regarding the nature of time seem to remove a large part of the trouble that appears in precognition experiments....[P]sychologists probably will witness a period of slow, but definite, erosion of the blandly exclusive attitude that has offered itself as the only appropriate scientific attitude in this field. The data from parapsychology will be almost certainly in harmony with general psychological principles and will be assimilated rather easily within the systematic framework of psychology as a science when once the imagined appropriateness of Newtonian physics is put aside, and modern physics replaces it....
>
> The year 2000 can come, and the twenty-first century can offer less terror and more joy, but only if psychologists have learned... how to recognize the reciprocities of inner and outer, through methods that are as far ranging and as deeply human as is the human stuff that is being studied.[20]

Epilogue: To Begin Again

The Challenge of the Extraordinary

I T'S BEEN FIFTEEN YEARS since my daughter's harp came back. I've opened the door to questions about reality that shake the foundations of the world as I've known it. The real cost of the journey has been to give up one variety of certainty. This means the loss of a familiar world that plays by the rules, in which cause leads reliably to effects we can specify, rationality triumphs in predictable ways, and we have some sense that we can gain control over our experience. Worse, the world opening up to me is too often inhabited by ideas I deeply mistrust and people who swallow every New Age fad, people whose credulity horrifies me.

I recalled my phone call to Harold the morning after we got that harp back. He wasn't home and I'd left a message: "Harold, we got it back! Call me!"

He'd phoned back that evening. "Well, Lisby, I bet you're

excited. I'm not—I said you'd get it back. But I am curious about one thing. What kind of condition was it in?"

I told him: superb condition. Astonishingly good condition. Not a scratch on it—it was barely out of tune. That harp had been out of its case for over two months. Usually, just moving it across a room was enough to require thorough retuning.

"Good," said Harold. "I been workin' on that."

I'd felt a jolt of dissociation. "You *what*?"

"I been workin' on that. The guy who stole it—he's a crook but he's a coward. He got so scared havin' that harp, he was tempted to junk it every day. So I just went in every morning and said, 'You keep that harp safe; that harp's a precious instrument.'" Harold paused, then casually added, "You know, thought forms can be very effective."

Thought forms can be very effective? Offhand, as though it were perfectly ordinary, Harold was telling me he'd kept that harp in good condition through *thought forms*.

With Harold making remarks like that, no wonder doubts about extraordinary knowing proliferate. But it was my experience with Harold and the harp that sent me down this long road propelled by a single question: What if? Harold got me thinking about a world that might contain something more than unmitigated magical thinking, a world where the barrier between mind and matter might be permeable, where people might be able not only to find a harp from two thousand miles away, but to literally affect its material reality. Investigating that world has stretched my credibility to its limits.

Where it leaves me, I'm not sure. Possibilities have opened up that mean my complacent view of reality will never be the same. The rules are up for grabs. I think the state I'm in now is akin to the loss of a child's world. I approached the experience of that harp returning with a child's eagerness to find magic. But if there's anything to mind-matter anomalies, we have to abandon a child's world of magic and wishful thinking and consider the subject with the sober scrutiny of adult thinking—thinking engaged by all the rational considerations we arduously develop in growing up. That's exactly what I've tried to do over the last fifteen years and in this book. And after that long journey, I have more questions than answers.

Once we open the door to mind–matter anomalies, who knows what the rules are? Even the most apparently objective data concerning anomalous mental capacities show up with quirks; the data just don't seem to play by the accepted rules of scientific inquiry. Left unexplained, those data invite a disturbing question. Do these quirks—the refusals to replicate or the erratic nature of the capacities being tested—result from trying to do science on illusory phenomena, on things that simply didn't exist in the first place? Or do they result from using methods that can't adequately address the essential nature of the phenomena being studied?

I've plowed through thousands of articles in which experimenters try to explain the quirks. Mostly they've focused on suggestions about how adjusting details of their experimental methods will solve the problem—choosing different statistics or altering minor elements of design. The running theme of those articles is simple: the overall approach isn't the problem. It's just that something hasn't yet been accounted for. Once that missing something is accounted for, the studies will submit to experimental control. The data will behave.

But the more studies I read, the more that approach strikes me as missing the forest for the trees. Not only does it lead to more boredom—endless articles packed with methodological quibbling—but, more important, it puts figuring out a way to play by the rules of conventional science ahead of asking whether anomalous mental capacities actually play by those rules. Maybe the quirks are in their nature—*because that's what makes them anomalous.*

More than a hundred years ago, William James identified the problem brilliantly, long before any course was set for experimental research into extraordinary knowing. He'd called for the scientific study of those capacities, to "enlarge the scope of science to include the study of phenomena that are random, non-repeatable, and dependent on universal personal capacities and dispositions." He'd called for a science that could handle all the ways anomalous mental capacities might not play by the rules. In naming the key variables as random and nonrepeatable, he was asserting that there would be quirks in a science of such capacities and that it would cut to the heart of conventional scientific method as he knew it—and as we know it still today.

All the professional intuitives with whom I've spoken assert that their seemingly extraordinary knowing is quintessentially characterized by its random, nonrepeatable quality and its absolute dependence on the highly idiosyncratic, deeply personal capacities and dispositions of the knower—just as William James predicted. When I asked Helen Palmer how reliable her readings were, she talked about the quirky nature of the state of mind she assumes to access information: "It's totally receptive and isn't geared to replicate the controlled reliability that we expect from the analytic part of our minds. Intuition is about recognizing internal impressions in an altered state of consciousness that simply doesn't work in the same way as linear thinking."

No wonder this kind of knowing slips out of scientific conversation. No wonder the experiments show up with quirks.

The official accounts from the Rhine Lab didn't occupy themselves with those quirks. It's worth noting, however, that Louisa Rhine did collect a huge file of anecdotal reports—hundreds upon hundreds of them—still sitting in boxes at the Rhine Lab, many of which offer lively portraits of these quirks. They're highly personal accounts, with plenty of subjective reflections on the weird qualities of apparently extraordinary knowing. At least so far, no one's figured out how to adequately study those reports. But they're there and waiting.

One of Rhine's quirky subjects especially fascinated me: Eileen Garrett, the midcentury doyenne of telepathy and clairvoyance whom I discussed briefly in Chapter 10. Of all such apparently gifted people, no one offered herself as willingly, regularly, and extensively for scientific investigation. She also funded numerous researchers, including Rhine himself, through her Parapsychology Foundation. Especially reassuring to me was her insistence on subjecting herself to her own constant battery of questions. How did her psychic abilities relate to ordinary consciousness and sensory experience? Did her knowing come from "another world" or from her own unconscious mind? Did it perhaps tap powers hidden in the vestigial animal brain? What tests could psychiatrists, psychologists, and neurologists use to verify her experiences? I found her insistence on open inquiry very appealing.

In 1934, Garrett visited the Rhine Lab for the first time, eager to make herself available as a subject in the ESP experiments. She and Rhine started off with the standard Zener-card-reading test. Much to her shock, her initial tests indicated no special ability of any kind. Eventually, she obtained impressive findings on Rhine's card-reading tests, but only after she'd worked at it and injected into her efforts what she called "an active emanation between two people or between an individual and an object," "vitality from the mind of the transmitter," and "the energy stimulus necessary for perception." As long as she focused solely on the cards, which she claimed "lacked personality," she could exhibit no extraordinary abilities. Once she focused on the minds of the transmitters, however, her scores rose considerably. In short, she could only access her extraordinary knowing by investing her work with personal meaning and connection.

As I returned again and again to my notes on connectedness, one of Freud's most famous pronouncements took on a new resonance for me. In *Civilization and Its Discontents,* he described a correspondence between himself and Romain Rolland, the French novelist and pacifist who'd won the Nobel Prize for literature. Rolland had taken issue with Freud's attribution of all mystical and religious feeling to infantile illusion. Rolland held no brief for institutionalized religion or even for religious faith, but he believed that there existed a subjective human state that Freud's analysis of religion dismissed too quickly. Freud's respect for Rolland was great, but he simply could not recognize the experience Rolland described as basic to human existence. As he explained,

> My friend ... was sorry I had not properly appreciated the true source of religious sentiments. This, he says, consists in a peculiar feeling, which he himself is never without, which he finds confirmed by many others, and which he may suppose is present in millions of people. It is a feeling which he would like to call a sensation of "eternity," a feeling as of something limitless, unbounded—as it were, "oceanic." ... The views expressed by the friend whom I so

much honour... caused me no small difficulty. I cannot discover this "oceanic" feeling in myself... If I have understood my friend rightly . . . it is a feeling of an indissoluble bond, of being one with the external world as a whole....

Normally, there is nothing of which we are more certain than the feeling of our self, of our own ego. This ego appears to us as something autonomous and unitary, marked off distinctly from everything else.... There is only one state—admittedly an unusual state, but not one that can be stigmatized as pathological—in which it does not do this. At the height of being in love the boundary between ego and object threatens to melt away. Against all the evidence of his senses, a man who is in love declares that "I" and "you" are one, and is prepared to behave as if it were a fact.'

It's fascinating. Freud was ready to permit the boundaryless quality of love, but he extended it only to sexual love. Only in that state, he said, do we see a nonpathological version of unboundaried human experience. That might have been one of Freud's most decisive articulations. It was certainly decisive for the future development of psychoanalytic theory. It led, among other things, to the irrevocable divergence of Jungian and Freudian thought.

Jung, like Rolland, embraced the "oceanic feeling" as a sensed reality. For Jung, understanding the unboundaried capacity of the human psyche was essential to understanding a person's nature. Freud, on the other hand, believed that the unboundaried quality of union experienced by lovers, far from being a sensed reality, was *"against all evidence of the senses."* With that as context, no wonder Freud deemed oceanic feeling as pathological. He located its roots in a wishful return to primitive, predifferentiated, infantile dependence on one's mother. Healthy ego development was a process of steady growth out of that symbiotic state. Maturity, he said, flowers with the establishment of strong and reliable ego boundaries that extricate the self from maternal symbiosis—and, incidentally, from the oceanic feeling as well.

Years after I'd first read that correspondence, I was in London with Ursula Vaughan Williams, widow of the English composer Ralph Vaughan Williams. She was an elegant and magnificent hostess, even as she approached ninety. She'd invited me to tea in the garden with some musician friends. One guest reminisced about another afternoon salon—held, she said, at the house of the Freuds.

No one there knew that I was a psychoanalyst. The woman who'd mentioned the salon kindly turned to me and asked if I knew who the Freuds were. "The professor from Vienna," she said, "and his daughter Anna." Several of the guests had attended salons at the Freuds' house regularly and they remembered the professor as un-failingly cordial. However, they also recalled the way he slipped away just as the music was about to start. I was interested but not surprised—Freud's disinclination for music was familiar lore.

But then the guests started talking about *why* he slipped away. One woman commented, "He didn't like how music made him feel. We spoke about it once. He was free in his admiration but it transported him more than he enjoyed. I believe he preferred to be more controlled in his feeling."

I thought about Freud and his rejection of the "oceanic feel-ing"—a transporting sensation if ever there was one. Then I thought of everything he had to say about fear and the ways we de-fend against it, the ways we remove ourselves from things that trig-ger fear—*angst,* as he called it. We remove ourselves physically but, more powerfully, we engage in all kinds of mental maneuvers that remove us psychologically. We rationalize, disavow, disclaim, and disaffiliate. We negate and we explain away. It's how we produce some of our best ideas. But it's useful to wonder about what goes into producing those ideas. When we recognize the defensive parts, we're freer to pick out what really has merit.

I wondered about Freud's disclaimers regarding the "oceanic feeling" and his insistence that the sense of boundarylessness was nothing but regression, a refusal to give up infantile yearning. His attitude was determined and his devaluation extreme, effectively removing the transporting experience of an "indissoluble bond with the world as a whole" from the realm of adaptive human func-tioning. But then there was the pointedness of the remark from Ursula's friend: "It transported him more than he enjoyed. I believe he preferred to be more controlled in his feeling." It made me wonder. Why was it so important to Freud to feel more in control of his feelings, not to surrender to a feeling of boundarylessness and connectedness?

Two years later, I returned to the subject, prompted by a fellow psychoanalyst. I was in London again, chatting with Adam Phillips, a British psychoanalyst who'd written a series of books that manage to put psychoanalysis back in the ranks of engaging literature. The titles were as enticing as their substance; e.g., *On Kissing, Tickling, and Being Bored* and *On Flirtation*. He's a literary fellow, often featured in the *London Review of Books*. Recently, he'd been editing a new translation of Freud's works, an alternative to James Strachey's 1950s translation known to every psychoanalyst as, simply, *The Standard Edition*.

Adam was quirky and charming. I'd told him about Harold and the harp, and he'd told me about his new translation. There was a wonderful freshness to the way he thought about Freud, and he couldn't ponder Harold without putting Freud into the mix. It was a treat to watch him put the two together. He finally smiled and exclaimed, "But just consider it—the Oedipal taboo was nothing. Compared to the taboo invoked by this quality of connectedness— now, *there's* a taboo. It suggests a capacity for connection that's far more fearful in implication than Oedipal love. It's far deeper, far more radical. Where are the boundaries? Where's Freud's concept of ego? It's overwhelming. Fascinating and full of promise but overwhelming."

Freud elucidated his worldview so brilliantly that it remains basic to the Western model of mind. He gave us the idea of nighttime eyes as a radically informative window into the unconscious. He also promoted the idea that we're deeply motivated by fear of the unconscious. But he went so far and no further. The unconscious he explored was quintessentially boundaried, with separateness as foreground. Despite his fascination with telepathy, he relegated perceptions rooted in boundarylessness to pathology along with their accompanying sensations—first and foremost, the oceanic feeling.

It's difficult to parse how much our fear of the unknown has affected our ability to study it, even to conceive of it. Who knows what's more conceivable than anything else? Is affecting the material reality of a harp really any more extraordinary than locating it over the phone from two thousand miles away? The fact that there are big hopes attached to how these questions get answered makes them crucial to consider. They readily unfold into bigger and bigger questions, each of which comes with hopes just as big and therefore just as subject to delusion.

Near the end of her life, Eileen Garrett was asked whether she really believed in all the psychic phenomena she'd dedicated her life to exploring. She promptly replied, "Monday, Wednesday and Friday, I do. Tuesday, Thursday and Saturday, I don't. On Sunday, I don't give a damn."[2]

Can minds touch each other in ways that transcend mind and space as we understand them? Can our notion of connectedness extend to contain all the anomalous possibilities suggested in this book? Can we work to develop these capabilities? What if, for example, the perceptions we now label extrasensory—transcending boundaries of time and space—could be reliably trained to deepen people's ordinary knowing of each other, extending our capacities for empathy and compassion? What if we could learn to reliably employ the apparently anomalous effects exerted by certain healers in ordinary medicine? What if we could approach solving our ordinary problems with access to the full spectrum of intuitive intelligence, routinely gaining information located at the apparently anomalous end of that spectrum? What if we took possibilities like that seriously—seriously enough to subject them to our best scientific scrutiny? These are the questions I've tried to address in this book, questions facing every individual who has ever had an experience, however dim or inchoate, of extraordinary knowing.

If there's anything real in anomalous mental capacities, the door has to stay open to these questions. If we don't investigate them seriously, a portion of our experience will remain walled off, never pushed to real consequence, never assessed in the ongoing context of life. To pursue the questions behind extraordinary knowing is to pursue a complete and free articulation of what it is to be human.

It's comforting to know that even Eileen Garrett had her

Tuesdays, Thursdays, and Saturdays. Keeping the questions alive doesn't mean deciding what's true. It just means keeping the conversation engaged. Maybe those Tuesdays, Thursdays, and Saturdays keep us doing our best science—while we entertain ideas that our science says don't deserve to be entertained. Maybe, like Garrett, the best we can do is go back and forth.

At the same time, one thing has changed for me. Those Sundays. It's been a long time since I've had a day when I don't give a damn.

Acknowledgments

MANY PEOPLE HAVE MADE the writing and publication of this book possible. If we have inadvertently omitted anyone, our sincere apologies. Heartfelt thanks to:

The experts in many fields who generously agreed to be interviewed and gave more time and energy to assuring that the finished text accurately represented their views: Daryl J. Bem, Ph.D., Cornell University; Judith Butler, Ph.D., University of California, Berkeley; Patrick Casement, who kindly allowed Lisby to recount an anecdote from his book *Learning from Life: Becoming a Psychoanalyst*; Phyllis J. Cath, M.D.; Susan Coates, Ph.D.; Paul Devereux, Ph.D., author and researcher; Norman D. Don, Ph.D., University of Illinois at Chicago; Larry Dossey, M.D.; Brenda J. Dunne, Robert G. Jahn, and their many PEAR Lab associates, Princeton University; Susan Fassberg, ConnectingDotz; Bette Flushman, M.A., IDS, Children's Hospital, Oakland; Paula J. Hamm, L.P.C.; John Huddleston; Deborah L.

Mangelus; Harold McCoy; Carole W. Morgan, Ph.D.; Rolf Nelson, Ph.D., Wheaton College; Helen Palmer; Stephen Palmer, Ph.D., University of California, Berkeley; Michael A. Persinger, Ph.D., Laurentian University; Adam Phillips; Harold Puthoff, Ph.D., Institute of Advanced Studies at Austin; Robert L. Pyles, M.D.; Dean Radin, Ph.D., Institute of Noetic Sciences; Michael P. Ripley, D.C.; Robert Rosenthal, Ph.D., University of California, Riverside; Michael J. Salveson; Rupert Sheldrake, Ph.D.; Huston Smith; Ellen Tadd; Montague Ullman, M.D.; and Garret Yount, Ph.D., California Pacific Medical Center.

Lisby's invaluable colleagues, including Susanna Bonetti, Carol Gilligan, Daphneae Marneffe, and Sue Stanley; the entire California Revels community; and her dear friends and tireless editors: Phyllis Cath, Charlie MacMillan, Michael Salveson, Rob Straus, and Kate Wenner.

Lisby's agent and friend James Levine and the staff at Levine Greenberg Literary Agency; editor Elizabeth Rapoport; and editors Toni Burbank and Julie Will and the publishing group at Bantam Books. In maintaining Lisby's vision and seeing her book to fruition despite significant odds, they have given Lisby, her friends, and her family a legacy they will treasure for years to come.

—Pamela Mayer, Rebecca Mayer, Meg Renik, and Byrdie Renik

Endnotes

Editor's Note:

The manuscript that Dr. Mayer completed just before her death contained a working draft of the following endnotes, but references were often in abbreviated form, a scholar's notes to herself. Although every effort has been made to provide the complete bibliographic information she intended, we apologize for the inevitable errors or gaps.

1 The Harp That Came Back

1. Shortly after finding my harp, Harold McCoy founded the Ozark Research Institute, whose mission is to conduct research into such phenomena as hands-on and remote healing, map dowsing, thought forms, and other fields of "thought power." ORI (www.ozarkresearch.org) currently has three thousand members in twenty-four countries.

2 Going Public with Private Knowing

1. Eva Brabant, Ernst Falzeder, Patrizia Giampier-Deutsch, *The Correspondence of Sigmund Freud and Sándor Ferenczi* (Cambridge, MA: Harvard University Press, 1993).
2. Elizabeth L. Mayer, "On 'Telepathic Dreams?': An Unpublished Paper by Robert Stoller," *Journal of the American Psychoanalytic Association* 49, no. 2 (2001): 638.

3 Disavowing the Extraordinary

1. William H. Eddy, "Galileo: Truth and Consequences," in *The Other Side of the World: Essays and Stories on Mind and Nature* (New Delhi, India: Tara-India Research, 2004).

4 States of Mind

1. Deb Mangelus may be contacted through her Web site: http://debmangelus.wordpress.com.
2. Ellen Tadd may be contacted through www.ellentadd.com, which provides information about classes, workshops, and personal consultations. See also Ellen Tadd, *Death and Letting Go* (Montague, MA: Montague Press, 2003), www.montaguepress.com.
3. John Huddleston may be contacted at (510) 548-4254/ (800) 891-2599, 2124 Kittredge Street, #733, Berkeley, CA 94704.
4. Helen Palmer may be contacted through www.enneagram.com for distance learning programs and an international schedule of personal and professional development trainings. See also Helen Palmer, *The Enneagram: Understanding Yourself and the Others in Your Life* (San Francisco: HarperSanFrancisco, 1991) and *The Enneagram in Love and Work: Understanding Your Intimate and Business Relationships* (San Francisco: HarperSanFrancisco, 1996).

5 Intuitive Intelligence

1. Ira Berkow, "Jordan Hovers Above the Rest," *The New York Times,* May 8, 1988.
2. Catfish Hunter as told to George Vass, "The Game I'll Never Forget," *Baseball Digest* 32, no. 6 (1973): 37.
3. Peter Bodo and David Hirshey, *Pelé's New World* (New York: W. W. Norton, 1977), 27.
4. Tony Jacklin in Dudley Doust, "Opening the Mystical Door of Perception in Sport," *The Sunday Times,* November 4, 1973.
5. Eugen Herrigel, *Zen in the Art of Archery* (1953; reprint, New York: Vintage Books, 1981), 31.
6. Jacques D'Amboise, "Wraparound High: What's Up There?" *Harper's,* October 1973, 9.
7. Janet Lynn Roseman, "Conversation with Isabel Allende," *Intuition,* June 1996; republished in Helen Palmer, ed., *Inner Knowing: Consciousness, Creativity, Insight, and Intuition* (New York: Jeremy P. Tarcher/Putnam, 1998), 120.
8. Diane Wood Middlebrook, *Anne Sexton: A Biography* (Boston: Houghton Mifflin, 1991), 82.
9. Howard Gardner, *Frames of Mind: The Theory of Multiple Intelligences* (New York: Basic Books, 1993).
10. Daniel Goleman, *Emotional Intelligence: Why It Can Matter More Than IQ* (New York: Bantam Books, 1995).
11. Andrew Newberg, M.D., Eugene D'Aquili, M.D., Ph.D., and Vince Rause, *Why God Won't Go Away: Brain Science and the Biology of Belief* (New York: Ballantine Books, 2001).

12. Ibid., 4–7.

13. Evelyn Underhill, *Practical Mysticism* (Alpharetta, GA: Ariel Press, 1914, first Ariel Press ed., 1986), 23.

14. Libby Bill, *Parnelli* (New York: Dutton, 1969), 171.

15. Richard Byrd, *Alone* (New York: Putnam, 1938), 85.

16. Patrick Vallençant, "Skiing the Steeps," *The New York Times Magazine*, January 25, 1981, 18–20.

17. Jiichi Watanabe and Lindy Avakian, *The Secrets of Judo* (Rutland, VT: Charles E. Tuttle, 1960), 33.

18. Charles Lindbergh, *The Spirit of St. Louis* (New York: Scribner, 1953), 289.

6 Starting—and Stopping—the Conversation

1. Werner Heisenberg, who won the Nobel Prize for physics in 1932, believed that the free exchange of ideas among scientists would lead to the quickest advances.

2. Marcello Truzzi, *The Zetetic* 1, no. 1 (fall/winter, 1976); Carl Sagan, *Cosmos* (New York: Random House, 1980) and later works.

3. See, for example, numerous examples in Dean I. Radin, Ph.D., *The Conscious Universe: The Scientific Truth of Psychic Phenomena* (San Francisco: HarperSanFrancisco, 1997).

4. The Editors of Time-Life Books, *Powers of Healing (Mysteries of the Unknown)* (Alexandria, VA: Time-Life Books, 1989), 87.

5. Louis T. More, *The Life and Works of the Honorable Robert Boyle* (New York: Oxford University Press, 1944), 121–122.

6. Ibid., 57.

7. Leonard Pitt, *A Small Moment of Great Illumination* (Emeryville, CA: Shoemaker & Hoard, 2006).

8. Society for Psychical Research, "Objects of the Society," *Proceedings of the Society for Psychical Research,* 1882–1883, 2.

9. Paul Roach, "Wandering Between Two Worlds: Victorian England's Search for Meaning," http://www.gober.net/victorian/reports/mesmersm.html.

10. Richard S. Broughton, Ph.D., *Parapsychology: The Controversial Science* (New York: Ballantine, 1991), 60.

11. Robert A. McDermott, Introduction to *Essays in Psychical Research (The Works of William James),* Frederick Burkhardt, General Editor (Cambridge, MA: Harvard University Press, 1986), xxxiii.

12. Ibid.

13. Broughton, *Parapsychology,* 64.

14. Ibid.

15. Richard Hodgson, British Society for Psychical Research, *Proceedings of the Society for Psychical Research* (1884), part IX.

16. Broughton, 96.

17. Ibid., 65.
18. "What Psychical Research Has Accomplished" (1892), in *Essays in Psychical Research*, 89–106.
19. Broughton, 65.
20. While James was a leader in setting this agenda, Robert A. McDermott, in his Introduction to James's *Essays in Psychical Research,* points out that it was an agenda shared by all the original members of the American Society for Psychical Research. *Essays in Psychical Research,* xix.
21. Eva Brabant, Ernst Falzeder, Patrizia Giampier-Deutsch, *The Correspondence of Sigmund Freud and Sándor Ferenczi* (Cambridge, MA: Harvard University Press, 1993), 211.
22. Freud's papers touching on "thought transference" include: "Dreams and Telepathy" (1922); "Some Additional Notes Upon Dream Interpretation as a Whole" (1925); "Dreams and Occultism" (1933); and "Psycho-analysis and Telepathy" (1941).
23. Brabant et al., 79.
24. Ibid., 81.
25. Ibid., 240.
26. Ibid., 274.
27. Ernest Jones, one of Freud's most ardent supporters, later described Freud's waffling on the subject as "exquisite oscillation." In 1911, he'd begged Freud not to accept an honorary membership in the British Society for Psychical Research because they'd moved away from their original mandate to focus on "spookhunting, mediumism, and telepathy." It's fascinating to speculate on how the direction of research into anomalous mental capacities might have changed had Freud followed that path at the turn of the twentieth century. (Source: http://sociologyesoscience.com/multicultural_psychology/secrethistoryofpsy-4.html.)
28. "Unpublished Letter on Parapsychology" to Hereward Carrington in *Psychoanalysis and the Future: A Centenary Commemoration of the Birth of Sigmund Freud* (New York: National Psychological Association for Psychoanalysis, Inc., 1957), 12. Freud politely turned down an offered membership in the American Psychical Institute, founded by Carrington.
29. For an overview of the work of McDougall and Rhine, I am indebted to the editors of Time-Life Books, *Psychic Powers (Mysteries of the Unknown)* (Alexandria, VA: Time-Life Books, 1987), 50.
30. Ibid., 50.
31. Ibid.
32. Hoyt L. Edge, Robert L. Morris, Joseph H. Rush, and John Palmer, *Foundations of Parapsychology: Exploring the Boundaries of Human Capability* (London: Routledge & Kegan Paul, Ltd., 1986), 31.
33. *Psychic Powers,* 53.
34. Ibid.
35. Ibid., 56.

36. For detailed historical summaries, see Richard Broughton, *Parapsychology,* 1991; Hoyt Edge et al., *Foundations of Parapsychology,* 1986; H.T. Irwin, *An Introduction to Parapsychology* (Jefferson, NC: McFarland & Co., 1994).

37. Paul Kurtz, "Committee to Scientifically Investigate Claims of Paranormal and Other Phenomena," *The Humanist* 36, no. 3 (May/June 1976): 28.

38. I also found references to projects at the University of Utrecht and the University of Amsterdam in Holland; the University of Arizona; the University of Coventry, the University of Hertfordshire, Liverpool Hope University College, Goldsmith's College in London, and University College Northampton, all in England; the University of Toulouse in France; Andhra University in India; Stockholm University and Gothenberg University in Sweden; and Adelaide University and the University of New England in Australia.

7 Tossing Out Meteorites

1. Michael Polanyi, *Personal Knowledge: Towards a Post-Critical Philosophy* (Chicago: University of Chicago Press, 1974), 138.

2. F. Paneth, "Science and Miracles," *Durham University Journal* 10 (1948–9): 49.

3. Drew Westen, "The Scientific Status of Unconscious Processes," *Journal of the American Psychoanalytic Association* 47 (1999): 1,066.

4. For a fuller account see Russell Targ and Harold Puthoff, *Mind-Reach: Scientists Look at Psychic Ability* (New York: Delacorte Press/Eleanor Friede, 1977), 19–24.

5. Hal Puthoff, Ph.D., "CIA-Initiated Remote Viewing at Stanford Research Institute," *Journal of Scientific Exploration* 10, no. 1 (1996): article 3.

6. As Hal Puthoff explained, that was the beginning, and the exercise rapidly turned into a far more interesting series of events than any of them could have anticipated. He said, "We now know, based on the declassified account of the CIA project manager, Kenneth Kress, that the initial CIA reaction was complicated. Kress described it in the winter 1977 issue of *Studies in Intelligence,* the CIA's classified internal publication. He gave a very convincing and detailed account there."

7. Russell Targ, "Remote Viewing at Stanford Research Institute in the 1970s: A Memoir," *Journal of Scientific Exploration* 10, no. 1 (spring 1996): 82.

8. David Bohm, *Wholeness and the Implicate Order* (London and Boston: Ark Paperbacks, 1983).

9. In the late 1970s, Hal was, in his words, devastated to learn that Pat Price had apparently been guilty of a serious security leak in relation to the remote-viewing research. A CIA agent had called Hal after a raid on files of an organization purportedly engaged in illegal activities. The raid had produced detailed debriefings of Pat Price about his participation in the CIA experiments. The material was extremely accurate. Hal was stunned. As he put it, "We trusted him. This was an unforgivable breach." Once

recovered from his shock, Hal went back over all the experiments conducted with Pat. Despite what he viewed as Price's unpardonable betrayal of security agreements, the evidence remained intact, thanks to the care of the original double-blind procedures.

Nonetheless, Hal's dismay remains palpable as he talks about it. I asked him about the organization that had been raided. The story resonates with ones I'm learning to find all too familiar. Some years before joining up with the CIA project, Pat had turned to a number of resources in search of ways to understand his apparently remarkable intuitive abilities—his ESP, as he called it. Mainstream psychology had little to offer and he finally joined a spiritually based group that had certain cultlike features. It also, however, offered guidance regarding development and use of intuitive talents. Apparently, for Pat, that was enough. Along with that guidance went a requirement that all activities be disclosed to a mentor in the organization. Pat succumbed, notwithstanding his signed security agreements. It is worth noting that there was no evidence that any of what he disclosed was ever revealed or used by the organization in any way.

10. Russell Targ and Hal Puthoff, "Information Transmission Under Conditions of Sensory Shielding," *Nature* 252 (1974): 602–607; Hal Puthoff and Russell Targ, "A Perceptual Channel for Information Transfer Over Kilometer Distances: Historical Perspective and Recent Research," *Proceedings of the IEEE* 64, no. 3 (March 1976): 329–354.

11. William G. Braud, "Psi-Conducive States," *Journal of Communication* 25 (1975), 142–152.

Braud's article still provides a suggestive outline for research in the field, as indicated by the following digest of the article's headings:

Relaxation, meditation, biofeedback, and several modes of altered consciousness are components of a psi-conducive "syndrome."

- One of the most obvious characteristics of persons in the psi-conducive state is that they are physically relaxed.
- A second characteristic "symptom" of the psi-conducive syndrome is reduced physical arousal or activation.
- The third characteristic is that psi receptivity is facilitated by a reduction in sensory input and processing.
- Another symptom of the psi-conducive syndrome is increased awareness of internal processes, feelings, and images (including dreams and fantasy).
- The fifth hypothesis suggests that psi is decreased with "action mode/left hemispheric functioning" and increased with "receptive mode/right hemispheric functioning."
- The sixth characteristic of the psi-conducive state is an altered view of the nature of the world.

- The final ingredient of the psi-conducive syndrome is that psi must be momentarily important.

Braud's list was further amplified by Joseph McMoneagle in *Remote Viewing Secrets: A Handbook* (Charlottesville, VA: Hampton Roads Publishing Co., 2000). In Chapter 5, "Who Makes a Good Remote Viewer," McMoneagle intriguingly notes, "The worst possible participants are the believers."

12. This account is based largely on Joseph McMoneagle, *The Stargate Chronicles: Memoirs of a Psychic Spy* (Charlottesville, VA: Hampton Roads Publishing Co., 2002).
13. McMoneagle, *The Stargate Chronicles*, 287–88, brackets mine.
14. Ibid., 120–123.
15. For the overview that follows, I am indebted to the detailed account in Dean H. Radin, Ph.D., *The Conscious Universe: The Scientific Truth of Psychic Phenomena* (San Francisco: HarperSanFrancisco, 1997).
16. Daniel Druckman and John A. Swets, *Enhancing Human Performance* (Washington, D.C.: National Academy Press, 1988).
17. Radin, *The Conscious Universe*, 215.
18. J. A. Palmer, Charles Honorton, and Jennifer Utts, "Reply to the National Research Council Study on Parapsychology," *Journal of the American Society for Psychical Research* 83 (1989): 31–49.
19. Monica J. Harris and Robert Rosenthal, *Interpersonal Expectancy Effects and Human Performance Research* (Washington, D.C.: National Academy Press, 1988).
20. Daryl J. Bem and Charles Honorton, "Does Psi Exist? Replicable Evidence for an Anomalous Process of Information Transfer," *Psychological Bulletin* 115, no. 1 (1994): 9.
21. In May of 1986, an assessment of the NRC report by Edwin May offered an expanded account of the fate of Rosenthal and Harris's review:

> The report selectively omits important findings favorable to parapsychology contained in one of the background papers commissioned for the Committee, while liberally citing from other papers supportive of the Committee's [negative] position. The principal author of the favorable paper, an eminent Harvard psychologist, was actually asked by the Chair of the NRC Committee to withdraw his favorable conclusions.
> This last point is particularly troublesome and reveals the political nature of what should have been a carefully conducted scholarly investigation that usually characterizes the National Research Council. Violating one of the basic tenets of science to report all findings, the NRC Committee asked Professor Robert Rosenthal to:
> ...omit the section of our paper evaluating the Ganzfeld research domains. I refused to do so but was so shocked and

disappointed by this request that I discussed this request with a number of colleagues in the Harvard departments of Psychology and Statistics. Without exception they were shocked, as I was.

In the end, censorship did not occur, and Monica Harris's and my paper is available in its entirety in a kind of preprint format from the National Academy Press.

Edwin C. May, "The American Institutes for Research Review of the Department of Defense's Star Gate Program: A Commentary," *Journal of Parapsychology* 60 (March 1996): 3–23.

22. Radin, *The Conscious Universe,* 101.

23. Dale E. Graff, *Tracks in the Psychic Wilderness: An Exploration of ESP, Remote Viewing, Precognitive Dreaming and Synchronicity* (Boston: Element Books, 1998); and Dale E. Graff, *River Dreams* (Boston: Element Books, 2000).

24. Edwin C. May, "The American Institutes for Research and Review of the Department of Defense's Star Gate Program: A Commentary," *Journal of Scientific Exploration* 10, no. 1 (spring 1996): 89, brackets mine.

25. Ibid., 90–91.

26. Ibid., 100–101.

27. Jessica Utts, "An Assessment of the Evidence for Psychic Functioning," *Journal of Scientific Exploration* 10, no. 1 (spring 1996): 23.

28. Ray Hyman, "Evaluation of a Program on Anomalous Mental Phenomena," *Journal of Scientific Exploration* 10, no. 1 (spring 1996): 29–40, parentheses mine.

29. Joseph McMoneagle, *The Stargate Chronicles,* 241–242.

8 Nighttime Eyes

1. Hal E. Puthoff and Russell Targ, "A Perceptual Channel for Information Transfer Over Kilometer Distances: Historical Perspective and Recent Research," *Journal of Electrical and Electronic Engineering* 64, no. 3 (March 1976): 329–354.

2. Stephen E. Palmer, *Vision Science: Photons to Phenomenology* (Cambridge, MA: M.I.T. Press, 1999), 266.

3. Arthur Koestler, *The Act of Creation* (1964; reprinted London: Arkana, 1989), 88.

9 Measuring the Power of Prayer

1. Kwang Y. Cha, M.D., Daniel P. Wirth, J.D., M.S., and Rogerio A. Lobo, M.D., "Does Prayer Influence the Success of *in Vitro* Fertilization-Embryo Transfer? Report of a Masked, Randomized Trial," *Journal of Reproductive Medicine* 46, no. 9 (September 2001).

2. Eric Nagourney, "Vital Signs: Fertility; A Study Links Prayer and Pregnancy," *The New York Times,* October 2, 2001.

3. Personal phone communication with Dr. Lobo's receptionist.

4. See, for example, Larry Dossey, M.D., *Healing Words: The Power of Prayer and the Practice of Medicine* (New York: HarperCollins, 1993).

5. Carl O. Simonton, Stephanie Matthews-Simonton, and James Creighton, *Getting Well Again* (Los Angeles: Jeremy Tarcher, 1978; New York: Bantam, 1980).

6. Bruce Flamm, "The Columbia University 'Miracle' Study: Flawed and Fraud," *Skeptical Inquirer* 28, no. 5 (September/October 2004).

7. Bruce Flamm, "The Bizarre Columbia University 'Miracle' Saga Continues," *Skeptical Inquirer* 29, no. 2 (March/April 2005).

8. The October 2004 issue of the *JRM* carried an erratum note that said "Dr. Lobo ... has requested that his name be deleted, as his name appears in error. He was not directly involved in conducting the research reported in the article...." Dr. Lobo is currently professor of obstetrics and gynecology and director of the fellowship program at Columbia University Medical Center. See Rogerio A. [removed], *Journal of Reproductive Medicine* 49, no. 10, (October 2004): 100A. lobo.

9. Kwang Y. Cha, "Clarification: Influence of Prayer on IVF-ET," *Journal of Reproductive Medicine* 49, no. 11 (November 2004): 994–995.

10. Mitchell W. Krucoff, M.D., Suzanne W. Crater, et al., "Integrative Noetic Therapies as Adjuncts to Percutaneous Intervention During Unstable Coronary Syndromes: Monitoring and Actualization of Noetic Training (MANTRA) Feasibility Pilot," *American Heart Journal* 142 (2001), 760–767.

11. Diane Hales, "Why Prayer Could Be Good Medicine," *Parade Magazine: San Jose Mercury*, March 23, 2003, 4.

12. Mitchell W. Krucoff, M.D., Suzanne W. Crater, et al., "Music, Imagery, Touch, and Prayer as Adjuncts to Interventional Cardiac Care: The Monitoring and Actualisation of Noetic Trainings (MANTRA) II Randomized Study," *The Lancet* 366 (2005): 211–217.

13. "Results of First Multicenter Trial of Intercessory Prayer, Healing Touch in Heart Patients," DukeMedNews, www.dukemednews.org/news/article.php?id-9136.

14. Wayne B. Jonas, M.D. and Cindy C. Crawford, B.A., eds., *Healing, Intention and Energy Medicine: Science, Research Methods and Clinical Implications* (New York: Elsevier Health Sciences, 2003), xvii.

15. John A. Astin, Ph.D., Elaine Harkness, B.Sc., and Edzard Ernst, M.D., Ph.D., "The Efficacy of 'Distant Healing': A Systematic Review of Randomized Trials," *Annals of Internal Medicine* 132, no. 11 (June 6, 2000): 903–910. See also the research on prayer and healing by Dale A. Matthews, M.D., of Georgetown University Medical Center: Dale A. Matthews, *The Faith Factor: Proof of the Healing Power of Prayer* (New York: Viking, 1998), and *The Faith Factor: An Annotated Bibliography of Clinical Research on Spiritual Subjects* (four volumes, no date found).

16. John T. Chibnall, Joseph M. Jeral, and Michael A. Cerullo, "Experiments on Distant Intercessory Prayer: God, Science and the Lesson of Massah," *Archives of Internal Medicine* 161 (November 26, 2001): 2529.

17. Ibid., 2530–2531, 2534.

18. Ibid., 2535.

19. Larry Dossey, M.D. and David J. Hufford, Ph.D., "Are Prayer Experiments Legitimate? Twenty Criticisms," *Explore: The Journal of Science and Healing,* vol. 1, no. 2 (March 2005): 109–117.

20. Morton T. Kelsey, *Psychology, Medicine and Christian Healing* (San Francisco: Harper & Row, 1988).

21. Ambrose and Olga Worrall, *Explore Your Psychic World* (1970; reprinted, Columbus, OH: Ariel Press, 1989), 12.

22. Ambrose and Olga Worrall, *The Gift of Healing: A Personal Story of Spiritual Therapy* (1965; reprinted, Columbus, OH: Ariel Press, 1989), 243.

23. Numerous examples are reprinted in *The Gift of Healing,* 229–230.

24. People have reported varying versions of Worrall's definition of faith. My preference is for this one, though in *The Gift of Healing* he defines it as "lack of resistance *to that which you hope to receive*" (196).

25. *Explore Your Psychic World,* 12.

26. *The Gift of Healing,* 17.

27. *Explore Your Psychic World,* 6, 82, 83, 88, 89.

28. Garret G. Yount, Ph.D., "The Qi Question: Is It More Than a Beautiful Form of Hypnosis?" *Spirituality and Health,* summer 2001, 36–38.

29. Wayne Jonas, M.D. and Cindy Crawford, eds. *Healing, Intention and Energy Medicine,* 275.

30. Garret Yount et al., "In Vitro Test of External Qigong," *BMC Complementary and Alternative Medicine* 4:5 (March 2004); online at http://www.biomedcentral.com/1472–6882/4/5.

31. Kenneth J. Hintz, Ph.D., Garret L. Yount, Ph.D., Ivan Kadar, Ph.D., Gary Schwartz, Ph.D., Richard Hammerschlag, Ph.D., and Shin Lin, Ph.D., "Bioenergy Definitions and Research Guidelines," *Alternative Therapies* 9, no. 3 (2003): A13–A30; Marilyn Schlitz, Dean Radin, Bertram F. Malle, Stefan Schmidt, Jennifer Utts, and Garret Yount, "Distant Healing Intention: Definitions and Evolving Guidelines for Laboratory Studies," *Alternative Therapies in Health Medicine* 9, no. 3 (suppl): A31–A43.

32. Richard Milton, *Forbidden Science: Suppressed Research That Could Change Our Lives* (London: Cox & Wyman, Ltd., 1994; Fourth Estate paperback, 1995), 5.

10 Listening Harder

1. Sigmund Freud, *Psychopathology of Everyday Life,* A. A. Brill, trans. (New York: New American Library Mentor Books, 1956), 156, quoted in Montague Ullman and Stanley Krippner, with Alan Vaughan, *Dream*

Telepathy: Experiments in Nocturnal Extrasensory Perception (Charlottesville, VA.: Hampton Roads Publishing Co., 1973, 2001), 23.

2. Daniel M. Wegner, Ph.D., quoted in "Dreams Ride on Freud's Royal Road, Study Finds," Anahad O'Connor, *The New York Times*, March 23, 2004; see also D. M. Wegner, R. M. Wenglaff, and M. Kozack, "Dream Rebound: The Return of Supressed Thoughts in Dreams," *Psychological Science* 15 (2004): 232–236.

3. Sigmund Freud, *Dreams and the Occult* in *New Introductory Lectures* (1922; New York: W. W. Norton, 1933), 24.

4. See Dean Radin's *The Conscious Universe: The Scientific Truth of Psychic Phenomena* (San Francisco: Harper Edge/HarperCollins, 1997), 68–73, for a detailed description of the Maimonides dream telepathy experiments.

5. Montague Ullman, Stanley Krippner, and Alan Vaughan, *Dream Telepathy: Experiments in Nocturnal Extrasensory Perception* (1973; Charlottesville, VA: Hampton Roads Pub. Co., 2001), xxv–xxvi.

6. Dean Radin, *The Conscious Universe*, 77.

7. Ibid.

8. Ibid., 78.

9. Eileen J. Garrett, *Adventures in the Supernormal* (1949; reprinted New York: Helix Press, 2002), 116–117.

10. Ray Hyman, "The Ganzfeld Psi Experiment: A Critical Appraisal," *Journal of Parapsychology* 49 (1985): 3–49; Charles Honorton, "Meta-analysis of Psi Ganzfeld Research: A Response to Hyman," *Journal of Parapsychology* 49 (1985): 51–91.

11. Ray Hyman and Charles Honorton, "A Joint Communiqué: The Psi Ganzfeld Controversy," *Journal of Parapsychology* 50 (1986): 351–364.

12. Dean Radin, *The Conscious Universe*, 85.

13. Ray Hyman, "Comment," *Statistical Science* 6, no. 4 (1991): 392.

14. Dean Radin, *The Conscious Universe*, 87–88. Among the replications were those produced by Professor Kathy Dalton and colleagues at the University of Edinburgh; Professor Dick Bierman at the University of Amsterdam; Professor Daryl Bem of Cornell; Dr. Richard Broughton and colleagues at the Rhine Research Center in Durham, North Carolina; Professor Adrian Parker and colleagues at the University of Gothenburg, Sweden; and doctoral student Rens Wezelman from the Institute for Parapsychology in Utrecht, Netherlands.

15. Marilyn J. Schlitz and Charles Honorton, "Ganzfeld Psi Performance Within an Artistically Gifted Population," *Journal of the American Society for Psychical Research* 86 (1992): 83–98.

16. Daryl J. Bem and Charles Honorton, "Does Psi Exist? Replicable Evidence for an Anomalous Process of Information Transfer," *Psychological Bulletin* 115, no. 1 (1994): 9.

17. Julie Milton and Richard Wiseman, "Does Psi Exist? Lack of Replication of an Anomalous Process of Information Transfer," *Psychological Bulletin* 124, no. 4 (1999): 387.

18. The back-and-forth proceeded not just with decorum but with rigorous scholarly debate. Lance Storm at Adelaide University in Australia and Suitbert Ertel at Georg August University in Göttingen, Germany, published a rebuttal of the Milton-Wiseman paper. Their meta-analysis looked at a grand total of seventy-nine studies and supported the conclusion drawn by Bem and Honorton. Milton and Wiseman shot back a refutation. See Lance Storm and Suitbert Ertel, "Does Psi Exist? Comments on Milton and Wiseman's (1999) Meta-Analysis of Ganzfeld Research," *Psychological Bulletin* 127, no. 3: 424; Julie Milton and Richard Wiseman, "Does Psi Exist? Reply to Storm and Ertel," *Psychological Bulletin* 127, no. 3 (2001): 434–438.

19. Daryl J. Bem, John Palmer, and Richard S. Broughton, "Updating the Ganzfeld Database: A Victim of Its Own Success?" *Journal of Parapsychology* 65 (2001): 207–218.

20. Paul Devereux has authored such fascinating examinations of the history of landscape as *Mysterious Ancient America: An Investigation into the Enigmas of America's Pre-History; Stone Age Soundtracks: The Acoustic Archaeology of Ancient Sites;* and *The Sacred Place: The Ancient Origin of Holy and Mystical Sites.* In the course of his research, he's also experienced a kind of extraordinary knowing:

> After eighteen years of vainly trying to understand the Neolithic landscape of the Avebury complex, I had a momentary flash in which I "understood" it at some level, and I found I was able to get past my interfering, rational, modern mind-set. I began thinking about Silbury Hill in the complex as a *living entity.* (I have since found out from ethnological sources that this is exactly how American Indians thought about sacred mountains—there are some fabulous early twentieth-century records about this in the ethnological literature referring to Indians in California and Arizona.) I have written at length about my Avebury experience in books and articles. By "clicking in" to this somewhat intrinsic mind-set and allowing Silbury Hill to act like a living teacher or mentor, I became able to "see"—indeed, it showed me—the landscape in a new and ancient way. This led to important archaeological observations that entered into the mainstream literature.

11 Three Seconds into the Future

1. Antonio Damasio, *The Feeling of What Happens: Body and Emotion in the Making of Consciousness* (San Diego: Harcourt, 1999).

2. For this analogy I am indebted (as for so many others) to my beloved conversation partner Michael Salveson.

3. Antonio Damasio, *The Feeling of What Happens,* 228.

4. Drew Westen, "The Scientific Status of Unconcious Processes: Is Freud Really Dead?" *Journal of the American Psychoanalytic Association* 47 (1999): 1061.

5. Ibid., 1066.

6. Ibid.

7. Endel Tulving, Daniel L. Schacter, and H. A. Stark, "Priming Effects in Word-Fragment Completion Are Independent of Recognition Memory," *Journal of Experimental Psychology, Learning, Memory, and Cognition* 8 (1982): 336–342.

8. This is the form of many dreams commonly reported as telepathic—a loved one in crisis and an image of the crisis matched by a coincidence in time that appears thoroughly uncanny.

9. Lloyd H. Silverman, F. M. Lachman, and R. H. Milich, *The Search for Oneness* (New York: International Universities Press, 1982); Lloyd H. Silverman and D. K. Silverman, "A Clinical-Experimental Approach to the Study of Subliminal Stimulation: The Effects of a Drive-Related Stimulus Upon Rorschach Responses," *Journal of Abnormal and Social Psychology* 69, no. 2 (1964): 158–172; Lloyd H. Silverman, " 'Mommy and I Are One': Implications for Psychotherapy," *American Psychologist* 40, no. 12 (1985): 1296–1308.

10. Silverman, " 'Mommy and I Are One,' " 1301.

11. J. R. Palmatier and P. H. Bornstein, "The Effects of Subliminal Stimulation of Symbiotic Merging Fantasies on Behavior Treatment of Smokers," *Journal of Nervous and Mental Disease* 168 (1980): 715–720.

12. Silverman, " 'Mommy and I Are One,' " 1301–1302.

13. Zoltán Vassy, "Methods of Measuring the Probability of 1-bit Extrasensory Information Transfer Between Living Organisms," *Journal of Parapsychology* 43, no. 2 (1978): 158–160.

14. Chip Brown, "They Laughed at Galileo Too," *The New York Times,* August 11, 1996.

15. Dean Radin, "The Future Is Now," *Shift: At the Frontiers of Consciousness,* Sept.–Nov. 2004, 38.

16. S. James, P. Spottiswoode, and Edwin C. May, "Skin Conductance Prestimulous Response: Analyses, Artifacts, and a Pilot Study," *Journal of Scientific Exploration* 17, no. 4 (2003): 617–641.

17. Edwin C. May, Ph.D., Tamas Paulinyi, and Zoltán Vassy, M.Sc., "Anomalous Anticipatory Skin Conductance Response to Acoustic Stimuli: Experimental Results and Speculation About a Mechanism," *The Journal of Alternative and Complementary Medicine* 11, no. 4 (2005): 695–702.

    The general public is invited to volunteer for ongoing studies at May's Laboratories for Fundamental Research in Palo Alto,

California, which are funded exclusively by private foundation grants. See http://www.lfr.org.

18. Bruce E. McDonough, Norman S. Don, and Charles A. Warren, "Differential Event-Related Potentials to Targets and Decoys in a Guessing Task," *Journal of Scientific Exploration* 16, no. 2 (2002): 187–206; Norman S. Don, Bruce E. McDonough, and Charles A. Warren, "Event-Related Brain Potential (ERP) Indicators of Unconscious Psi: A Replication Using Subjects Unselected for Psi," *Journal of Parapsychology* 62 (1998): 127–145; Charles A. Warren, Bruce E. McDonough, and Norman S. Don, "Partial Replication of Single-Subject Event-Related Potential Effects in a Psi Task," in E. Cook, ed., *The Parapsychological Association 35th Annual Convention: Proceedings of Presented Papers* (1992): 169–181; Charles A. Warren, Bruce E. McDonough, and Norman S. Don, "Event-Related Brain Potential Changes in a Psi Task," *Journal of Parapsychology* 56 (1992): 1–30.

19. Daryl J. Bem, "Precognitive Habituation: Replicable Evidence for a Process of Anomalous Cognition," a modified version of a presentation given at the 46th Annual Convention of the Parapsychological Association, Vancouver, BC, August 2–4, 2003. See http:/dbem.ws/Precognitive%20Habituation.pdf.

20. This experiment was not available online, and it has since been completed.

21. Daryl J. Bem and Charles Honorton, "Does Psi Exist? Replicable Evidence for an Anomalous Process of Information Transfer," *Psychological Bulletin* 115, no. 1 (1994): 4–8.

22. Personal communication from Daryl Bem, June 2006.

23. Jean Laplanche and Jean-Baptiste Pontalis, *The Language of Psycho-Analysis,* Donald Nicholson-Smith, trans. (New York: W. W. Norton, 1993).

24. Daniel Goleman, *Social Intelligence: The New Science of Human Relationships* (New York: Bantam Books, 2006), 42–43.

25. See, for example, Dean Radin, "Event-related EEG Correlations Between Isolated Human Subjects," *Journal of Alternative and Complementary Medicine* 10 (2004): 315–324; Dean Radin, *Entangled Minds: Extrasensory Experiences in a Quantum Reality* (New York: Simon & Schuster, 2006); Alex Sabell, G. Clarke, and P. Fenwick, "Inter-Subject EEG Correlations at a Distance— The Transferred Potential," in Charles S. Alvarado, ed., *Proceedings of the 44th Annual Convention of the Parapsychological Association* (New York: 2001), 419–422; Jiri Wackermann, "Dyadic Correlations Between Brain Functional States: Present Facts and Future Perspectives," *Mind and Matter* 2, no. 1 (2004): 105–122.

12 Quantum Uncertainty

1. Freeman Dyson, "One in a Million," *New York Review of Books* 51, no. 5 (March 25, 2004).

2. Adrian Parker, "We Ask, Does Psi Exist? But Is This the Right Question and Do We Really Want an Answer Anyway?" *Journal of Consciousness Studies* 10, no. 6–7 (2003): 128.

3. "The Center as It Enters a New Decade," *Frontier Perspectives* 7, no. 1 (1998); 2003 Mission Statement, The Center for Frontier Science at Temple University.

4. Quoted from PEAR Lab's mission statement on their homepage on Princeton University's Web site at www.princeton.edu/~pear/.

5. Robert G. Jahn and Brenda J. Dunne, *Margins of Reality: The Role of Consciousness in the Physical World* (New York: Harcourt Brace Jovanovich, 1987), 88.

6. Ibid., 89.

7. Robert G. Jahn, "Information, Consciousness and Health," *Alternative Therapies in Health and Medicine* 2, no. 3 (1996): 34.

8. Ibid., 35.

9. Ibid. See also Brenda J. Dunne and Robert G. Jahn, "Information and Uncertainty in Remote Perception Research," *Journal of Scientific Exploration* 17, no. 2 (2003): 207–241.

10. Elizabeth Lloyd Mayer, "Subjectivity and Intersubjectivity of Clinical Facts," *International Journal of Psychoanalysis* 77 (1996): 709–737.

11. For further discussion, see Robert G. Jahn and Brenda J. Dunne, "A Modular Model of Mind/Matter Manifestations," *Journal of Scientific Exploration* 15, no. 3 (2001): 299–329.

12. Evelyn Fox Keller, *A Feeling for the Organism: The Life and Work of Barbara McClintock* (New York: W.H. Freeman, 1983).

13. F. David Peat, "Non-Locality in Nature and Cognition." Source: http://www.fdavidpeat.com/bibliography/essays/nat-cog.htm.

14. For a full discussion, see Dean Radin, *Entangled Minds* (New York: Simon & Schuster, 2006).

15. Michael Brooks, "Entanglement: The Weirdest Link," *New Scientist* 181, no. 2440 (March 27, 2004): 32.

16. Matthieu Ricard and Trinh Xuan Thuan, *The Quantum and the Lotus*, Ian Monk, trans. (New York: Crown Publishing Group, 2001): 89.

17. Ibid., 89.

18. Brenda J. Dunne, York H. Dobyns, Robert G. Jahn, Roger D. Nelson, "Series Position Effects in Random Event Generator Experiment," *Journal of Scientific Exploration* 8, no. 2 (1994): 197–215.

19. William James, "The Confidences of a 'Psychical Researcher'" (1909) in *Essays in Psychical Research* (Cambridge, MA: Harvard University Press, 1986), 374–375.

20. Gardner Murphy, "Psychology in the Year 2000," in Lois B. Murphy, ed., *There Is More Beyond: Selected Papers of Gardner Murphy* (Jefferson, NC: McFarland & Co., 1989).

Epilogue: To Begin Again

1. Sigmund Freud, *Civilization and Its Discontents* (1930) *Standard Edition* 64–66. (London, Hogarth Press, 1961).
2. Reported by Garrett's granddaughter, Lisette Coly, in Sioban Roberts, "Legendary Psychic's Journal Gets Reincarnated," *The National Post* (Toronto), April 7, 2001.

Index

Act of Creation, The (Koestler), 151
Adelaide University, 279n. 38,
    286n. 18
Advances in Mind-Body Medicine, 92
AIR (American Institutes for
    Research), 122–23, 127–28
    CIA/AIR report, 122, 123,
    125–26, 197, 281n. 21
Allende, Isabel, 61
Alternative Therapies in Health and
    Medicine, 92
American Institute of Mathematics,
    91
American Journal of Psychology, 75
American Physical Society, 94
American Psychological
    Association, 91, 262
American Society for Psychical
    Research, 262
American Society of Dowsers, 2
Andhra University, 279n. 38
Annals of Internal Medicine, 165
anomalous cognition (extraordinary
    knowing). See also
    clairvoyance; evidence of
    anomalous cognition; dreams;
    telepathy
  attunement and, 23–24
  conceptual models and, 214–15,
    245–50, 252, 258

conditions of occurrence, ix, 9,
    23–24, 51–52, 59–60, 76–77,
    101, 137, 138–39, 145, 169,
    171–72, 186, 193, 219, 224–36,
    238, 258–59, 280n. 11
  cultural disapproval of, 25
  developing ability, 9
  as elusive state, 42
  fear of, 8, 13, 17, 23, 97–101,
    104, 126, 127, 206–7, 270
  history of research, viii, 4–5,
    69–95
  as intuitive intelligence, 9
  knowing through connectedness,
    xi, 66, 67, 68, 142–43, 147,
    148–50, 173, 234–36, 256–57,
    267
  "nighttime eyes" and, 150, 186,
    187, 189, 195, 201, 215, 239, 270
  paradox of, 42, 46, 60–61,
    134–35, 259–60
  Patrick Casement's story, 20–22
  poker player's abilities, 39–42
  popularity, nineteenth century,
    72–82
  positions on, by scientists, viii–ix,
    133–51
  scientific disavowal of, 28–38, 73,
    83, 122, 123, 125–26, 213–14,
    230, 240

short anecdotes, 5–7
silence among academics about,
    95–96
source of, 51
unconscious mind and, 9, 14,
    223–36
anomalous knowing. See anomalous
    cognition
APA (American Psychoanalytic
    Association), 2
American Psychologist, 20, 191
anomalous cognition discussion
    group, 14–16, 22–23, 96, 101
exclusion from, 222
ganzfeld studies and, 121
Archives of Internal Medicine, 166
arts, peak moments and, 61, 67
Aserinsky, Eugene, 189
Asimov, Isaac, 93
athletes, peak moments and, 61, 67
Atwater, Frederick, 114–15
Avakian, Lindy, 67

Backster, Cleve, 105
Banks, John Gaynor, 168
behaviorism, 83, 222
Bem, Daryl, 121, 201–3, 240, 253,
    285n. 14
ganzfeld studies and, 202–3,
    286n. 18
precognition hypothesis, 229–32,
    234
Bem, Sandra, 229
Berger, Hans, 190
Berkeley Psychic Institute, 50
Bierman, Dick, 285n. 14
Birth of Pleasure, The (Gilligan), xiiin
Blavatsky, Madame, 75–76
*BMC Complementary and Alternative
    Medicine,* 180
Body and Mind (McDougall), 85
Bohm, David, 112
Bowditch, Henry Pickering, 75
Boyle, Robert, 70–72, 92

Braud, William, 114, 115, 193, 194,
    280n. 11
Broch, Henri, ix, 237–38, 239–40
Brooks, Michael, 257
Broughton, Richard, 203, 285n. 14
Buber, Martin, 58
Butler, Judith, 135, 136
Byrd, Richard, 67

Carrington, Hereward, 82
Casement, Patrick, 20–23, 28, 134
Cath, Phyllis, 134, 135–36
Center for Frontier Sciences,
    Temple University, 240
Cha, Kwang, 154, 156, 160
Chang, Kenneth, 213
Charpak, Georges, ix, 237–38,
    239–40
Child, Irvin, 191
children
    Freudian theory and, 81
    telepathy and, 13–14
Christmas Revels, xiii
CIA (Central Intelligence Agency).
    See also Star Gate
    CIA/AIR report, 122, 123,
        125–26, 197, 281n. 21
    declassification of Star Gate
        documents, 122, 279n. 6
    Harold Puthoff and, viii, 109–11,
        279n. 9
    remote viewing and anomalous
        cognition studies and, viii, 106–7,
        109–19
Civilization and Its Discontents
    (Freud), 267
clairvoyance, 42, 45, 55, 78, 79
    card identification studies, 87–92
    Eileen Garrett and, 196
    harp story, vii, xi, 1–3
    Paula Hamm's experience, 15
    short anecdotes, 5–6
    the Worralls and, 168–72
Clark, Jimmy, 67

Clark University, 79
Coates, Susan, 14–15, 28
complementarity, 239
"Confidences of a 'Psychical
    Researcher', The" (James), 261
Conscious Universe, The (Radin), 226,
    285n. 14
Copernicus, Nicolaus, 37
Cornell University, Bem lab, 229,
    285n. 14
Crawford, Cindy, 164–65, 178–79
Crookes, Sir William, 73
CSICOP (Committee for the
    Scientific Investigation into
    Claims of the Paranormal), 93
Curie, Marie and Pierre, 73

Dalton, Kathy, 285n. 14
Damasio, Antonio, 214, 217
d'Amboise, Jacques, 61
D'Aquili, Eugene, 64–66, 68, 150,
    172, 185–86, 223
Death and Letting Go (Tadd), 276n. 2
Debunked! (Charpak and Broch), ix,
    237–38, 239–40
déjà vu, 220
Devereux, Paul, 204–5, 245, 286n.
    20
    ganzfeld experiment, 208–11
DIA (Defense Intelligence Agency),
    106, 116, 124
discrimination (of mind), 52
"Does Prayer Influence the Success
    of *in Vitro* Fertilization-Embryo
    Transfer?" (Cha and Wirth),
    153
"Does Psi Exist?" (Storm and Ertel),
    286n. 18
Don, Norman, 229
"Do Paranormal Phenomena
    Exist?" (Chang), 213
Dossey, Larry, 162, 167
dowsers/dowsing, xi, 2–3, 4, 170
Doyle, Sir Arthur Conan, 85

dreams
    Freud's theory, 186–88
    Honorton research, 192–93
    Maimonides dream lab
    experiments, 189–92
    prescient, 7, 221
    REM sleep and, 189
    telepathic, 16–20, 188–93, 236,
    287n. 8
    unconscious mind and, 187–89,
    191, 220–21
Duke University, viii
    McDougall at, 83–84
    Medical Center, distant healing
    studies, 162–64
    parapsychology lab, 86, 89, 171,
    192
Dunne, Brenda, 242, 245, 246, 249
Durt, Thomas, 257
Dyson, Freeman, vii–ix, 237–40,
    254

Eddy, William, 37
Einstein, Albert, 257
Emotional Intelligence (Goleman), 62
Enhancing Human Performance
    (NRC), 119–20
Enneagram, The (Palmer), 276n. 4
Enneagram in Love and Work, The
    (Palmer), 276n. 4
"Entanglement: The Weirdest
    Link" (Brooks), 257
entrainment, 234–36, 257
epistemology, 135
Erdelyi, Matthew, 249
Erikson, Erik, xii
Ertel, Suitbert, 286n. 18
ESP (extrasensory perception), vii,
    xii. *See also* anomalous
    cognition (extraordinary
    knowing); telepathy
    academics and scientists accepting
    existence of, 230
    coinage of term, 89

failure of scientific investigation,
ix
Freud on, 13
history of research, viii
magicians believing in, 240
Pat Price and, 109, 280
positions of scientists on, viii–ix
psychologists disavowing, 230,
240
Zener Cards and testing at Rhine
Lab, 87, 89, 90, 91, 267
ESP: A Scientific Evaluation (Hansel),
225
evidence of anomalous cognition
(extraordinary knowing)
anecdotal, vii, 85, 266
Bem experiments on
presentiment, 229–31
Boyle's investigation of Irish
healer, 70–72
brain-imaging by Newberg and
D'Aquili, 64–66, 68, 150, 172,
185–86, 223
Braud's outline for research,
280n. 11
card identification studies, 36,
87–92, 238, 267
category error, 159, 160, 165
Cha-Wirth study of intercessory
prayer on IVF-ET, 153–60,
183–84, 283n. 8
critics and attacks on, 90–92,
93–96, 119–23, 159–60, 166–67,
197–99
cultural fear and, 8
distant healing studies, 155–56,
161–84
Don presentiment experiments,
229
empirical data, 38
ganzfeld studies, 120–21,
194–211, 223
history of research, 69–95
intuition studies, 24

Juilliard telepathy study, 200–201
Maimonides dream lab
experiments, 189–92
MANTRA and MANTRA II,
162–64
meta-analysis, 198–99, 202–3,
286n. 18
methodological problems of
distant healing studies, 161–65
methodology for testimony, 76
Murphy on, 262
Pearce-Pratt experiments, 88–89
PEAR Lab research on
anomalous mind-matter
interaction, 241–45
presentiment studies, 224–36
problems of testing, viii–ix, 79,
186, 219, 236, 239, 265–66
protocols by Yount, 178–80,
182–83
protocols for ganzfeld studies, 195
published, viii
qigong and distant healing
studies, 173–83
quality of research, 4–5, 70, 154,
178–79
Radin experiments on
presentiment, 227–28
remote viewing (Star Gate),
107–28
replication difficulties, 177–78,
180, 199, 203, 285n. 14
research centers, 95, 279n. 38
research on knowing, 61–62
Rhine's experiments, 86–92
Sagan on type of evidence, 70
scientific discussion, nineteenth
century, 72–82
SRI experiments, 105–6
twin studies, 24
Vassy experiments on
presentiment, 224–25, 227
"Experiments on Distant
Intercessory Prayer," 166–67

extraordinary knowing. See anomalous cognition (extraordinary knowing)

Extra-Sensory Perception (Rhine), 89, 90

Extra-Sensory Perception After Sixty Years (*ESP-60* [Rhine]), 91–92, 96, 122, 123

faith healing, 167–73, 238, 284n. 24

Faraday, Michael, 184

Fassberg, Susan, 192

Feeling of What Happens, The (Damasio), 214

Ferenczi, Sándor, 80–82

Flamm, Bruce, 159–60

Flushman, Bette, 29–30

fortune telling (predicting the future)
  Bem experiments, 229–31
  entrainment and, 234–36
  "feeling the future," 231
  Freud's signal anxiety and, 232–34
  Radin experiments, 227–28
  Vassy experiments, 224–25, 227

Frames of Mind (Gardner), 62

Freud, Sigmund, 79–82, 84
  Angstsignal (signal anxiety), 232
  Civilization and Its Discontents, 267
  dreams and telepathy, 188, 189
  dream theory, 186–88
  fear and the human psyche, 101–2
  free association, 259
  music and, 269–70
  religion and rejection of "oceanic" feeling, 267–70
  Standard Edition (of works), 270
  "thought transference" and belief in anomalous cognition, 13, 14, 278n. 27
  the unconscious and, 14, 80–81, 102, 215–16, 217–18

"wild analysis," 253

From Eros to Gaia (Dyson), 237

Fromm, Erich, 189

Frontier Perspectives, 92

Fullerton, George Stuart, 75

Galileo, Galilei, 37, 38

ganzfeld studies, 120–21, 124–26, 194–211, 223, 236
  artistically gifted people and, 200–201
  author's experience with, 205–8
  autoganzfeld experiments, 199, 200
  Devereux's experience with, 208–11
  history of research, 194
  meta-analysis, 198–99, 202–3, 286n. 18
  protocol, 194
  replication of, 199, 203

Gardner, Harold, 61–62

Gardner, Martin, 93

Garrett, Eileen, 196, 266–67, 271–72

Georg August University, 286n. 18

Gestalt psychology, 136–38
  anomalous cognition and, 140–42
  chalice and profiles, 137, 142
  Dalmatian photograph, 144
  Eureka experience and, 151
  figure-ground perception and, 136–37, 140, 143–46, 148, 239

ghosts, 78

Gift of Healing, The (Worrall and Worrall), 168, 169, 284n. 24

Gilligan, Carol,, xi–xiii, 13–14, 101

God
  intercessory prayer, healing, and validating, 157, 165, 166–67
  role in distant mental intention, 160, 183–84
  in science, 159, 160

Goleman, Daniel, 62, 235

Gothenberg University, 279n. 38, 285n. 14

Greatrakes, Valentine, 71–72, 92

Greenson, Ralph, 17

habituation, 230–31

Hall, Granville Stanley, 75

Hamm, Paula, 15

Hansel, C. E. M., 225

Harris, Monica, 120–21, 281n. 21

Harvard University, 79

healing, treatment, and diagnoses. *See also* qigong (Chinese energy healing)
  bone cancer in physician, 5
  Boyle's investigation of Irish healer, 70–72
  Cha-Wirth study of intercessory prayer on IVF-ET, 153–60, 183–84
  distant healing studies, 155–56, 161–84
  faith healing, 167–73, 183–84
  female physician and smell of disease, 32–33
  intention and distant healing, 156–57
  methodological problems of studies, 161–65
  music-imagery-touch therapy (MIT), 162–64
  neurosurgeon's story, 11–13, 34–35
  nurse's assistant and premature infants, 28–30
  research areas, 164
  Robert Pyles's experience, 15–16
  sports doctor, Michael Ripley, 30–32

Healing Light, The (Sanford), 168

Healing Words (Dossey), 162

Hebard, Arthur, 105

Heisenberg, Werner, 69, 253, 277n. 1
  uncertainty principle, 254–55

Herrigel, Eugen, 61

Honorton, Charles, 121
  anomalous cognition and, 192
  death of, 201
  ganzfeld studies, 194–201, 202, 286n. 18
  Juilliard telepathy study, 200–201, 227
  paper with Bem, 202–3
  Psychological Research Laboratories, Princeton and, 192–93

Horney, Karen, 189

Huddleston, John, 46, 50–53, 63, 68, 101, 276n. 3
  fear confronted by, 130
  state of mind during readings, 169, 185

Hufford, David J, 167

Hunter, Catfish, 61, 147

Hyman, Ray, 123, 125–26, 197–99

ICRL (International Consciousness Research Laboratory), 107, 204–5, 245–46, 251

IEEE (Nature and Proceedings of the Institute of Electrical and Electronic Engineer), 114, 133–34

In a Different Voice (Gilligan), xiiin, 14

Infinite in All Directions (Dyson), 237

INSCOM (U.S. Army Intelligence and Security Command), 115

Institute for Advanced Studies, Austin, 106, 122

Institute of Noetic Sciences, 227

International Journal of Parapsychology, The, 92–93

Interpretation of Dreams, The (Freud), 80, 187

intuition, 9, 26–36
  accessing abilities, 138–39, 170, 171–72

defining intuitive, 63
dowsing and, 170
female physician and smell of
    disease, 32–33
medical disavowal of, 28–36
non-Western cultures and, 130
nurse's assistant and premature
    infants, 28–30
secrecy about use of, 28–33,
    97–101
sports doctor, Michael Ripley,
    30–32
statistician's abilities, 97–101
ubiquity of, 52–53
intuitive intelligence, 9, 63–64, 66
intuitives, professional, 43–55, 58.
    See also Huddleston, John;
    Mangelus, Deb; Palmer, Helen;
    Tadd, Ellen
    accessing abilities, 53–55
    fear confronted by, 101, 129–30
    state of mind during readings,
    51–52, 53–55, 67–68, 138–39,
    146–47, 185
IONS Noetic Sciences Review, 93

Jacklin, Tony, 61
Jahn, Robert G., 240–49, 251, 252,
    259
    model for mind-matter inaction,
    245–50, 252, 253, 261
James, William, 74–75, 77–78, 79,
    84, 261, 262, 265–66, 278n. 20
    death of, 79, 83
"Joint Communiqué, A"
    (Honorton and Hyman),
    198–99
Jonas, Wayne, 164–65, 178–79
Jones, Ernest, 278n. 27
Jordan, Michael, 61
jorei, 178. *See also* qigong
Josephson, Brian D., 213–14
Journal of Communications, 114
Journal of Parapsychology, 92, 198–99

*Journal of the American Society for
    Psychical Research,* 93, 124, 200,
    238
Joyce, James, xii
*JRM (Journal of Reproductive
    Medicine),* 153, 155, 158,
    159–60, 283n. 8
JSE (Journal of Scientific Exploration),
    93, 123
Juilliard telepathy study, 200–201
Jung, Carl, 51, 81, 82, 268

Kleitman, Nathaniel, 189
Koestler, Arthur, 151
Kress, Kenneth, 279n. 6
Krippner, Stanley, 190, 191
Krucoff, Mitchell, 162–63
Kuhn, Thomas, 130–31
Kurtz, Paul, 93
Kyo, Sekai Kyusei, 178

Laboratories for Fundamental
    Research, 108, 287n. 17
Laurentian University, 205
life after death, 104
Lindbergh, Charles, 67
Liverpool Hope University College,
    279n. 38
Lobo, Rogerio, 154, 155, 156, 158,
    160, 283n. 8
Lodge, Sir Oliver, 73, 85

magicians, 240
"magnetic circles," 74
Maimonides Medical Center, Sleep
    Lap, 189–92
Mangelus, Deb, 43–46, 63, 67–68,
    101, 204, 276n. 1
    state of mind during readings,
    138, 149, 185, 219
MANTRA and MANTRA II,
    162–64
May, Edwin, 107, 121–22, 123–24,
    228, 281n. 21, 287n. 17

Mayer, Elizabeth
    experience with Deb Mangelus,
        43–46, 63, 204
    experience with Ellen Tadd,
        47–50, 63
    experience with Helen Palmer,
        53
    experience with John
        Huddleston, 50–53
    fear response in, 206–8
    finding her sister's watch, 58–60,
        62–63, 145, 207, 215
    ganzfeld experiment, 205–8
    gestalt perception and, 139
    harp story, vii, xi, 1–3, 14, 20, 44,
        45–46, 63, 159, 168, 204, 215,
        262–63, 270
    ICRL and, 245–46, 251
    patients' anomalous cognition
        experiences, 7–9, 11–13
    psychoanalysis practice and
        career, 1–2, 245, 250–51
    as scientist, vii–viii
    study of anomalous cognition,
        early, 4–9
McClintock, Barbara, 252
McCoy, Harold, 275n. 1
    abilities of, 215, 243
    accuracy of, 45–46
    feelings about psychic ability,
        101
    harp story, vii, 2–3, 4, 14, 38, 63,
        135, 159, 204, 214, 270
    harp story and "thought forms,"
        262–63
    how dowsing works, 170
    refusal to accept payment, 168
    state of mind during readings, 60,
        137, 170, 185, 219
McDermott, Robert A., 278n. 20
McDougall, William, 83–84, 85, 86
McMoneagle, Joe, 114, 115, 123,
        124, 126, 127, 185, 193, 219,
        280n. 11

meditation
    anomalous cognition and, 68, 172
    brain-imaging of, 64, 66–68, 150,
        172, 185–86, 223
mediums, 74, 75–76, 78, 104
    Margery of Boston, 85
Mesmer, Franz, 73–74
Mesmerism, 73–74
Milton, Julie, 203, 286n. 18
mind-machine interactions, 242–43
Mind Science Foundation, 200
Minot, Charles Sedgwick, 75
Miraculous Conformist, The (Stubbe),
        71
Mitchell, Edgar, 227
Morgan, Carole W., 16, 19
Moyers, Bill, 141
Murphy, Gardner, 84, 91, 191, 262
Mysterious Ancient America
        (Devereux), 286n. 20

National Academy of Sciences,
        121
National Institutes of Health
    Chinese herbs study, 174
    Office of Alternative Medicine,
        164
    study on qigong and cancer stem
        cells, 182
Nelson, Rolf, 143–46
Network: The Scientific and Medical
        Network Review, 93
neuropsychoanalysis, 218
Newberg, Andrew, 64–66, 68, 150,
        172, 185–86, 223
New Life Clinic, Baltimore, 168
New York Times: Science Times, 213
"Non-Locality in Nature and
        Cognition" (Peat), 255–56
NRC (National Research Council),
        119, 124–25
    ganzfeld studies and, 120–21,
        124–26, 135, 194, 201–2, 281n.
        21

NSC (National Security Council), 116

Okada, Mokichi, 178
oneness, 66, 67, 68, 142–43, 147, 148–50, 173, 183–84
  entrainment and, 234–36
  love and, 268
  "Mommy and I are one" experiments, 221–23
  nonlocality and, 256–57
  Tao, 183
On Flirtation (Phillips), 270
On Kissing, Tickling, and Being Bored (Phillips), 270
On the Revolution of Heavenly Bodies (Copernicus), 37
Order of Saint Luke, 168
Ozark Research Institute, 275n. 1

Palmer, Helen, 46, 59–60, 63, 67, 101, 276n. 4
  fear of abilities and, 129
  reliability of readings, 266
  state of mind during readings, 138–39, 149, 169, 185
Palmer, John, 203
Palmer, Stephen, 143, 145–46
paradigm shift, 130–31
Parapsychological Association, 228, 229
Park, Bob, 94
Parker, Adrian, 193, 194, 285n. 14
past lives, 47, 51
peak moments, 60–61, 67
PEAR (Princeton Engineering Anomalies Research) Lab, 241–45, 258–59
Pearce, Hubert E., 88
Peat, F. David, 255–56
Pelé, 61
Perls, Fritz, 142
Persinger, Michael A., 205, 208
Phantasms of the Living, viii, 76

Phillips, Adam, 270
phrenology, 73
Pickering, Edward Charles, 75
placebo effect, 156
Planck, Max, 131
Polanyi, Michael, 103
Pratt, Joseph, 88
prayer
  anomalous cognition and, 68, 172
  brain-imaging of, 64, 66–68, 150, 172, 185–86, 223
  Cha-Wirth study, 153–60
  MANTRA and MANTRA II, 162–64
  studies of intercessory, 165
"Precognitive Habituation" (Bem), 229
Price, Pat, 109–11, 112, 114, 279n. 9
Princeton University, 95, 252
Principles of Psychology (James), 74
"psi," 114
"Psi-Conductive States" (Braud), 280n. 11
Psychic Entertainers Association, 202
Psychological Bulletin, 121, 201–2
  Bem-Honorton paper, 202–3
Psychological Research Laboratories, Princeton, 192–93, 200, 224
"Psychology in the Year 2000" (Murphy), 262
psychoneuroimmunology, 158
Puthoff, Harold
  gestalt perception and, 141, 151
  remote viewing/Star Gate and, viii, 104–14, 115, 116–19, 121–22, 126–28, 133, 185, 226, 279n. 6, 279n. 9
  unconscious mind and intangible spheres, 260–61
Pyles, Robert, 15–16

qigong, 164, 174. *See also* jorei
  external, 175, 177
  internal, 175
  qi and concept of God, 183–84
  Yount distant healing studies,
    173–83
quantum phenomena, 253–58
  Bell's theorem, 257, 258
  entanglement, 257–58
  EPR paradox, 257
  intangible dynamics and, 41–42,
    251, 254
  nonlocality, 255–57
  uncertainty principle, 254–55
  unified theory, 257–58

Radin, Dean, 225–29, 285n. 14
Randi, James, 93
remote viewing/remote perception,
    36, 106, 107–28, 185, 243–44.
    See also May, Edwin; Puthoff,
    Harold
  article in *IEEE,* 133–34
  Dean Radin and, 226
  efforts to discredit, 119–28
  Joe McMoneagle, 115–19
  military intelligence and, 114–19
  Pat Price and, 109–11, 112
  Severodvinsk Shipyard and
    Typhoon submarine seen, 116–18
  spying and, 111–19
  Star Gate, 115–19, 120, 121, 122,
    125, 126
Remote Viewing Secrets
    (McMoneagle), 280n. 11
replication difficulties, 79
Rhine, Joseph, viii, 84, 122, 123,
    192, 196
  coins term *extra-sensory perception,*
    89
  debunking of medium by, 85
  parapsychology lab, 86–92
  wife, Louisa, 85
Rhine, Louisa, 85, 266

Rhine Research Center, 86–92,
    266–67, 285n. 14
Ricard, Matthieu, 258
Richet, Charles, 78–79
Ripley, Michael, 30–32
Rolland, Romain, 267–68
Rosenthal, Robert, 120–21, 281n. 21

Sacred Place, The (Devereux), 286n.
    20
Sagan, Carl, 70, 93
SAIC (Science Applications
    International Corporation),
    106, 122, 125–26
Salveson, Michael, 183
Sampson, Harold, 204
Sanford, Agnes, 168
San Francisco Bay Revels, xiii
Schlitz, Marilyn, 200–201, 226–27
Schmeidler, Gertrude, 105
science
  evidence as basis of, 103
  Gestalt psychology and, 142–43
  ignoring evidence and cultural
    bias in, 103, 133–34, 213–14
  intangible dynamics and, 247–48
  paradigm shift and, 130–31
  paradox of anomalous experience
    and, 137–38
  perception of reality and, 140
  quantum phenomena and, 254
  religion separated from, 159, 160,
    167, 183
  resistance to new ideas, 128–29,
    130–31, 232
  studies and category error, 159,
    160, 165
  tossing out meteorites and, 103,
    234
Science and Spirit, 93
"Scientific Status of Unconscious
    Processes, The" (Westen),
    217–18
séances, 74

Secrets of Judo, The (Watanabe and
    Avakian), 67
Shanghai Jiao Tong University, 95
Sheldrake, Rupert, 119
signal anxiety, 232–34
Silentium Altum (Worrall), 171–72,
    186
Silverman, Lloyd, 221–23
Skeptical Inquirer, 93–95, 159
Skinner, B. F., 83
Smith, Huston, 141, 151
Social Intelligence (Goleman), 235
Soviet parapsychology, 106–7
Spiritualism, 74, 79, 85
Spottiswoode, James, 228
SPR (The Society for Psychical
    Research), viii, 73, 100, 238,
    278n. 20, 278n. 28
  American presidents of, 75, 84
  Freud's letter, 82
  investigation of mediums, 75–76
  Sir Arthur Conan Doyle and, 85
  William James and, 74–75,
    77–78, 79
SRI (Stanford Research Institute),
    viii, 105, 109, 226
  International, 107
Stanford University, 79, 105
Stapp, Henry, 258
Star Gate, 115–19, 120, 121, 122,
    125, 126, 127
Star Gate Chronicles, The
    (McMoneagle), 126
Stockholm University, 279n. 38
Stoller, Robert J., 16–20
Stone Age Soundtracks (Devereux),
    286n. 20
Storm, Lance, 286n. 18
Strachey, James, 270
Structure of Scientific Revolutions, The
    (Kuhn), 130–31
Stubbe, Henry, 71
"Subjectivity and Intersubjectivity
    of Clinical Facts" (Mayer), 245

subliminal priming, 219–20
  experiments, 221–23
Sufi folk tale, 150
Swann, Ingo, 105–6, 107, 114

Tadd, Ellen, 46, 47–50, 63, 68, 101,
    276n. 2
  state of mind during readings,
    149, 185
Targ, Russell, 114, 115, 133
"Telepathic Dreams?" (Stoller),
    17–20
telepathy, 36, 83
  author's ganzfeld experiment,
    205–8
  card identification studies, 87–92
  Devereux's ganzfeld experiment,
    208–11
  dreams and, 17–20, 188–93, 236,
    287n. 8
  Eileen Garrett and, 196
  experiments, and interference
    with the unconscious, 236
  Freud and, 13, 14, 79–82
  ganzfeld studies, 194–211, 236
  Juilliard study, 200–201
  short anecdotes, 5–6
  Susan Coates's experience, 14–15
  unconscious mind and, 20
  veridical crisis apparitions, 77
Theosophical Society, 75
"They Laughed at Galileo Too,"
    226
Thoreau, Henry David, 51
thought transference, 13, 14, 78. *See
    also* telepathy
trances, 78
Truzzi, Marcello, 70, 154

Ullman, Montague, 189–92
unconscious mind
  anomalous cognition and, 9, 210,
    258–59
  artistically gifted people and, 201

associative memory, 219
dreams and, 187–89, 191, 220–21
Freud's psychoanalytic theory
 and, 80–81, 102, 215–17
Honorton and, 202
implicit memory, 218
Jung's universal unconscious, 51
mental activity occurring in,
 216–17
model for mind-matter inaction,
 245–50, 252
"Mommy and I are one"
 experiments, 221–23
procedural memory, 218
signal anxiety and, 232–34
subliminal priming, 219–20
telepathy and, 20
Westen's work on, 103–4
Underhill, Evelyn, 66
universal unconscious, 51
University of Amsterdam, 279n. 38,
 285n. 14
University of Arizona, 279n. 38
University of California, 258
 Palmer Lab, 143–46
University of California at Berkeley,
 1
University of California at San
 Francisco
 Brain Tumor Research Center,
 173
 Medical Center, 174
University of Coventry, 279n. 38
University of Edinburgh, 95, 193,
 203, 285n. 14
University of Freiberg, 95
University of Hertfordshire, 279n.
 38
University of Toulouse, 279n. 38
University of Utrecht, 279n. 38,
 285n. 14

"Updating the Ganzfeld Database"
 (Bem, Palmer, and
 Broughton), 203
Utts, Jessica, 123, 124–25

Vallençant, Patrick, 67
Vassy, Zoltán, 224–25, 227, 228–29,
 231
Vaughan, Alan, 191
Vaughan Williams, Ralph, 268
Vaughan Williams, Ursula, 268–69
Vedic medicine/Vedic tradition, 95
veridical crisis apparitions, 76–77,
 100–101
veridical hallucination, 76

Watanabe, Jiichi, 67
Watt, Scotty, 114, 115
Wegner, Daniel M., 188
Westen, Drew, 103–4, 217–19
Wezelman, Rens, 285n. 14
Why God Won't Go Away (Newberg
 and D'Aquili), 64–66
Why Religion Matters (Smith), 141
Wirth, Daniel, 154, 156, 160
Wisdom of Faith with Huston Smith,
 The (PBS series), 141
Wiseman, Richard, 227, 286n. 18
World's Religions, The (Smith), 141
Worrall, Ambrose and Olga,
 168–72, 183–84, 186, 284n. 24

Yeats, William Butler, 75
Yount, Garrett, 173–83
 protocols developed by, 178–80,
 182–83

Zener, Karl, 87
Zener Cards, 87, 88, 267

About the Author

Known as Lisby by her many friends and colleagues, Elizabeth Lloyd Mayer was an internationally known psychoanalyst, researcher, and clinician, the author of groundbreaking papers on female development, clinical technique, the nature of science, and intuition.

A graduate of Radcliffe College, she received her doctorate from Stanford University and graduated from the San Francisco Psychoanalytic Institute, where she later became a training and supervising analyst. She was associate clinical professor of psychology at the University of California, Berkeley, and in the psychiatry department at the University of California Medical Center, San Francisco. She was also a fellow of the International Consciousness Research Laboratories at Princeton and on the research faculty of the Institute for Health and Healing at California Pacific Medical Center. She maintained a private practice in Berkeley for thirty years.

Dr. Mayer served on the editorial boards of many of the major journals in her field, including the *Journal of the American Psychoanalytic Association*, *International Journal of Psychoanalysis*, *Gender and Psychoanalysis*, *The Psychoanalytic Quarterly*, and *Contemporary Psychoanalysis*. She was the first winner of the American Psychoanalytic Association's prestigious Menninger Award.

A contralto with a long-standing interest in traditional folk and classical music, she was a founder of the California Revels and its artistic director for many years. The mother of two daughters, she was also the producer of an award-winning video series on music education for children and was named Alameda County's Woman of the Year for Arts and Culture in 1995.

Dr. Mayer died on New Year's Day, 2005, shortly after completing *Extraordinary Knowing*.